Praise for *401 Killer Marketing Tactics*

"As one of the world's Marketing Geniuses, I have marveled for the 30+ years that I have known Tom—I have been an admirer. This book is his best work yet!"

Beryl J. Wolk, Chairman of IMC, Pennsylvania Entrepreneur of the Year 2003

"Tom's ideas aren't just the makings of a marketing plan. His thoughts form the basis of a business model that cuts to the heart of your business. It begins as a virus within the four walls of your store, spreads within your internal customers and eventually becomes pandemic."

Robert A. Funk, Founder/Chairman/CEO of Express Personnel Services

"No one knows the strategies and tactics of successful marketing like Tom Feltenstein. Taking the fight to the streets in the local market is becoming more important in the retail business and Tom's approach will help you win the battle with your competition where the customer is. If you care anything about growing your business and top line sales, this book is a must read."

Kevin E. Dunn, Retired Division President, McDonald's Corporation/President - Dunn Enterprises

401 Killer Marketing Tactics to Increase Sales, Maximize Profits, and Stomp Your Competition

Tom Feltenstein

McGraw-Hill

New York   Chicago   San Francisco   Lisbon
London   Madrid   Mexico City   Milan   New Delhi
San Juan   Seoul   Singapore   Sydney   Toronto

Copyright © 2005 by Tom Feltenstein. All rights reserved. Printed in the United
States of America. Except as permitted under the United States Copyright Act
of 1976, no part of this publication may be reproduced or distributed in any
form or by any means, or stored in a data base or retrieval system, without the
prior written permission of the publisher.

1 2 3 4 5 6 7 8 9 0   DOC/DOC   0 9 8 7 6 5 4

ISBN 0-07-144137-9

Printed and bound by RR Donnelley.

McGraw-Hill books are available at special quantity discounts to use as
premiums and sales promotions, or for use in corporate training programs.
For more information, please write to the Director of Special Sales, Professional
Publishing, McGraw-Hill, Two Penn Plaza, New York, NY 10121-2298.
Or contact your local bookstore.

This book is printed on recycled, acid-free paper containing a
minimum of 50% recycled, de-inked fiber.

TABLE OF CONTENTS

Introduction

Marketing Is a Way of Life

The marketing battle is hard, unrelenting work, but it can also be fun. It costs money, but any business or organization can afford it, no matter how small its budget, how unique its activity, or how ferocious its competition.

Furthermore, you should think of marketing your business and yourself as a way of life, not an expense. That's how it was a century ago when Mr. Miller at the general store remembered every customer's birthday with a lagniappe, a small gift of appreciation. That was marketing at its most fundamental and effective. Since then, we've forgotten the wisdom of it—we've become impatient and allowed ourselves to think too big.

Today most companies spend huge sums on advertising, with ever-diminishing returns. Fewer and fewer people notice ads anymore because they're everywhere, even on a piece of fruit, and therefore are as invisible as wallpaper. Like bombing campaigns, advertising makes you feel as if you're accomplishing something, but it can't win the war. The competitive battle is won in the streets, in your neighborhood, and within your four walls. And the prize is not a sale, but a relationship.

"The only reason to be in business is to create a customer."

This quote by Peter Drucker, author and father of American management theory, should be posted on every cash register and every telephone in every business in the land. Creating customers, not just generating sales, is the focus of this collection of promotional tactics I've assembled during three decades working with hundreds of companies, large and small. You don't need all these tactics, just the right ones at the right times.

Everything I've learned about how to grow a business began at the knee of Ray Kroc, the man who founded and built McDonald's. As a marketing executive at McDonald's in the 1970s, I had the privilege of watching how common-sense practices—treating your employees as allies, making your customers feel important, keeping your place of business clean and welcoming, being a good neighbor—always win out over flashy, expensive media campaigns.

Whether you're starting a new venture or your business has been around for generations, chances are that you're reading this because your competition has more marketing experience or muscle than you. But that fact can work in your favor. Marketing techniques change quickly, and most of your competition will be relying on principles that have been out of date for years. You will be amazed at how many simple, affordable, and effective marketing tactics your competitors ignore or don't even know about.

If you're willing to forget what you think you know for a few minutes and plunge into these pages, you can outwit and outmarket the hotshots and the big guys. You'll do it by building a broad and loyal customer base, which will ensure a long-running, profitable business.

While some of these tactics may not suit your particular activity, you'll find more than enough of them that will fit and work well. With true commitment, careful execution, and continuous follow-up, they will work their magic, and your business will flourish.

Tom Feltenstein
West Palm Beach, Florida

1
Planning the Battle — The Basics

"Without promotion, something terrible
happens—nothing!"
  —P. T. BARNUM, circus impresario

This book is a working manual of promotional ideas and programs for your business, based on the guiding principle that everything you need in order to grow your business is within your four walls and your neighborhood. This is a gold mine of tactics (the building blocks of the marketing plan of any organization) that, when selected, assembled, and tailored by you, will help you meet your specific objectives. They work best when they are executed consistently as part of an overall plan of action that is intended to last from several months to a year. I strongly recommend that you develop a firm marketing plan before you begin your promotional activities.

When I sit down to speak with new clients, they are often surprised when I start off my marketing discussion by talking about their internal customers, better known as their employees. Employees' lives are enriched when they sense commitment and caring from those whom they work for and with. When their work is fulfilling, they become your partners in business. Without the support and buy-in of your employees, all the slick advertising and creative promotional ideas in the world will never achieve the results you seek.

Your internal customers should be involved in your total marketing effort, not simply by doing what you want them to do the way you want them to do it, but by having their input on the tactics you implement solicited. A truly devoted employee is one who honestly believes in the company and is faithful to its mission and its products or services. This

1

book includes ideas dedicated to helping you partner with, motivate, and reward your staff in order to achieve maximum results.

The tactics in this book are based on decades of successful promotion planning experience. They are targeted to specific audiences made up of the members of your community you should be trying to reach: those within your local trading area, or roughly a 10-minute drive from your front door. Whether you serve food or install carpeting, sell cars or fix teeth, run a hospital or run a pet shop; whether you're big or small, independent or part of a chain; whether you're in the suburbs, a shopping mall, a downtown, or a hotel, you'll find tactics that you can either use off-the-shelf or adapt to fit your own situation and budget.

Avoid trying to shoehorn a tactic into an insufficient budget. For example, suggestions for print or radio advertising are to be used only if your budget can sustain an effective media schedule. If a tactic recommends four weeks of advertising and you can afford only one, it might be better to choose a different tactic that costs less.

As you plan your activities, be sure to record all materials needed, the steps necessary to undertake the promotion, and the costs involved. Maintain a precise promotional calendar to help keep you current, properly budgeted, and on schedule.

Promotions should be exciting, enjoyable experiences for your customers, your staff, and you. Keep this goal foremost in your mind. Your own enthusiasm and showmanship will add an air of electricity that will buoy your staff, reenergize your existing customers, and attract new customers.

2

How to Choose the Right Tactics

At the beginning of most of the promotions and tactics in this book is a statement of the objective. This is the short- or long-term effect that the tactic is designed to achieve. Once you have created your marketing plan and decided upon your objectives, you should then choose from among the appropriate tactics.

In alphabetical order, here are some objectives to consider:

- *Awareness.* This is the first step in bringing in new customers. The potential customer must know or be reminded of your existence, your location, your product or service, your price range, and what makes you different from the competition.

- *Building a mailing list.* This involves collecting the names and addresses of all customers who walk through your door. You will use this list time and again to implement many promotional activities. Do everything you can to collect this information, and maintain and update it continually.

- *Community goodwill.* This is the creation of a positive image of your business or organization in your community. No matter how large or small your business or organization may be, you put out an image that reflects on you positively or negatively. Promotions aimed at community involvement show your genuine caring and sharing.

- *Excitement.* These are promotions that make you stand out from the crowd. Exciting promotions will create a loyal customer base.

- *Frequency.* These are promotions geared toward establishing your business as the place to go in your category. Bringing in new customers and keeping the old ones is important, but once you have gained customers' loyalty, the goal is to keep them coming back as often as possible.

- *Generating PR.* Public relations, also called publicity, is an effective and inexpensive way to get your message out by getting the media (radio, television, newspapers, magazines) interested enough in what you are doing to tell their audiences about it. Once you've been noticed the first time, it becomes easier to get press attention for future promotions.

- *Generating traffic.* These promotions are designed to attract people into your operation. People may be coming in simply to pick up an entry blank for a contest, but it's likely that they will make some purchase as a result, either then or later.

- *Keeping staff busy.* These are promotions that are designed to help you face slow periods. They keep your staff busy and build business during down times. Most important, they prevent you from having to lay off employees. The knowledge that you are working to help your staff keep their jobs will create staff loyalty and goodwill.

- *Image.* This involves the perception the public has of your business. Is it a fun place to take the kids, a special occasion destination, a place the community can count on for special events, a business that makes customers feel like family? The image you have established in the community should drive the promotions you choose. If you want to change your image, choosing the proper promotions can make it easy.

- *Increasing sales.* These are promotions that are designed specifically to build a higher check (and a higher profit) per customer through the suggestive selling of add-ons or selling up to higher-priced products or services. Many of the staff incentives you will find in this book are also designed to increase sales.

- *Promoting activity during slow periods.* These promotions are different from those described under "Keeping Staff Busy," in that they aim to build your normal and usual business during off times, rather than to expand your activities and services. They can also keep your staff busy!

- *Staff incentives.* The attitudes and actions of your employees will be the first (and possibly last) impression that customers get. A harmonious, exciting, and pleasant working environment, in which individuals' needs are paramount, will keep your business running smoothly and leave you and your management with time to implement other promotional activities.

- *Stimulating trial.* These promotions are designed to get people to try you out. Customers who already know about you may not have been motivated to try you. Promotions that are designed to stimulate trial offer something that is special enough to give potential customers the push they need.

3

Ten Steps before Launching Any Promotional Tactic

You could open this book to any page, pick a tactic, and give it a try. However, that's not making marketing a way of life, and it won't get you to use these promotional tactics in the most effective manner.

There are a number of steps you should go through, even if you think you already know what you're doing, to ensure success each and every time. In doing so, you may be surprised by what you will learn about your business, the people you've hired to work for you, and your role and perception in the community.

Determine Objectives Is your goal to stimulate trial purchases by new customers or to stimulate more frequent purchases by current customers? Are you aiming to increase your average transaction, enhance your image, boost employee productivity or morale, stimulate community awareness, or a combination of these? These are all important goals, but you need to determine which ones you want to achieve first, second, and so on, and which are most easily and effectively executed.

Be Specific If your objective is to get new customers to try you out, what is a reasonable goal—an increase in new customers of 5 percent, 10 percent, or 15 percent? Would it be reasonable to shoot for an increase in customer frequency from three purchases a month to four? If your objective is to increase your average sale, what is a reasonable increase based on your current pricing? If your objective is employee morale, how much can you reduce employee turnover by running this promotion?

Be Realistic in Your Goals   Success is rarely achieved in one fell swoop. Remember, this is a way of life. Each incremental improvement builds on the last. If you get too ambitious, you and your staff will quickly become frustrated and disappointed, and you will be less enthusiastic next time. Set your goals high enough to make a difference and low enough to have the best chance of success.

Set Your Strategy   Once you've established your objectives and selected some tactics, you must decide how to make those tactics successful. What can you afford, and how can you maximize your results?

Consider Various Aspects   Consider such aspects as timing, frequency, capitalizing on local events, seasonal population variations, competitive challenges that call for extra effort, variable costs of materials, labor, real estate, and other factors that are unique to your situation.

Create a Plan   Create a carefully thought-out plan for each promotion, and make sure that each promotion is slotted into its proper place in your long-term objectives.

Zero In on Your Target   What type of customer does your business attract—upscale, blue-collar, families, singles, ethnic groups, and so on? Ideally, the group or groups that are predominant in your neighborhood (within a 10-minute drive of your front door) should be most attracted to your concept. Once you've zeroed in on your target audience, review your tactical options and pick those that would most appeal to that audience and would be the most appropriate.

Calculate Your Payout   Almost every promotional tactic that is intended to increase sales should have a measurable result and produce a profit. You should know how many new customers you need in order to cover the costs of your promotion. How many of those new customers must you convert to regular customers to consider the promotion a success? If you do your homework ahead of time, you'll be able to tell how realistic your objectives are and what, if any, adjustments are necessary for next time.

Improving employee morale or improving the image of your business is more difficult, but not impossible, to measure. Ask yourself, or your bookkeeper or accountant, "What does it cost us to hire and train a new employee?" or "How much traffic will an improved image generate?" In most cases, you can find a way to track the results of a promotion.

Remember, if you can measure it, you can manage it. Or, as Yogi Berra once said, "If you don't know where you're going, you might end up someplace else!"

Check the Calendar   You shouldn't be mailing announcements today for a promotion that starts tomorrow. You don't need New Year's noise-makers delivered in January. Leave extra time to make sure that each element of your promotion is in place in time. Leave time for creating, producing, and implementing each element. Make a promotion calendar or schedule showing each phase and pad the time a little to allow for the inevitable changes and delays.

Refine Your Products and Services   Be sure that the service or product you offer is right for your target customers—that you're offering the right varieties, with the most customer appeal, the right pricing, and the right presentation. Keep track of what is most popular, what's producing the most sales, what's producing the largest profit margin.

Compare what you know with what your competitors are offering. Survey your customers by questionnaire or one-on-one conversations. Take the temperature of your market, and be a good listener by leaving your ego and your preconceived ideas out of it.

Polish the Brass   Go a step beyond your regular maintenance proce-dures. Make sure that your selling, operating, and customer areas are attractive; that your physical space is clean and tidy; that any background music appeals to your audience; that unpleasant sounds or odors are neutralized; that fading paint, broken door handles, and any other flaws are corrected. It all sells, even sparkling bathrooms. You may not see the grimy windows or the litter because you pass them every day and they've become invisible, but your customers will.

Check the Logistics   You can execute your tactics with minimum diffi-culty by making sure that you have the technical know-how, the space, and the resources to handle the promotion without disrupting customer service or staff efficiency. Plenty of otherwise successful promotions have been ruined by insufficient or poorly trained staff, poor product quality, or equipment failure.

Practice run-throughs, when appropriate, help iron out any kinks and increase the chances of a smooth promotion.

Cheerlead Hold a team meeting of all your employees and explain the objectives, the rationale, the implementation, and the fun of your upcoming promotion. Let employees know what is expected of them, what is in it for them personally, and how much you care about their job satisfaction and feedback. They are your customers, too, and you should work just as hard to earn their loyalty. It's the right thing to do, and it pays.

Plan Your Analysis Successful promotional activity is a learning process. You take lessons away from each effort, and you build on them. Setting specific objectives allows you to measure the success of your promotion. For example, before your promotion even begins, you might prepare brief customer and employee questionnaires that you can use afterward to solicit reactions. Review every aspect of your promotion, and gather the information you need to make your next promotion even more effective.

4

Must-Do Business Tactics

Whether you've just invented a new product on your kitchen table and are ready to build a business around it, or you are involved in a mature business that needs a kick in the pants, or your business finds itself facing a competitive threat, there are some basic steps to take first. In the following pages, you'll find some steps that are obvious, and some that you might not have considered as important as they are. Take the best and leave the rest.

You'll also find a menu of the various basic tactics that most businesses use successfully. Use these pages to familiarize yourself with the tools at your disposal.

Think of this process as basic training for your marketing battle, or the systems checklist before launch. The marketing way of life requires us to constantly reexamine, reconsider, and reinvent. If you absorb the information in these pages, you won't have to guess which tactics will work best for you. You'll know.

1. Have a Business Plan

How well do you know your business? If you're like many busy entrepreneurs, managers, and owners, you might have trouble answering some basic questions, such as

- What are your business's greatest strengths and weaknesses?
- What are your biggest challenges and opportunities?
- Who are your current customers, and why are they patronizing your business?
- Who are your competitors' current customers, and why are they patronizing their businesses?

- What changes or new programs would have the greatest potential to boost your sales?

If you haven't already done so, you should develop a business plan based on facts, not hope and speculation. Prayer may comfort your soul, but it is not an effective promotional tactic.

Facts include customer attitudes, as measured by a questionnaire or survey; employee attitudes, also measured by a questionnaire and by interviews; an analysis of your sales, broken down by product or group or category or time of day or time of year and measured against previous months and years; an analysis of profit margins, broken down; the demographics of your market area; your competition; and so on. You can never know enough about your business. Measure it so that you can manage it.

Out of all this information comes a blueprint for building your business. Use it regularly to be sure that you are headed in the right direction. Build your marketing plan into it. Be sure to include both top- and bottom-line goals and objectives—and stick to them!

2. Declare Your Personality

Every business, like every individual, has its own unique character—its own brand personality. Coca Cola is "The Real Thing." Pepsi, on the other hand, has positioned itself as new and hip: "The Choice of the New Generation" or "Generation Next." Southwest Airlines is in the freedom business, and Ben & Jerry's sells earth-friendly ice cream.

What's your business's character? And how can you tap into the positive aspects of your business's identity to improve your marketing?

You may think you know your business's personality, but many business owners and operators either don't know it or have forgotten it in the distraction of everyday business. Nothing is more basic than the idea or mission that defines your business's reason for being.

Your unique selling proposition must be precise, and you should take some time to write it out. It describes your exact position in your market and category. It describes the clear and compelling promise that you make to your customers about the benefits to them that are delivered by your product or service at your business.

Your brand personality captures the feel of your business and the psychological bond you want to establish with your customers. And, by remaining faithful to the core brand personality in your tactical programs, you will solidify your position in the minds of your potential and current customers.

A brand personality statement sets your business apart by identifying how customers feel about you, how you differ from the competition, and how your physical surroundings emphasize your personality. To develop a brand personality, you can begin by creating a working list using such factors as age, gender, emotional qualities, intelligence, sense of humor, and any other characteristics that identify a unique quality of your business.

In developing your brand personality, you must find inherent drama in your concept—the reasons why people want to patronize your business. Then translate the drama into meaningful benefits: a good time, quality service, quality products, speed, comfort, convenience, expertise, a pleasurable atmosphere, and value. Finally, state those benefits as if you were describing a real personality—in as many words as you need—to round out the character of your business.

For your exercise in developing a brand personality, you should condense your thoughts into descriptions and then into a short essay of three or four paragraphs. This is hard, and you may want to hire a writer to do it for you, or someone you know who can look at your business objectively and articulate what he or she sees.

3. Naming Names

There are good names for your company, and there are names that may make it harder for you to establish your brand personality and run your promotions. If your business is named after yourself or the owner and the name is something unpronounceable, consider changing it.

Be sure your name doesn't confuse people, and that it is uniquely yours. Consult the Yellow Pages, do a Google search on the Internet, play with names and ideas, and try to come up with something that reflects the concept you are trying to get across and is easily differentiated from other types of businesses.

Bad names abound; you can see them everywhere. AAAA Systems tells you absolutely nothing except that the company wanted to be first in the phone book. Fitness Superstore is not a neighborhood, customer-friendly name. Neither is Unique Carpet.

Virgin Atlantic Airways is a brilliant name because it suggests something new and fresh, and it tells you what the company does and where it does it, all in three words. Butch's Auto Body is a good name because it suggests strength and determination, and it's easy to remember. Floribunda is a wonderful name for a flower shop because it suggests lushness and luxury. Bagel Barrel is a good name for a bagel shop because it suggests the coziness of a general store and gives a feeling of abundance and freshness. Starbucks is a great name because it's edgy and forward-looking, like the company's coffee.

Consider giving your business a sense of place: Peace Valley Internal Medicine sounds like a calm place to get a checkup, Peddler's Village sounds like a fun place to shop for an unusual gift, and Painted Earth Landscaping sounds like a creative company that could turn your lawn into a piece of art. (Sorry, all these names are taken.)

Names matter. Take the time to think about yours. If you can afford it, consider hiring a brand expert to help.

4. The Color of Success

When you are designing your selling, work, production, or other business spaces, color should play a major role. If you haven't painted your walls in a long time, your old color scheme may be sending a message that you don't intend—that your business is a tired concept that's out of date. Walk into any business today that has a color scheme of burgundy and gray and you know immediately that nothing exciting has happened there since the 1980s.

I once helped an independent linen store whose walls hadn't been repainted in decades, and that was selling the latest linens, towels, and curtains in all the new colors but still used black and white for its brochure. We repainted the store and put together a color catalog, and the linen store's sales jumped 10 percent.

Color palettes change with fashions, and certain colors are associated with particular moods. Blues and greens are emotionally soothing and physically cool. Reds, yellows, and oranges are emotionally exciting and physically hot. A doctor's office, where patients may be upset or nervous, should opt for cool or soft colors. A nightclub should opt for hot or bold colors. Color should be an essential decision in developing your brand personality. Check out your competition to see what they're doing. A professional can also help you choose the colors that are right for your business.

5. Logo Logic

The graphic symbol that represents your business should reflect the identity you're trying to project. To be effective, it must be readable, clear, and bold. Your logo should not look like another company's recognizable image unless that is an important aspect of your product or service. If you're in the business of selling sports memorabilia, for example, your logo might benefit from using a typeface that mimics a sports team's.

Colors should be consistent with what you have chosen for your business. Use your logo wherever possible—on matchbook covers, communication boards, direct mail, letterhead, shopping bags, and so on.

A consistent image-creation program ties all of these elements together to create excitement, freshness, and the mood that's appropriate for your type of business.

6. It's All in the Business Cards

A business card is a miniature advertisement that doesn't have to compete with any other ads or editorial content. It's usually handed from one person to another, so you know that the content is being read. Spend some time creating a card that will enhance your image, leave a positive impression, and tell your story in a few words.

Business cards can double as mini-brochures, especially if you have them done on folded stock, so that you get extra space to tell your story. And tell the story—hours of operation, special features, even a photo, if it makes sense. If you're a family business that's been around for decades, say so.

One of the most successful marketing tactics is to make sure that every employee has his or her own business card, right down to the person who sweeps the floors. Marketing to your staff is every bit as important as marketing to your customers. The members of your staff are your marketing ambassadors. Encourage them to use their cards, to give them away every chance they get. Suddenly you've got a salesperson in every barbershop, gas station, and family event in your neighborhood. This will make your staff feel important, valued, and loyal.

7. Stationery with Staying Power

If you do direct mailing, the look and feel of your stationery can be a powerful marketing tool. This is another area where you should consider hiring a professional. Your stationery conveys the overall character of your operation to those who have not yet patronized your business. Make sure your stationery is consistent with your business cards, your color scheme, and your brand personality.

All of these printed materials should have full contact information, including your web site and e-mail address, and any imagery that helps define who you are and what you do.

8.   Themes and Slogans

Choose a group of words that summarizes your company or its prime benefits. Pick one that you can live with—you should use the theme as long as possible. It can be informational, inspirational, even funny.

"Don't leave home without it" and "We bring good things to life" are well-known examples. A Philadelphia-based publishing company, Xlibris, which provides publishing services directly to writers, says it is "Where writers become authors." A disaster-recovery service that cleans up smoke and water damage has a great slogan: "Like it never happened."

Here are a few clever slogans, collected by a newspaper in Edmonds, Washington:

"Nobody knows the truffles we've seen." Truffle merchant.

"Your pane is our pleasure." Window-cleaning company.

"Take a spin with us." Laundromat.

"Let us steer you in the right direction." Butcher.

"We dry harder." Concrete products company.

"Let us remove your shorts." Electrician.

"We're number one in the number two business." Septic service.

"After the first whiff, call Cliff." Septic service.

"We don't want an arm and a leg . . . just your tows!" Towing company.

"Get your buns in here." Pastry shop.

"It's great to be kneaded." Massage therapist.

"Spouses selling houses." Husband and wife real estate agents.

"We're easy to get a lawn with." Turf farm.

"We curl up and dye for you." Hair salon.

Even a slogan is a promotional tactic if it's memorable. Once again, check out your competition and see what others are doing, and consider hiring a copywriter to give you some ideas.

9. The Whole Package

Your business is just like a box of Valentine's chocolates. What you're selling, in most cases, is a commodity—like chocolate and sugar. But it comes in a heart-shaped box covered in shiny red paper, wrapped with a bow, and lined inside with tissue, and the intricately shaped candies are neatly arranged in their own cubbyholes in fluted wax paper cups, all in a shiny gold plastic tray. Opening it is an experience: It feels special, and there are delightful surprises once you've gone through the ritual. You should think of your business the same way.

Back in the days when McDonald's was smaller and closer to its roots, store managers had to wash and polish the outsides of their buildings once a week. Starbucks is a success story because the company put the millions it could have spent on advertising into decorating its stores.

The elements that go into making an experience special and leaving your customers wanting more include your staff, your physical location, your delivery vehicles, your promotional pieces, and your products and services. How you package yourself will either attract or repel customers.

Look at your business as a total package, from the curb to the bathrooms. Think about all of it, from the design and traffic flow right down to the look of your printed promotional pieces.

10. Maintaining Your Edge

Customers form instant opinions about your business based on how you maintain your establishment. You may not notice what's worn out, or dirty, or smudged, but your customers will, even if it's only on a subliminal level. Everything counts.

Put a fresh coat of paint on your building, or at least touch up the trim. Repaint the stripes on your parking lot. Work your way through all the zones of your business. Try to imagine what it's like to see it for the first time. If you're having trouble doing that, ask someone else to do it for you.

Are there cigarette butts ground out in front of the door? Is there gum stuck on the sidewalk? Is there trash in the gutter? Is the glass greasy with fingerprints? Is the awning torn, faded, or dusty? Are your signs clean and freshly painted, or have letters disappeared in the latest windstorm? Are the restrooms always spotless and well stocked?

Pay careful attention to maintenance, and customers will come back and will recommend your business to new prospects.

11.   Size Matters

The size of your business may influence whether people buy. Bigger is not always better. For some customers, bigger is off-putting.

If you want to see a large selection of door chimes, you'll definitely want to go to a giant home improvement store where part of an entire aisle is devoted to every imaginable type of door chime. But you might not want to go to the trouble of looking for a place to park and fighting the crowds just to buy a small house plant for Mom on Mother's Day.

As the owner of a small business, you can defeat the big guys by focusing on providing a caring, warm environment and a good product or service selection. Establishing yourself as the friendliest, most personal place in town will win out over the big guys any day.

12.   The Price Should Be Right

Although good customer service executed with a smile is the single most important reason that customers patronize one business rather than another, price is a factor for about one in seven.

Look at the competition in your business category, look at your market, and decide where you are in the pricing universe—low, medium, or high. If your current pricing is high, you'd better be offering your customers something extra to justify it, and you'd better be in a market that supports premium pricing. If your current pricing is low, and you intend to keep it that way, brag about it.

In any case, make sure that your pricing levels fit your market and your concept.

13.   Internal Customer Attitude Check

It is a basic principle of promotional tactics that motivated, smiling employees attract loyal customers. Yet one of the hardest concepts to get across to business owners is that your employees and your staff should be treated as customers. You can do all the clever marketing in the world, but if your staff isn't on board, if your employees aren't engaged and enthusiastic, the results will be unsatisfying.

You should be asking your employees on a regular basis, by way of employee satisfaction surveys, what they think about everything you do and how they feel about working for you.

Start with input from every single manager in your business. It's their neighborhood, it's their career, and they should have a sense of ownership in any plan you come up with.

Managers always have something to complain about. Let them. Everybody needs to vent, and you need to leave your ego at the door. You want the truth, not a response that makes you feel good. You want a candid evaluation from every internal customer, from your top-line managers right down to the guy who vacuums the floor. What do they really think about the product or service, the pricing, the atmosphere—all of it?

Managers are notorious for having great ideas but either feeling uncomfortable about speaking up or simply not having time to do so in the rush of everyday business. You want to give them a sense that you really want their opinion on what the opportunities in the business are and what the strengths and weaknesses are. Even if you don't agree with all of their opinions, you've made your managers your partners.

When you get down the ladder to your staff, you must make sure that your internal customer survey gives your employees an opportunity to give you an anonymous opinion about what they think about your business. These are the people who make or break you.

At the start of this process, you may be nervous: "The staff is just going to slam us." That's not always the case, but if people do slam you, you might deserve it. The insights that come out of these surveys frequently surprise business owners and managers.

You might even think, "My people aren't that bright," only to discover that they are not only bright, but caring and filled with valuable knowledge and insight. You just never asked them.

You can find standard forms online that you can either use as is or customize to suit your particular business. One vendor is AllBusiness.com. There are services that allow you to set up a survey online, although doing it in person is the only way to guarantee participation. Ask around, do some research, and find the form that's right for you.

The internal customer survey must be self-administered and absolutely confidential. If it isn't, you're wasting time. The answers won't be honest or useful. Put a staff member in charge of this process and hold an all-company meeting. Tell the members of your staff why they're being asked to fill out the survey, that their feedback will be taken seriously, and that the survey will be totally anonymous.

To demonstrate that you mean what you say, have your employees drop their completed surveys into a preaddressed FedEx box that is sealed in their presence for shipping to a research company or some other objective consultant for tabulation. There are many companies that do this for a reasonable fee.

Don't try to tabulate these results yourself. You'll defeat the purpose, and you won't get honest answers. Build trust and you get trustworthy employees.

In your survey, ask your employees how they feel about themselves; how they feel about the company as an employer; and what they think about the marketing, about the culture, and about diversity in the workplace. You may not want to change some things, but you should know what your staff thinks before you go out and spend a fortune on your next set of uniforms or new office equipment.

How do your employees feel about the salary and benefits you offer compared to those offered by other companies in the area? Of course, they're going to think their salary and benefits are lower, but often that issue can be handled very simply. If you know they're misinformed, you can go out and do a little research yourself. If you're right, hold a staff meeting and show your employees in black and white that the grass is not really greener on the other side. You may, in this situation, even find that you're able to reinforce some of the benefits that you do offer, benefits that your staff may not know about or understand.

If they're right, maybe you have a clue to the reasons for your high turnover, low quality of staff performance, or any of a host of other issues.

Ask your employees in this survey if they see your business as a place they would recommend to friends or associates as a place to patronize. If your employees would not recommend you, you have a huge opportunity for improvement.

These surveys should give a total score for the store (or store by store, if you have more than one outlet). However, within each store, they should be broken down by category or employee activity. In the food service business, which employs more people–12 million–than any other industry, you would want your results broken out to reflect attitudes in the back of the house (kitchen staff), the front of the house (dining room and bar staff), and management. In an auto dealership, you'd break it down by service (garage and service desk separately!), parts, sales (used and new), accounting, and so on. Even the people who manage your parking lot should be included and reported. Be creative and look inside your four walls to see who your internal customers are, what categories they naturally fall into, and how they can be surveyed.

What you do with the results of this survey is study your business to see the big picture, and a lot of smaller pictures that make it up. Look for opportunities to correct problems and build on advantages. Listen with an open mind.

See my book *The 10-Minute Marketer's Handbook* and visit my web site www.tomfeltenstein.com for more details on the survey.

14. Customer Attitude Check

As well as taking an employee survey, you should be regularly taking the temperature of your customers with a customer attitude profile survey. There are many forms that can be found through marketing supply companies that specialize in this area.

In a busy retail operation, the survey should be done over a several-day period, so that you have a representative sample of your customers. If you are in a retail business that is open seven days a week, do your survey on two weekdays and two weekend days. In most companies, business is heaviest later in the week, so the best days would be Thursday, Friday, Saturday, and Sunday. If you are in the food service business and you're open for lunch and dinner, your survey should be done at both times. It should be done during each marketing part of the day.

In any sort of retail business, the survey should be done during your busiest periods, without cutting corners or taking shortcuts. If you happen to be in a business that offers a product or service that is purchased with less spontaneity, the same idea applies, with some creativity.

The information you get from this survey is a demographic breakdown of your customers: their age range, their ethnicity, the number in a party (if you are a restaurant), how often they patronize your business, whether they are male or female. The survey tells you who your target audience is. If you know who your customers are now, you know which part of your neighborhood you should market to, without shouting over the heads of people who aren't your prospects. This survey will provide real statistical data—it is far more accurate than trying to estimate your target audience based on who is coming through the front door.

You will use this information, such as frequency, to determine the number of visits required for any frequency discount. If your survey shows that you have a frequency per customer of 2.6 visits per month, you might set your frequency premium at four visits a month to encourage a 50 percent increase. Many business owners have a tendency to set the number of visits required for a frequency premium high, often at 10, hoping that this will, in time, result in a large increase in sales. You want your promotions to be easy and accessible. You want your customers to get the benefit sooner rather than later.

In some industries there are national databases that calculate the average national frequency of visit in each category. If, when you get your survey results, the national average for your category of business is 2.67, and your frequency is lower than that, you have room for improvement.

In massaging this information, break down the frequency results into subcategories: what percent patronize once a month, twice a month, and so on. If 10 percent of your customers visit your business four times a week, they are already above-average visitors without any incentive. Don't focus your marketing on them. If 15 percent visit once a week or more, your goal might be to move them up to the next category: visiting two to three times a week, or even four times a week. That would have a huge impact on sales.

The survey should also collect information on customer satisfaction. How many of your customers rate you excellent on product quality, service, and atmosphere? How do your customers rate you versus your competitors? It may reassure you and stroke your ego to know that your customers say you're great on your own, but those results often conflict with what your customers say when they rate you against the competition. If only 25 percent rate your business better than your competitors' on quality and service, that means that three out of four of your customers think that you're the same or worse. You're lacking a competitive edge when your customers have four places to choose from and there isn't much that's distinguishing you.

Interviewing customers is something that many business owners and managers hate doing. They may respect their customers' privacy, or they may be afraid to hear bad news, or they may be uncomfortable having that sort of conversation with people. But customers love to talk about themselves and their experiences. You can use a simple card with 20 questions on it and a check-off system, with ratings from best to worst. This often works well in busy places so long as your staff is trained to encourage customers to fill out the cards.

Customers in businesses in upscale categories prefer being interviewed. You can hire interviewers, but the people that consultants hire for these positions often aren't up to snuff, and they don't know your business. Make sure that you're training interviewers well about exactly how you want the survey done.

It's useful to train one employee for that responsibility, someone who normally works in a different location or doesn't usually have contact with customers. This helps reduce the possibility of skewed results caused by customers who have a personal knowledge of your staff.

Always conduct your survey after customers have had their transaction experience. Let them know that you're doing a survey, and ask politely if they will fill out the form or answer the questions. Select attractive young men and women with good people skills to collect your data. Be sure you design a survey or an interview that takes just a couple of minutes to complete.

See my book *The 10-Minute Marketer's Handbook* and visit my web site www.tomfeltenstein.com for more details on the survey.

15. Time Flies

Life has speeded up, people are busier than they've ever been, and customers consider the reception they receive in most businesses deplorable. People hate slow service, even when it isn't. They also resent being rushed, even when they aren't. Being left on hold or made to wait has lost more sales for more businesses than any other single cause.

Make sure someone acknowledges customers within moments of their encountering your business. Even "Hello. How are you? I'll be with you in just a moment" is better than risking the impression that you don't care. Mary Kay, the late cosmetics mogul who built an empire creating customers one at a time, put it best when she said, "Everyone has an invisible sign around their neck that says, 'Make me feel important.'"

16. Ready When They Are?

Unless you're in a mall or some similar selling environment, there are no rules that say that you can be open only the same hours as your competition or the rest of the world.

You can often steal business from your competitors by opening earlier or later. If longer or different hours meet your market and concept criteria, you may be surprised at the result. A dentist I know decided to work on Sundays and discovered that patients really appreciated being able to schedule appointments that didn't conflict with their work. They told their friends, and his business grew. A hair salon I know of decided to open Mondays only because none of its competitors did. Soon, Monday became the most profitable day of the salon's week.

17. Phoning It In

We all know what the problems are with phone etiquette and service. So it's hard to understand why so many businesses ignore this critical gateway. When a potential customer has a bad experience phoning you, you rarely get a second chance.

Have some friends pretend to be shoppers and phone your business with questions. Make sure that your phone system is easy to use and that a real person is always available to answer a question. Is your staff answering correctly, paying attention to customers, solving problems, and creating customers? Are messages taken accurately and answered promptly? Does your phone system have a special busy message with some sort of background music? Give callers who are on hold information about your hours of operation, specials, your web site, and so on. If you depend on the phone for a significant part of your incoming business, make it a top priority.

18. Mail Bonding

From the day you open your business, you should be building a customer mailing list. There are many tactics in this book that help you to do that efficiently and gracefully, without invading your customers' privacy. This database is a central tool in your promotional program. Such targeted marketing is highly efficient, is easily measured, and produces high returns.

Be sure to enter all this data into a flexible computer program on a timely basis. Don't let little slips of paper pile up in a shoebox until you have so many that nobody has time to enter them. You'll want to collect the usual information, including email addresses, and you will learn the importance of other data, such as birthdays and buying habits. The longer your list becomes, the larger your profits.

Send mailings to your list on a regular basis, and be sure to update your database with address changes. Even if a customer moves out of your trading area, if that customer continues to hear from you, she or he will often feel special enough to make the trip—and to bring friends!

Repeat mailings reinforce your bond. Studies show that customers on average need to be "touched" six times by your marketing before they become motivated enough to purchase.

19.   Your Window on the World

You don't have to be in the retail business for windows to matter—the same visual impact theory applies. There's no reason that an auto mechanic has to have ugly, static windows. It's all part of marketing and promotion.

Retailers should change their window displays often. This creates excitement and projects one of the most important concepts in marketing: "New!" Use your windows to announce promotions and special events.

Decorate seasonally and use awnings, shutters, lights, plants, pictures, signage, and so on to create the appropriate mood. Your "face" should be attractive, inviting, exciting, and fresh so that people will be curious to know what's inside the package.

20.   Signs of Life

Are your walls cluttered with crookedly taped out-of-date community announcements, or covered with the same tired pictures of covered bridges that have been there for years, or simply blank because you never had the time to decorate? Your four walls are one of your most important promotional tools, even the walls of your bathrooms. You control the walls, every customer sees them, and they are where you get to create the perfect atmosphere, announce specials, engineer clear traffic flow, and generally make the customer's experience a pleasure and your sales grow.

Posters, banners, and reader boards are great marketing tools. They act as silent salespeople to encourage impulse purchases. Design them attractively, in keeping with the image of your business and decor, and place them where they'll be seen.

21.   Outside the Box

We live in a forest of signs and advertisements. It's hard to stand out, but it can be done with careful thinking and planning. A well-lit, attractive outside sign is always worth the investment; it makes your business easily identifiable at night, and it serves as a continuous advertisement even when you're closed.

Think creatively. A restaurant I know of faced having to go to court to get zoning permission to erect a sign at the curb. Rather than go to war with the town, the manager had a couple of dozen auto shades made up with the business logo prominently displayed. All employees were instructed to park their cars facing the street, and to place the shades in the windows with the logos facing out. The effect was even more exciting than a plain sign would have been.

Signage should always be clear and well maintained. Nothing says careless like burned-out bulbs, missing letters, torn banners, and peeling or faded paint.

22. Spreading the Wealth

There are so many ways today to get your services and products to market that there is no excuse for most businesses to ignore as many of them as they do. Your wares can be sold in the stores of others. If a bookstore can sell coffee, why couldn't a coffee shop sell books? If you market earth-friendly detergents, couldn't you find a plumber who'd like to make a little extra money selling septic-safe laundry soap? The possible combinations are limited only by your imagination.

You can market just about anything by telephone, so long as you aren't violating do-not-call registries or otherwise offending potential customers. If you are in the carpet business, why not recruit a cheerful, competent staff member to sit down with the phone book and call every lawyer in town offering a free estimate and an attractive discount on office carpeting? If you are an electrician, you could call every small retailer in town and offer a free safety and surge inspection, with a discount on some basic service. You can also follow up on any of these calls with a faxed offer. Make sure it has an expiration date that is no more than a month away.

Direct mail is a major way to stimulate sales, not just make people aware of you. Mailings should always offer something of value if customers act within a specific period. Product lists, service menus, and special deals are all part of a mailing program.

Part of your marketing plan should be to grow your distribution so that it is as wide as possible.

23. More than Lip Service

Hundreds, possibly thousands, of books have been published on the subject of customer service, but many companies still just don't get it. Good customer service, and all that it entails, is the key to success. "Make me feel important" is all that customers ever want in a business transaction. Every study confirms that consumers put this at the top of their list of factors when they are deciding where to buy. No matter how fabulous your product may be, poor service will drive away customers. Alternatively, people who get good service will remember you and come back even when the product didn't exactly meet their needs or expectations.

Most studies show that 40 percent of customers who have a bad service experience tell their friends. Less than half that number tell their friends about a good experience. If you can get rid of the bad service, you're already winning. If you can replace it with consistently good service, you're batting a thousand!

24. After-Marketing

A sale is only the first step toward creating a customer. What you do after that is what creates loyalty and repeat business, the easiest sales increase to generate. It's much more costly to get a new customer than to stimulate an existing customer to become a more frequent buyer.

This is the key to a loyal customer base and to referrals. Maintain a V.I.P. list of regular customers and mail to them regularly. Send them birthday cards. Offer them special services or products aimed just at them. Send them thank-you letters for referrals.

Make sure your staff members thank customers for coming. If you offer any kind of valet service, don't forget that attitude and efficiency are the last and lasting impression that your customers will be receiving about your business.

25. Complaints Are Your Best Friend

The great Russian novelist Leo Tolstoy wrote, "All happy families resemble one another, but each unhappy family is unhappy in its own way."

Every complaint that your business receives should be viewed as a golden opportunity because every unhappy customer gives you a chance to show how uniquely you care about his or her satisfaction. Every employee should be fully aware that you have a policy of never arguing, rarely disagreeing, and always trying hard to fix whatever's wrong. Burn it into your culture that 90 percent of unhappy customers never complain, at least not to you. Instead, they don't come back, and then they tell all their friends.

Ford Motor Co. once did a study that found that satisfied customers tell 8 people and dissatisfied customers tell 22. The Internet has probably increased that statistic by many times. Handling complaints is an essential promotional tactic. Do everything you can to address each and every one. Make sure that your staff is empowered to make decisions when a supervisor isn't available to do it for them.

Ritz-Carlton Hotels gives its front-line employees spending authority up to $2,000 to take care of their customer's needs. A member of the housecleaning staff can offer a guest a complete refund on the room if the guest is dissatisfied. When a guest in one of the hotel restaurants isn't pleased with the meal, the server can refund her money on the spot and give her a certificate for a free dinner in the future.

One of the highest values that customers look for in a transaction, and in the businesses they deal with, is a no-risk satisfaction guarantee. Make sure you give it, and forget about the cost because whatever the cost is, you'll usually end up making more on the goodwill you've created. It's surprisingly easy to turn an unhappy customer into a loyal customer.

When employees are empowered to make customer service decisions on the spot, their self-esteem and company pride go up. The person who has a complaint feels better and is likely to become a repeat customer.

Too often we put an employee behind the front desk or counter, make the desk too high, the information confusing or wrong, and the room too hot or too cold, then wonder why the employee can't function. Why not understand what the customers want, set the standard, and involve the employees in creating the process? With this approach, everyone becomes warm and friendly, and everyone knows how to up-sell.

26. Hire Eagles, not Turkeys

Ross Perot once said, in discussing how to hire good people, "Eagles don't flock. You have to find them one at a time."

When discussing this most important aspect of marketing, I often hear the same tired responses: "You can't get good help." "Nobody cares about customer service anymore." "I can't afford to hire the good people." "These kids today. . . ."

I know it's hard to find eagles in the huge flock of turkeys that are out there looking for "a job." All the turkeys have learned to dress up like eagles. So we hire them thinking that they're eagles, and when they start acting like turkeys, we figure it's a training problem. Then, when the training program doesn't help, we figure it's a motivational problem, and we institute a motivational program. But if that eagle really is a turkey, things won't improve, and we end up with a trained, motivated turkey.

You should be constantly on the lookout, one by one, for people who shine, and try to keep them as long as possible. Whatever business you're in, it should be a caring business. Look for people who are naturally gifted in the art of relating.

You will find a number of tactics in this book for doing just that: giving a bonus to employees who find a successful candidate, asking your customers to recommend people, and going out yourself and handing job application invitations to people who give you good customer service elsewhere.

Every person who works in your business is a sales representative, even the receptionist in a law firm or a dentist's office. Each and every person who is in contact with your customers must be trained to sell your products and services with a smile.

27. Sampling Is Simple

No matter what business you're in, sampling will help customers remember you. This is standard procedure in many food-related businesses, but the same principle applies in many other businesses.

Sampling does not always have to take place within your establishment. If you are in the food business, you can deliver samples to area businesses at lunchtime. If you own a bookstore, you can give away free copies of novelty books or magazines or the local weekly newspaper. Often you can partner with a vendor who will give you a special price for samples to be given away. Look around your business and try to find something of value that your customers would appreciate having and would be likely to come back and buy in the future.

Keep tabs on how well the samples are received, and measure the sales of the item being sampled while the promotion is taking place and in the weeks after.

28. Credit Where It's Due

The easier you make the purchase, the more people will buy. It's worth the cost and paperwork to accept as many credit cards as possible. Nothing is more of a turnoff or an embarrassment to a customer than being short of cash and having to write a check.

If your business is small and you haven't been able to justify the setup costs for a credit card machine, consider partnering with another business to process your credit card sales. Even service businesses like lawyers and accountants should be able to accept credit cards.

29. High Finance

Individual charge accounts for customers create increased business. Especially in an upscale establishment, a customer's ego will be stroked when he can simply sign for the check. Giving credit can be tricky, so make sure you carefully credit-check anyone to whom you offer a charge account. And make sure you manage your receivables so that charge accounts don't get too big before you discover you've got a deadbeat on your hands.

30. A Word from Our Sponsor

One of the biggest mistakes that businesses make is advertising poorly, in the wrong media, at the wrong time, with the wrong message. More money is squandered on bad advertising than on any other aspect of marketing. Too often, businesses shout over the heads of potential customers, or target the wrong group, or send inefficient or confusing messages.

Avoid the shotgun approach—mass communication. If you own a sporting-goods store, why would you spend thousands of dollars to run a boring ad in a large newspaper that reaches thousands of people who live outside your trading range? Yet marketers do this all the time.

Don't guess about advertising. Consider hiring a professional to help you create great ads, and make sure that every single ad you run includes a specific offer, such as a discount or a free sample, with a specified time limit. This is crucial to advertising promotions.

An ad that says, "We're the friendliest veterinarian in town," is never going to be as successful as an ad that says, "Come in by the end of the month and get a free month's supply of tick repellent." Or if friendliness is one of your strong points, tell people, "Come and visit us, and if our staff doesn't smile, your purchase is free." Then, make sure your staff smiles!

31. Communing with the Community

You will find a number of promotional tactics in this book that involve partnering with or reaching out to your community. The more you get involved in your community, the higher your profits will be. This takes time and legwork more than money. Schools, charities, hospitals, religious institutions, and nonprofits of every stripe are good places to start. Consider adopting a favorite charity and collecting toys or food during the holiday season.

32. Coalitions of the Willing

One of the most overlooked opportunities in marketing is the chance to leverage your business with another noncompeting business. The possibilities are unlimited, from cross-promotional display signs and circulars, to special offers for specific products and services, to event partnerships, to sharing mailing lists and advertisements.

Potential cross-promotion partners include high-customer-count businesses such as gas stations, video stores, department stores, movie houses, and sports arenas. Choose quality operations that are traditionally respected for their products and service. Businesses should be conveniently located within the same trading zone, preferably only a few blocks away.

Cross-promotion partners will usually involve an equal trade-off: You distribute a realtor's business card or flyer, and the realtor provides newcomers to the community with your brochure and a special invitation.

The benefits are manifold. You can quickly increase your marketing base, cut your marketing costs, and gain goodwill.

33. Going Public

Another frequently overlooked and even more frequently misunderstood opportunity is free publicity for an event or promotion. Charity promotions and benefits will get you noticed. If you cannot afford a public relations agency, you can become your own. Call your local newspaper or radio station. Tell it about what you think is newsworthy. If the newspaper or radio station agrees, it will help you out.

Study your local press to see what areas it is most interested in. If you live in a military town, consider special events for military families that the media might cover. If you have an employee with an unusual story, call the local papers to tip them off, and invite the reporters to come to your store or business for the interview. When the photographer shows up, make sure that you or your employee is sitting in front of a big sign for your business.

If you received a shipment of merchandise and discovered a tarantula hiding inside, that's news. If your shop manager just won an award for a short story he wrote, it's potentially news. If you've invented a new flavor of ice cream, that's news. If you're an accountant who discovered an overlooked tax deduction, that's news.

Look around your entire business and try to find reasons that the public would like to know about something you or members of your staff have done. People stories are the bread and butter of local newspapers, radio, and television.

34. Join This

More than ever, people are joining clubs and associations that reflect their interests. Your own memberships will serve to involve you in community events and help you to make real friendships. Clubs and associations almost always call upon the services of businesses owned by their members before going outside for these same services.

Encourage your employees to do the same, and, if you can, offer to pay any dues. There are clubs or groups for every possible interest: pets, gardening, history, alternative health, children's issues, educational, writing, music, religion, sports, business, and community. Get involved and connected, and people will think of you when they need your product or service.

35. Team Efforts

Sponsoring sports teams is a time-honored way to get your name in front of a lot of potential customers. Members of the team you sponsor will frequent your establishment and recommend it to others. You can sponsor a team with cash, or you can provide a product or service that the team needs or a venue for its off-field events.

Organized youth sports are among the fastest-growing activities in the country. Boys' lacrosse, for example, is the fastest growing of all youth sports. If there isn't a team in your community, try starting one. For every player on a sponsored team, there are numerous family members who will learn about your business and become potential customers.

36. The Word on Word of Mouth

When was the last time you saw a mass-market advertising campaign for Starbucks? How about Paul Newman's food company? Or the Virgin Group of companies? What about the restaurant chain Cheesecake Factory, or Tommy Bahama clothing? These companies don't emphasize their advertising. They don't need it. The fuel that's made them grow and prosper is word of mouth, that fabled quality that all truly successful businesses seem to have.

How you get word-of-mouth commitment from your customers is by opening yours. Talk to your customers, and listen to what they have to say. When they give you advice, try not to dismiss it offhand, but hear it, digest it, and take away that which makes sense.

Ask your happy, loyal customers for referrals. You may be surprised to learn that they are glad to oblige. After all, they discovered your great business, and this gives them a chance to look smart in the eyes of their friends, relatives, organizational comrades, and business associates. When they do oblige, make sure to thank them with gusto, both verbally and in deed. Give them a gift, a discount, something of true value. Reward good behavior and it will reward you.

In short, build community by making sure that you and your staff are constantly creating relationships that last.

37.   Take a Flyer on Flyers

If they are done well, designed well, and distributed properly, flyers and other handouts announcing special events and promotions are a cheap, easy way to generate excitement and sales. Remember to maintain your brand personality, logo, and so on throughout. Use as much color as you can afford, and hire an expert if you don't feel confident that you can produce the best result. In various sections of this book, you'll find some tips about different kinds of offers to put on flyers that'll get great results.

Make sure you distribute your literature in such a way that it won't be considered a nuisance. Depending on your type of business, doorknob hangers and other literature can be delivered to front doors and tucked under windshield wipers. Look for special occasions with tie-ins to your business, such as sporting or entertainment events, and put your flyers on cars in the parking lot.

But be cautious! Make sure that the high school kid you hired didn't either dump them all in the trash or put them where they will annoy people. A great promotional tactic is only as good as its execution.

38.   What's the Book on You?

General brochures, catalogs, and price lists are where you get to tell your whole story, talk about your products and services, and project your business's personality in an uncluttered environment. It's where potential customers can take their time to get to know you. And brochures often get passed on to other potential customers. People can get these printed materials directly from you at your place of business or by mail, or they can pick them up at other locations, such as clubs, churches, or chambers of commerce, and from promotional partners.

These documents should be professionally produced and should be as crisp and clear and pleasing to look at as possible. Effective copywriting and graphic design are specific talents, and if you lack them, find someone who has them.

Imagery is the most powerful tool you have, so choose your pictures and graphics carefully. You should be able to "read" what the picture shows from a distance. Muddy, low-contrast, out-of-focus pictures send exactly the wrong message. Use pictures to help tell your story and convey the friendliness, excitement, or other mood that you want to project. Some great choices are smiling people, a view of your place of business, attractive photos of products, maps, and so on.

This is not the time to skimp. Your brochure should be as inviting as your storefront, lobby, or other "face" that you show the public. A poorly produced brochure is *not* better than none at all.

39. Spread the Good Word

As a businessperson, you are an expert on something, whether it's the law or how to install wallpaper. So tell this to the world, or hire a ghostwriter to help you. Figure out what knowledge you have that the general public would be most interested in, and write an article about it for your local newspaper. If you make bagels, write an article about the history of bagels and how they're made today versus the old days. If you are a tree trimmer, write about tree health and care or the varieties of trees that prosper in your zone. If you cut hair, write about how styles have changed over the years, or whatever happened to Brylcreem.

Write the article and pitch it to all your local publications, even the little weeklies and throwaways. If any of them bite, instead of being paid for your writing, ask to be allowed to mention your business name and phone number.

Even if no one wants your articles, have them printed up to look as if they were printed in a newspaper, with justified columns, and print up some copies to give away to your customers.

40. Winning Is Everything

Contests and sweepstakes are guaranteed excitement builders, if they are done properly. There are an unlimited number of permutations on this basic theme and an unlimited number of affordable ways to make the payoff have real value and increase your sales. You will find many such promotional tactics in the following pages. You can even buy fortune cookies with customized messages inside, such as discounts on purchases. Each customer gets a cookie, breaks it open, and wins whatever discount the slip says. Consider what a different level of energy is created when you compare "Ten percent off this week" with "Come in, have a cookie, and find out if you got up to 20 percent off your purchase." You mix the discounts to achieve the result you want—a few 20 percents, some 15s, and a lot of 10s. This tactic often encourages people to buy more because they know that the discount is good only for that day, so they load up.

Contests call attention to your business, and they also give you an excuse to collect names and addresses for your customer mailing list. Always try to fashion these promotions so that people must come to your business in order to participate.

41. Little House in a Hurry

Booths, kiosks, stands, and the banners and other displays that go along with them are ways to take your business on the road at very low cost and high visibility. These inexpensive, portable structures should be kept ready for use when you need an additional location in a hurry.

Charity events, fairs, sporting events, street festivals, flea markets, and so on are great places for customers to sample your product, receive a brochure, and talk to a salesperson, and for you to sell your products and services. Often a percentage of your proceeds will go to the event in exchange for allowing you to participate. Consider it cheap advertising.

42. Be Cooperative

If you sell products made by others, your vendors often will be happy to furnish free advertising materials about their products or share the cost of producing your ad materials. Cooperative ad programs are common. Look for products that you think you could stimulate sales of with a little help from the vendor. Look for opportunities to link this promotional tactic with another, like a special event or a charity drive. Vendors will also often give free prizes for contests and sweepstakes.

Consider this technique when planning any of your promotions.

43. A Classified Act

An unusual place for many businesses to advertise, but one that is highly targeted and often successful, is in the classifieds. A great-looking display ad in the classifieds stands out and is an inexpensive way to announce special promotions and events.

If your target audience is largely male, try the car ads. They are largely read by men. Try running an ad in the help wanted section, the other most-read classifieds in the paper. Look at the classified listings in your local papers and see if there are other categories that might appeal to your customer base.

44. Putting On a Display

Traditional display ads in the main sections of the newspaper are a prime marketing medium for small businesses, but they are often prohibitively expensive. Test this kind of marketing cautiously, and be sure to track your results carefully to see if the return is worth the investment. When an ad seems to work well, save it and reuse it from time to time. Don't change successful ads just for the sake of changing them. One of the cardinal rules of promotion is to find what works and keep doing it until it doesn't.

Investigate whether your local newspapers offer zone advertising. Some publications offer to run your ads only in certain geographical locations at cheaper rates. This could be a good idea because buying the full press run probably means that you're reaching an audience that includes many people who aren't in your trading area.

Also, don't overlook the small weekly newspapers that are common in every community. Their ad rates are very cheap, and they are well read by people who are interested in the most local news.

45. Looking Slick

Magazine advertising requires a longer planning cycle, so it can be difficult to use it for special promotions unless you are well prepared far ahead of time. Magazine ads (magazines are known as "slicks" because of their shiny paper) add to your credibility, but they can be quite costly. Many publications put out regional editions that can target your market at a lower cost.

Don't forget to consider trade and other categories of publications as well as consumer magazines. Look for places that your competition may have overlooked.

46.   Yellow's not Mellow

Advertising in the Yellow Pages can be tricky and expensive, and you don't necessarily have to be there unless your competition is. If you do advertise against your competition, make yours the largest ad you can comfortably afford because the larger ads appear in the book ahead of the smaller ones.

Save money by *not* using bold type. Also, do *not* be talked into using color. Studies show that it makes no difference in effectiveness. Every Yellow Pages ad should have a clear, short headline, and it should make an offer or guarantee.

Your display ad in the Yellow Pages should be carefully thought out because you have to submit it months before the books are printed and distributed, and it's there for a whole year. Read your contract carefully, and make sure the ad is the best it can be. Study the Yellow Pages and see which ads you think are the most effective.

47.   On Deck

Marketing companies compile coupons from groups of area businesses into deck cards and mail the entire packet to target areas or groups. These can be effective and relatively inexpensive, but make sure that your card is well designed and makes a specific offer, such as a trial buy-one-get-one-free offer. And always make the offer good for a limited time. That's what motivates potential customers to act.

48.   Wish You Were Here

Postcards are the best, cheapest, and most effective way to maintain a conversation with your existing customer list. Most marketing experts recommend a mailing program in which you send a postcard once a month for six to nine months. Always make a special offer, and always make it time-limited.

Postcards are also a very effective way to speak to individual customers. A simple thank-you with a special offer is appreciated by your audience and increases loyalty. Every business that knows its customers' names and addresses and can track their buying habits should always be thanking customers every time they make a purchase.

49. Letter Perfect

While slightly more costly, direct-mail letters serve a function similar to that of postcards, but they give you more space to tell the story and make an offer. Use direct-mail letters for longer-term follow-ups. You can combine your pitch with a plug for your favorite community charity (no politics or religion!). "Don't forget Toys-for-Tots this Christmas, and come see us for our preseason specials on photo albums to keep those treasured memories from getting mislaid."

50. Things Are Looking Up

There are some very exciting promotional tools that are a little more work and expense, but that really grab the public's attention: balloons, blimps, and searchlights. These boost foot traffic for special events and promotions.

For example, try releasing hundreds of balloons with flyers attached in a crowd of people after the theater or at a stadium. It will be unexpected, and it will get a lot of attention in a short period of time.

51. Isn't That Special

An entire industry exists to supply businesses with every conceivable type of advertising specialty with your name on it, and many of these can be powerful promotional tools. One of the simplest and most successful of these specialties, which you can order yourself from a local printer, is scratch pads. Scratch pads always get used, and each sheet is a new ad. The pad often sits on a counter or desk, so the message and your name are being constantly reinforced, burned into the memory of the potential customer.

Calendars, refrigerator magnets, pens and pencils, plastic drinking cups, and sunshades for your car dash are just a few of the more common items offered. Search on the Internet for suppliers and look for items that are useful and inexpensive to give away to your customers.

52. Stick to the Script

Create scripts that your staff can use when making sales calls or just answering the phone. You may want to hire an experienced copywriter to help with this because you don't want your script to be too wooden or to contain any false notes. Scripts should include key sales ideas, questions, and suggestions for closing a sale.

Remember one of the first rules of selling: People like to talk about themselves. Make sure your telephone people are asking customers about themselves, their needs, and their wants.

53. Take-One Boxes

Any stationery supply store sells brochure display holders that you can load up with your flyers or other printed materials and place in locations that are frequented by your prospects. Be sure to offer a bring-this-with-you special for discounts or free samples. Track these sales carefully to make sure that your flyers are in the right places. This is an excellent cross-promotion tactic to use with other noncompeting retailers.

54. Ride the Airwaves

Radio commercials can be very effective, especially in smaller markets, where airtime is less expensive and competition among stations for audiences is less crowded. Ads run 30 to 60 seconds in length and may or may not have background music.

Use radio as part of a campaign to carry out a particular theme or promotion. Prerecord your commercials and present them to the radio station in cassette form or as an electronic file. If your business will plug the radio station in return, the stations may help with the commercial or provide it for you.

Radio is all about repetition. It takes up to two dozen impressions over a very short period of time to get listeners to remember your message. Running one spot a day over a period of weeks is wasted money. If you can't run an aggressive program, don't bother. Try something else.

55.   The Case for Cable

Billions and billions of dollars are poured into producing and broadcasting lavish television ads, and most of that money is wasted because the environment is so cluttered that no one remembers much of what they've seen, and most viewers use the remote to avoid watching the ads. However, there is a very strong case to be made for local cable advertising. It remains a fairly well-kept secret that you can buy television time inexpensively on major cable channels like A&E or Bravo or the Food Channel, and have your ad piped only into specific neighborhoods of your choosing.

Most cable providers will produce your commercial on videotape for a relatively low cost—as little as $2000—or sometimes for free in exchange for your commitment to an ad campaign. Your cost to air an ad each time can range from as little as $25 to as much as several hundred dollars. As with radio, you will need to run a solid three-month program of constant repetition. The beauty of cable is that you can segment your market by neighborhood and related interest. For example, if you run a home decorating business, you'll want to buy time on Discovery or The Learning Channel near home improvement shows.

Make sure that your ad attractively and clearly conveys the theme and value of your business, and especially be sure that you let people know which community you're in. Television viewers are impressed by TV ads that feature their neighborhood businesses.

56.   The Gifted Approach

Gift certificates are an easy, cheap, effective promotional tool that can be used in many ways: to reward loyal customers, to reward employees, and to encourage new trials. They can be promoted during the holiday season or used as special mailings for customers' birthdays and other occasions. You will find many tactics later in this book that rely on gift certificates.

If you have a product or service that is high profit and a good seller, direct your gift certificates toward those purchases to spur additional sales.

57.   Basket Cases

If they are done well and attractively, gift baskets are a great way to introduce people to your product line and ring up additional sales during holiday periods. Be sure to include coupons for discounts to get those customers to return for additional purchases.

Gift baskets can also be used to win goodwill with local charitable and other organizations, introducing potential new customers to your brand, your product line, and your commitment to the community.

58. Firing Up the Troops

You will find a number of tactics in this book that are aimed at motivating your staff. Too many businesses overlook the enormous promotional potential of their employees. Your employees should be fully engaged in your promotional plans, and you should solicit their experience, advice, and feedback. After all, they are your front-line troops. They are seeing the battle up close.

One way to win your employees' attention and commitment is to encourage them to come up with promotional ideas on a regular basis. Once a month, pick the best idea and try it out. Reward the winning employee with a cash bonus. Remember, reward good behavior, and it will reward you.

59. Delivering the Goods

Home delivery is not just for pizza anymore. Too many businesses see this as a vague opportunity, but don't want to go to the trouble of trying it out. It may be true that delivering a bottle of Aunt Hattie's Maalox and her favorite shampoo is time-consuming for a busy drugstore and, by itself, not profitable. But think about the loyalty you create by doing so, and think about the number of people that Aunt Hattie might tell, and about where she will shop for other products that she might not have realized you can offer.

To deliver your products, you can hire unemployed retirees, many of whom would be happy to make a little money, get out and about, meet some of their neighbors, and perform a valuable service. And when your sign is on the vehicle, your business is being advertised with each delivery.

Delivery people should be independent contractors who provide their own cars, auto insurance, and gas. Hire people who smile and relate well to others. Charge $1 for delivery, and pay the delivery people the minimum wage plus the delivery fee and tips. Provide a separate phone line for delivery call-ins. With the delivery, always include a list of your other products and a coupon that is good for a discount on some other product. Save the customer's contact information and remember to send a thank-you card, a follow-up letter, and even an occasional phone call to see if there's anything else the customer might need.

To promote this program, provide menus or product lists to offices and use them as doorknobbers in your local area.

60. Ready–Set-to-Go

Most food businesses should have take-out service, and nearly all businesses that sell consumer goods of any kind should offer call-in service that allows orders to be phoned in for pickup. Use the same menu or price list that you do for delivery. Provide a coupon with every order— for example, offering a free beverage with each $5 worth of carry-out food. Use the same methods mentioned in Tactic 59 to promote the new take-out service.

61. Easy Does It

Whatever you do, make, or sell, be sure that it's easy for your customers to buy it. Be easy to find, easy to call, easy to order from, easy to deal with, and easy to pay. Look at all your systems, processes, advertising, promotions, traffic flow, and signage—look at every aspect of your business with one thought in mind: How can I remove every conceivable obstacle or hindrance to creating a customer, building a relationship, making a sale?

Use mystery shoppers (people who pose as customers to test your service or products) frequently. If you can't afford to hire a professional mystery-shopper service, recruit friends and acquaintances, or consider swapping the job with another business, with your employees mystery-shopping that business while its employees mystery-shop yours.

62. Deliver What You Promise

One of the biggest mistakes businesses make in the marketing wars is to put money, time, and human resources into a promotional campaign and then forget to train their front-line staff to deliver. Great marketing can kill your business if you aren't prepared.

In 2003, McDonald's reported the first quarterly loss in its history, right after it had spent more than $100 million on a campaign that said, "Come in and see us smile." During this campaign, and as part of my consulting work, I visited 45 McDonald's, and I didn't see a single server smile.

McDonald's spent 4 percent of its revenues on advertising to drive customers to its stores, only to be confronted by unsmiling, unmotivated servers.

If your employees are not happy with their work environment, how can you expect the customers who come through your doors to be satisfied? Your employees pass their attitude right along to the customer. It's up to you to hire good people and treat them well, so that they will pass on enthusiasm and excitement, rather than boredom and discontent.

63. Shop the Competition

Too many businesspeople neglect to keep tabs on their competition. How in the world will you know where you stand in your market and your category if you don't keep a weather eye on the other guy?

Do competitive shopping, but go with an open mind. We all have a tendency to look for everything that the competition is doing wrong. It makes us feel better and superior, and it helps confirm that what we are doing is right.

Here's a better idea: Send your employees out to do your competitive shopping. Give them the assignment to come back with 10 things that the other guys are doing right. Think about that. What could you possibly learn from paying attention to what your competitor is doing wrong? What you really want to know is why those customers are in his store instead of yours.

Your employees will come back with ideas that they can incorporate into their work. Furthermore, you will get a better result from your internal customers, your employees, than you will if the boss goes out and comes back to tell the employees what she learned. If that happens, the employees will not have bought into it or internalized it.

Don't do this once and forget about it. Make it a regular program. Send your staff out once a month or once a quarter, whichever is appropriate for your business.

64. Making History

How many times have you said to yourself, "I need to do a promotion, but I can't remember the details of the one we did last year that worked so well"?

Keep a notebook or a folder on your computer that includes every marketing promotion you have ever run, along with a close analysis, a cost sheet, and a copy of the promotional piece and other materials. Yes, it's work. By the time a promotion is over, you're sick of it and ready for a break.

But nothing tells you what works better than what worked well. We tend to want a cool new idea, something that'll get us excited. Instead, you could take an old idea that worked well, tweak it, and do it again. You may be bored with it, but your customers may not be. Sometimes the same promotion at the same time of year works better than the cool new idea. What's the goal, to increase your sales or relieve your boredom?

65. Move the Goal Posts

A famous study done in the early twentieth century tried to find a system that would motivate new employees to reach certain performance standards. What was learned should be incorporated in your business.

A group of new, unskilled employees were given a production quota that was hard to achieve in a set period of time. Predictably, the group missed the mark. A second group, also unskilled, got progressive goals—the bar was raised a little more each week. As the workers' proficiency increased, the goals were raised. At the end of the same period of time, the second group had met the ultimate goal.

Every business operator should attack each of his goals with the same measured approach. Home runs are great, but the game is really won by singles and doubles and good fielding and relentless pitching, inning by inning.

66. Seven Steps to Success

There are seven steps to creating a killer marketing plan. You should check yourself against these steps every time you run a promotion or other marketing effort:

1. Gather data.
2. Analyze them.
3. Set goals.
4. Develop strategy.
5. Implement the plan.
6. Track the progress.
7. Evaluate the result.

67. Fish When the Fish Are Biting

Most businesses focus on fixing what they think is wrong. If you try to increase sales on Monday and Tuesday, when business is going to be slow anyway, you squander the opportunity to fish when the fish are biting. If weekends are your busy time, run your promotions to improve the opportunity you already have, when people already have an urge to spend.

If Mother's Day is your busiest day of the year, run a promotion. Unless you're truly swamped, why wouldn't you take advantage of the opportunity to introduce new customers to your business? A busy day like that is a terrific opportunity to promote something else. Make sure to have flyers and coupons to give to each customer to keep them coming back.

68. Give Them a Break

Give your staff a break between promotions. It's hard to keep getting pumped for one promotion after another if you don't have a rest. Your customers need a rest also.

Make sure your promotions are timed properly, or you'll set yourself up for failure. Motorists aren't interested in an air-conditioning tune-up in the dead of winter.

69. No Risk, Big Gain

Turn the tables on the risk factor. Your customers are accustomed to bearing the risk. Surprise them by bearing it yourself. It pays in first-time trials and loyalty. People will buy merchandise with a spotty record for quality if they know that they can always return it. If you are the first in your field to assume the risk, you gain a big advantage over the other guys.

Most businesses veil their guarantees. They make customers ask and squirm. If you emphasize the no-risk guarantee and give customers something valuable as a bonus, you've got the makings of a sale, and of a repeat customer.

70. Lieutenant MAC

One of the most difficult tasks in coordinating promotional activities is managing the personal selling required at the customer level by staff and management. Communication from the support team down to the staff often takes a circuitous path and, like the childhood game of whispering down the lane, results in miscommunication, or no communication at all.

One way to fill this gap is to have a marketing activities coordinator, or Lieutenant MAC. This is an individual whom you employ on a part-time to full-time basis to administrate, manage, and report to you on any marketing plan and the tactical maneuvering it requires. This person is specifically assigned to drive your carefully conceived plan so that it runs as smoothly as it would if 100 percent of your time could be spent on marketing alone.

71. The Multicultural Wars

Diversity marketing—reaching out to specific ethnic groups—is basic Marketing 101. In your hiring, your visual ads (whether print, TV, or Internet), and your radio ads, you need to show consumers that you're reflecting your customer base. If you show only white people in your ads, or only men, or only women, you are telling some customers that they are not important to you, that you don't value them and don't want their business.

Ethnic self-identifiers live in a world that already excludes them. That's not a message you want to send consumers. Diversity should be in every aspect of your marketing. Note that diverse markets—African American, Hispanic, Asian—are growing faster than the traditional white market.

You have to match marketing with your operations in order to be successful. Make sure that your staff understands and buys into why this is so vital. The worst thing you can do is drive diverse markets to your front door, only to offend them or turn them off once they're there.

5

Marketing to Your Internal Customer

In the previous chapter, I outlined some basic ways to take the temperature of your staff and get them engaged as your partners in business. Here are a few more general tactics for hiring and retaining good employees, and for getting your managers and staff to focus on the marketing lifestyle. In later chapters, you will find some tactics that are intended to reward staff as part of specific promotional techniques.

72.   Recruit 24/7

Best For   All business types

Objective   Hire better staff members and keep them longer

Target   Staff (internal customers)

You should always be recruiting, all the time, even when you don't need anyone. Because sooner or later, you will. Many years ago, the manager of a small rural hotel was sitting quietly at the front desk late one night when a couple arrived. They seemed somewhat tired and bitter, and the manager assumed that this was due to the harsh weather conditions outside. The gentleman, a man of some stature—maybe in his mid-fifties—approached the desk and asked the manager for a room. The manager kindly replied, "Sir, because of the harsh conditions outside, we are filled to the brim! Let me check if one of our suites is available." He checked, but there was not a single room available in the entire hotel. The gentleman glanced at his wife and let out a sigh.

The manager stood up and said, "Sir, there is not a room that I could find for you, but I can see that you are tired and in need of some rest.

Please take my room for the evening, and make yourselves comfortable." Not waiting for a reply, the manager stood up and walked the couple to his modest but well-kept room. The gentleman told him, "You know, one day I am going to call you, and you will be the manager at my hotel." The manager nodded politely as he brought the luggage into the room.

A few months later, the manager received a phone call from the gentleman asking if he would be interested moving to New York to manage his hotel. The gentleman, it turns out, was the owner of the greatest hotel in New York City—and now, because of his superb hospitality, the former manager of the small hotel is the manager of the Waldorf-Astoria.

Have some business cards printed up with your contact information and the following statement: "You were really terrific. If you're ever looking for another job, please give me a call." The next time you encounter great customer service and think, I wish my employees were like that, hand that person one of those cards.

One of the best places to recruit is from your competitors. Visit the other businesses in your category and neighborhood. Study their staffs, and when you see someone you wish was working for you, discreetly give that person one of your cards.

You should recruit seven days a week, constantly. Don't wait until you need somebody. That's when you make choices out of desperation rather than inspiration.

73. Create a Unique Training Manual

Best For   All business types

Objective   Train and motivate internal customers (employees)

Target   Staff

Marketing to your staff is not just about telling them what to do and how to do it. Every year American companies fill our landfills with truckloads of unread, unabsorbed training literature and videos. Be creative and avoid making a job out of doing the job. Here are a couple of examples to start you thinking.

At Hard Rock Café, they've taken the training manual and turned it into a comic book. The company is marketing to, and hiring, young people who are visual and who want to have fun. It even recruited some of its employees to help write the content and draw the comics. As a result, the staff of Hard Rock Café has a direct interest in the training and motivation of new hires.

An unexpected side benefit: The comic book training manuals have become collector's items, and some Hard Rock employees keep them on their coffee tables at home because they think they look cool.

Maybe a comic book isn't your style. Nordstrom's, which is considered one of the world's best retailers for staff competence and customer service, gives every new employee a handbook that is, in fact, a printed card that keeps it simple and dignified:

"Welcome to Nordstrom. We're glad to have you with the company. Our number one goal is to provide outstanding customer service. Set both your personal and professional goals high. We have great confidence in your ability to achieve them. Nordstrom Rules: Rule #1–Use your good judgment in all situations. There will be no additional rules. Please feel free to ask your department manager, store manager, or division manager any question at any time."

74. Back-Office Data

Best For   All business types

Objective   Create a statistical picture of where your business has been over the last three years, to use as a baseline to measure how well your promotions are working

Target   Managers

At least once a year, take your spreadsheets and other bookkeeping data and plot them on graphs. Look at the trends. I recommend plotting a three-year trend. If you do only two years, the results may be skewed by unusual events like a blizzard, road construction, or some other nonrepeating factor over which you have no control. This helps you see where the predictable peaks and valleys are for scheduling your promotions. You may think you know where those peaks are, and you may be right. But more often than not, business managers find hidden surprises in these charts.

Break your sales down as much as you can—by part of the day, transaction size, weekday versus weekend, product or service, and so on. This will show you where you're hurting and where you need a boost. It will also help you measure whether you were successful in your marketing goals.

Look at your product or service mix. What are your best sellers? Which items contribute the highest profit? If you're going to do a promotion to attract new customers, the best things to promote are your most popular products or services. Your existing customers already like them, so new customers will probably like them as well and are more likely to become repeaters.

What is your most profitable product? When you design staff incentives, you want to encourage your employees to sell your most profitable items or services. They may tend to sell the items that increase the ticket the most, but that you hardly make any money on.

6

Grand Opening/ Reopening Tactics

Overview and Timetable

A. Before Developing Opening Activities

As you plan your grand opening or reopening, analyze your trading area for marketing opportunities. Your success depends on local residents supporting your business for years to come, and it is vital that you be as relevant and meaningful to them as possible.

When formulating promotions, be sure to pay close attention to current activities that are going on within the community. As you develop your plan, pay attention to these objectives:

Stimulate trial

Increase frequency

Create excitement

Build your image

Specific programs will follow this overview and timetable.

B. Basic Activities and Materials

Giveaways are an important part of a successful opening. Have on hand balloons, hand puppets, buttons, and so on. Distribute "Be My Guest" cards—door openers for people who are hard to reach—to local retailers and V.I.P.s to generate a trial visit after your opening.

Display an "Opening Soon" banner at least two weeks before your opening. Display a "Now Open" banner during your first two weeks of operation and a "Grand Opening" banner throughout the Grand Opening celebration. The banners should be at least two- color and large enough to create visual awareness. Outdoor pennants add excitement and are easily noticed, but you may want to order two in case of vandalism or damage from weather.

C. Timetable

1. Get Ready

Ninety days before opening:

> Conduct and analyze a trading area background study.
> Begin staff recruitment and training.

Sixty days before opening:

> Develop grand opening promotional plans and staff incentives.
> Order premiums (giveaways).
> Order "Be My Guest" cards.
> Complete staff recruitment and training.
> Order generic grand opening displays.
> Buy grand opening media (if applicable).

Thirty days before opening:

> Develop public relations activities.

Fourteen days before opening:

> Display "Opening Soon" banner outside.
> Confirm all grand opening activity and incentive programs with your staff.
> Plan V.I.P. event and distribute "Be My Guest" cards.

2. Get Set

At opening:

> Host the V.I.P. event.
> Start two-week operational dry run prior to grand opening.
> Display "Now Open" sign.

3. Go

Fourteen days after opening:

Begin grand opening activities.
Display all grand opening generic and promotion elements.
Display grand opening banner.
Execute all activities.

4. Keep Going

Twenty-eight days after opening:

Evaluate grand opening activities.
Remove promotional display elements.
Continue monitoring operations.
Set six-month marketing goal.
Develop six-month marketing plan.

Two months after opening:

Implement six-month marketing plan.
Evaluate and monitor plan regularly.

75. V.I.P. Pre-Grand Opening Cocktail Party and Press Conference

Objective   Generate PR, increase awareness, create excitement, build your image

Target   Prominent members of the community, celebrities, politicians, and the press

In addition to inviting members of the community, extend invitations to the families of your staff as a gesture of goodwill. Consider this event a final operations checklist that ensures that all staff and all equipment are properly prepared, and that you are ready to open for business. You'll need a photographer; you may be able to get one to take photos for free in exchange for the invitation.

If you are in a nonfood business, you should hire a caterer to provide the best and most interesting food and beverages you can afford. If you are in the food-service business, try to offer your finest, including wine, if applicable. At the same time, keep it simple so that you don't put too much strain on your new facilities and staff.

Materials Press kits, company biographical information, "Be My Guest" cards. Optional: Flowers for female guests.

Timing

Four weeks prior:

> Set program goals and determine costs.
> Prepare press kits.
> Determine the people you wish to invite.

Three weeks prior:

> Send out invitations with "Be My Guest" cards to V.I.P.s.
> Send press releases, kits, and "Be My Guest" cards to press.
> Obtain photographer.
> Contact caterer to furnish food and beverage for event.

One week prior:

> Order flowers (optional).
> Plan food or other offerings.
> Go over details of food and beverages with caterer or chef.
> Discuss program with employees.

One day prior:

> Contact press to remind them of the event.
> Contact photographer to remind him or her of the event.
> Wine and food arrive for the event.
> Review program with employees.

Start:

> Flowers arrive and are arranged (optional).

76. Sample VIP Invitation Letter

(On your letterhead)

Dear (V.I.P.):

Just a short note to introduce myself. I'm _____, the owner of _____ at 1234 Main Street. As you may have noticed, we are getting ready to open in a couple of weeks. In fact, we are already planning our Grand Opening activities, and we would like you to join us.

On (day of week), (date), (time), the evening prior to our official opening, we are planning a cocktail party and press conference to introduce you and other prominent members of the community to our store. We would be very pleased if you would attend. A "Be My Guest" card is enclosed, which you need only present at the door. You are welcome to bring a guest. Just give me a call at (phone number) to let me know how many will be attending in your group.

I look forward to meeting you.

Sincerely,

Your Name

Title

Grand Opening Day Activities

The following programs are held on the designated grand opening day, which should ideally be a Saturday, when people are out shopping and doing errands anyway. The purpose of this program is to stimulate a trial visit and create an air of excitement.

77. $100 Ribbon-Cutting Ceremony

Construct a ribbon by taping one hundred $1 bills together or attaching the bills to a standard ribbon, and drape it across the front door of your restaurant. Contact a local dignitary to officially open the restaurant by cutting the ribbon, and present the ribbon to a local charity. Promote the donation given to the charity, learn as much about the charity as you can, and promote it through your press releases and PR.

78. High School Band

Ask the local high school band to participate in the opening ceremonies. In exchange for its appearance and cooperation, offer a contribution of $100 toward new instruments and uniforms.

79. Radio Remote

If possible, arrange to have an on-air radio personality in front of your store. Offer "Be My Guest" cards for his or her family, too, to encourage participation. Give the DJ T- shirts and coupons to give away.

80. Celebrity Appearance

Arrange to have a dignitary or celebrity appear to hand out photos and autographs. Make this arrangement with one of the V.I.P.s at the V.I.P. dinner party. It pays to get friendly.

81. Caricature Artist

Arrange to have a caricature artist on hand to draw caricatures of your customers. If customers don't want to buy them, arrange a discounted price and buy them yourself to hang around the store. To promote future visits by the "models" and their friends and family, make sure customers see you hanging up the caricatures.

82. Magician

Hire a magician to go around performing magic tricks. He should, with regularity, pull coupons from behind the ears of customers to promote future visits.

83. Million-Dollar Legacy

Best For   Most business types.

Objective   Increase awareness, increase community goodwill, create excitement, generate PR, build your image, stimulate trial

Target   Church groups, community leaders, existing and potential customers

This is a clever, thought-provoking tactic that draws a lot of attention on a limited budget. Let local residents in the community determine what the community will need in 100 years. Your business will deposit between $200 and $300 with a local bank. At average interest rates, the account will yield about $1 million in a hundred years. The bank should be able to determine the exact amount of the deposit that will be necessary to ensure a $1 million yield. Make the account a trust, payable to the person, group, or cause selected by the community. Have the bank draw up the trust, and make sure the exact yield is not guaranteed.

Use advertising and in-store materials to promote the event to members of the community. Make it clear that, as a newcomer to the community, you're depending on the people to decide who will receive the legacy.

Your advertising should explain how the program will work: Community members are invited to vote for the delegate—the person who will decide who will receive the trust after 100 years—with a limit of one vote per visit. Locals must come to either your business or the participating bank, ask a staff member for a ballot, vote for the chooser, and place the ballot in a sealed ballot box.

The counting of the ballots should be done by a local accountant under the supervision of local elected officials. Include newspaper editors and the banker who will handle the trust fund. The timing of the ballot counting should be arranged to generate the maximum possible publicity.

There should be a delay of a week or so between the announcement of the chooser and the announcement of his or her choice for the final recipient of the legacy. Officially, this is to give the chooser time to make a decision. Unofficially, it is to draw out the promotion and generate as much public interest as possible.

Your establishment could serve as a collection point to receive suggestions from the community and pass them on to the chooser. Local radio stations could also generate call-ins from listeners. Public speculation should be encouraged.

The final announcement of the recipient should come during your grand opening ceremonies. The chooser should announce the choice and explain how the choice was made. The banker should explain the mechanics of the trust fund. You or your manager should speak about being a new member of the community and how you hope to continue to be a good neighbor in the future. The date of the granting of the trust fund to the recipient should also be announced.

The chooser should present the trust fund to the recipient in a formal ceremony, again held at your establishment, with involved parties, including the media, invited as guests. Light refreshments should be served.

After the promotion, photos of the grand opening and the presentations should be posted around the business.

Materials   Ballots, ballot boxes, newspaper ads, press releases, posters

Timing

Six weeks prior:

Order ballots, ballot boxes.
Prepare advertising and buy media.
Prepare press releases.
Make initial contact with local bank.

Four weeks prior:

Begin advertising.
Mail/fax/email press releases.
Put out ballots and ballot box at participating bank.
Contact press and city officials for participation.

Two weeks prior:

Contact accountant to serve as ballot counter.
Arrange radio and newspaper announcement of chooser.

One week prior:

Announce chooser.
Follow up with a personal congratulatory phone call.
Begin acting as a collection point for community suggestions.

Grand opening:

Chooser announces recipient. Speeches are made.

One week after:

Trust is presented to recipient at a casual party at your business.

Follow up:

Decorate your business with memorabilia of the event.

84. Door Prize Contest

Objective Build mailing list, create excitement, generate PR, generate traffic, stimulate trial

Target Existing customers and potential new customers

This program is implemented prior to the actual grand opening. It offers any person a chance to win a special secret door prize by filling out an entry form during a pre-grand- opening visit.

After all the entries are collected, hold a drawing and contact the winner. Announce to the community and the media that the prize—a most unusual presentation—will be given at the grand opening ceremonies.

During the presentation, the winner and family are blindfolded and the comical prize is presented—an actual car door with a large bow and ribbon attached. Take off your winners' blindfolds and, after the laughter subsides, present the actual prize, something of real and ongoing value, such as a book a month for a bookstore, a dinner a month for a year for a restaurant, or something similar, as appropriate.

Materials   Entry blanks, entry box, auto door, blindfolds, 12 or 52 coupons, posters

Timing

Two weeks prior:

> Order or create entry blanks and entry box.
> Locate old car door.
> Order coupons.

One week prior:

> Conduct a staff meeting and explain the contest. Keep the door prize secret even from the staff, or it will surely leak.
> Display posters, entry forms, and entry box in a visible location.
> Contact news media via phone and press releases.

End date:

> Enter all names and addresses of entrants into a computer for your customer mailing list.

7

Four Walls
Promotions

85. Store Remodeling or Grand Reopening

Best For Retailers, restaurants.

Objective Create excitement, build your image, stimulate trial

Target Existing customers and potential new customers

Place ads in local papers to encourage existing and potential customers to see what's new at your place. Put a "Grand Reopening" banner outside to create awareness and bring in street traffic. If your budget allows, develop a special sweepstakes. Create an added-value offer, or use one of the tactics in this book, for special week-long savings on product items. Develop a special-events program for a Saturday opening, and create a party atmosphere with balloons, streamers, and so on. Use flyers as well as newspaper ads to promote the day. Here are some suggested activities:

Schedule local music groups for a happy hour of two to three hours.

Post special pricing during this event.

Provide free balloons, crayons for kids, Frisbees, and so on, as door prizes.

Offer inexpensive beverages, such as five-cent drinks. You may be able to make a deal with your local soft-drink bottler.

Place searchlights outside your store. They are great attention-getters, visible up to five miles away.

Materials Newspaper ad, flyers, sweepstakes promotional materials, balloons, streamers, posters, crayons, Frisbees, searchlights

Timing

Two weeks prior:

Set program goals and determine costs.
Write copy for flyers, ads, and posters.
Print posters.
Print flyers.
Buy media for one week and one day prior to event.
Arrange for searchlights.
Buy door-prize items and decorations.
Arrange for local musicians.

One week prior:

Distribute flyers.
Discuss program with staff and arrange staff schedule.
Talk to soft-drink bottler or other vendor.
Send out press releases.

One day prior:

Run second newspaper ad.
Decorate store and set out posters.

86. Connecting the Dots

Best For   All business types

Objective   Identify the neighborhoods or geographic areas that your current customers are coming from

Target   Current customers

A device that will let you identify your principal trading area, your neighborhood, is a dot map. Nothing tells a story more clearly than a picture. Buy a map of your area and attach clear plastic overlays. If you're measuring different parts of the day, use a different overlay for each part. This works for any sort of business.

If you're in the retail business, put the map in your lobby on an easel, and as each customer arrives, have someone ask that customer where she came from and place a self- sticking dot on that location on the map.

If you aren't in a retail business that lends itself to asking customers this question directly, put the map in a prominent place in your office or other workplace so that employees can see it, and have someone put the dots on it at the end of each day or week. Nothing tells the story of where your market is like a map.

This tactic is simple and enormously valuable, and customers and employees get a kick out of it. Everyone loves maps, people love seeing where everyone else comes from, and people love to be asked about themselves.

Make sure your staff understands how important this is and how it works.

When you're done, you have a starkly visual picture of your principal trading area. If you use different overlays for different parts of the day, week, or month, you can then tell what patterns there may be. Your business may be drawing from the commuters heading south on the main road in the morning, but from your backyard on the weekends. Armed with this information, you know exactly where to spend your marketing time and dollars.

87. Surprising and Delighting

Best For   All business types.

Objective   Increase goodwill, build loyalty, increase sales.

Target   Current customers.

Any day, at any time, you have the power to surprise and delight a customer. Remember to do it, and do it often. Get a reputation for giving something away—a product or a discount—when you don't have to. It's cheap marketing. Your customer will have his day pleasantly interrupted, he will tell a bunch of his friends, you will have increased your bond with him, and all of this will generate additional sales.

Your ability to do this is limited only by your imagination. If you're in the auto repair business, when a customer's car reaches 100,000 miles, you could give her a 10 percent "senior-vehicle" discount on certain services. That will keep your customer coming back.

If you are a lawyer, call up a client and offer a free consultation on a will or some other basic service that you think he might not realize that he needs. In the food or restaurant business, there's always something you can give away, even if it's just a cup of coffee or a glass of wine. The simple touch goes a long way. Remember, it's all about "Make me feel important!"

88. Make It Easy to Complain

Best For   All business types.

Objective   Improve customer service by handling complaints faster and better.

Target   Current customers, staff.

Nothing drives a customer away faster than to have a complaint and be told by an employee that the manager is out today, or the owner isn't around, or she'll take a message. Surveys find that about 70 percent of customers will remain loyal if it takes just one contact with your business to resolve a problem, but that only a third will remain loyal if it takes three or more tries.

As an owner or manager, this should be a great concern to you. You want to know about complaints and deal with them quickly. Every complaint is an opportunity. When there's a problem, silence is not golden.

A radical but commonsense idea is to put the manager's or owner's home or mobile phone number right on your business cards or other printed material, so that your customers find you when they need you.

If you're in a retail business, put out on the counter a stack of business cards with all the usual information and this statement: "If you have any comments at all about the store, please call me at home." Then list your off-hours contact number.

Your employees won't help noticing the walk-in customers eyeballing those cards and sticking them in their pockets. It creates accountability for your staff, and it lets your customers know that you care about their satisfaction.

89. Make Everything Come Up Roses

Best For   All business types.

Objective   Create excitement.

Target Current and prospective customers.

Flowers are an inexpensive way to freshen your look, whether you operate a professional office, a retail store, or a service business. Everyone loves flowers. They make people, both customers and employees, feel good. Flowers can be changed to reflect the changing seasons and to create excitement. People remember a beautiful display; it makes your business appear more prosperous, and some of your customers will tell their friends.

Here's the formula for how many flowers you will need for your business: Too many is exactly the right amount. Make your displays lush and unforgettable. A way to do this and save money is to make a deal with a florist to give away its brochure, share a mailing list, or engage in some other swap that will make it worthwhile for the florist to offer you a discount. If you give the flower supplier a place for its sign, it will put extra effort into making the display attractive. It's cheap advertising for the florist, too!

8

Existing Customers

90. Gift Certificates

Best For Most retailers and restaurants.

Objective Increase frequency.

Target Existing and prospective customers.

Gift certificates provide a twofold opportunity. They offer an additional product for you to sell to your customers—a gift—and an effortless way for the recipients to make a purchase, since they are already at your business. Having chosen a gift at your business reinforces your image in the purchaser's mind.

When the gift certificate is redeemed, you have achieved one of your most important goals: a trial visit from a new customer. By making sure that the new customer receives the best possible service and experience, you are on your way to developing a new loyal customer and enhancing the loyalty of the customer who purchased the gift.

Customers who are redeeming gift certificates should be tastefully reminded that they made their first visit because of the gift and that they can also purchase gift certificates for others.

91. Customer Wall of Fame

Best For Most business types.

Objective Build customer loyalty.

Target Current customers.

Your staff, servers, drivers, and cashiers provide especially good service to their best customers. It's only natural. Take the time to formally thank those customers, which will increase their loyalty and also give your staff some welcome recognition.

Ask your team members to put together a list of candidates for a Customer Wall of Fame. Put it in as prominent a place as is appropriate. As you add names, mail a note of thanks signed by you and your team members, e.g., "Thanks for being such a great customer. We're glad you chose us!" Make sure you mention that the customer has made it to the wall of fame. His curiosity is likely to spark a return visit.

92. Happy Birthday Program

Best For   Most retail businesses, all restaurants.

Objective   Build mailing list and database, increase community goodwill, increase sales.

Target   All customers.

Place a receptacle box and registration forms by your register, front desk, or customer greeting area. Have your staff encourage guests to join the birthday program, and reinforce this with in-store displays.

Each month, enter the data yourself or send the registration forms to your service provider for manual data entry and processing. Customers receive a free item during the month of their birthday. The birthday postcard can be highly personalized and can incorporate actual photos of your location and staff.

Materials   Registration cards, receptacle box, envelopes to send the cards to the data capture company.

Timing

Four weeks prior:

Prepare photos of staff that will be on the card. Order the receptacle box and printing of the registration forms.

Three weeks prior:

Email photos to the service provider for design of piece. Pre-address envelopes to send the filled-out cards to the service provider.

One week prior:

Discuss program with staff.

Start:

Collect registration information and mail to service provider.

Ongoing:

Continue to send in new submissions each month.

93.   Birthday Tactics in General

Best For   Most retailers and restaurants.

Objective   Increase awareness, increase goodwill, build mailing list, generate traffic, increase sales, stimulate trial.

Target   Existing and potential customers.

Birthdays, like holidays, are a promotional opportunity, as current and potential customers alike are generally in a festive mood. People like to feel special, and a birthday remembrance from a business can generate warmth and build loyalty.

Customers' birthdays are one of your best reasons for establishing a mailing list and keeping it up to date. Even when a customer moves out of your local trading area, a birthday remembrance can bring her back to you.

Birthdays are especially effective for children, who will often beg their parents to patronize your establishment.

94.   Birthday Club

Best For   Most retailers and restaurants.

Objective   Increase awareness, build mailing list, generate traffic, increase sales, stimulate trial.

Target Existing customers and potential new customers.

Have your staff encourage customers to fill out a Birthday Club registration card, located in a take-one box. Patrons return the cards to a staff member, who puts them in a Birthday Club collection box. The sign-up cards are bundled each week by month of birthday and put into your database to trigger a birthday-card coupon mailing.

If you are in the food-service business, offer something like a cake for four to six people. This way, your birthday offer has the potential to bring in many more new customers.

The birthday cards should read: "Congratulations on your Birthday. To make it even more special, we have a gift (or cake) waiting for you! Just call to let us know when you're coming in. And have a Happy Birthday."

Both the sign-up cards and the birthday cards should be attractive two-color pieces. Be sure to transfer the names of the Birthday Club members to your master mailing list for other mailings.

Materials Take-one boxes, Birthday Club registration cards, preprinted birthday cards, registration card collection box.

Timing

Four weeks prior:

> Design attractive take-one boxes, Birthday Club registration cards, and birthday cards.

Three weeks prior:

> Print registration cards and birthday cards.
> Order take-one boxes.

One week prior:

> Explain promotion to staff.

One day prior:

> Set out take-one boxes with registration cards.
> Set up collection box.
> Review program with staff.

One week after:

Meet with staff to obtain feedback in the form of customer comments and staff suggestions.

95. Seasonal Tourist Retention Program

Best For   Lodging, food, and entertainment businesses

Objective   Increase frequency, build mailing list.

Target   All customers.

Many consumers take their vacation at the same time of year, every year, for their entire lives. Being there to remind them about your business about three months or so before they arrive, when they are most likely to be making travel decisions, is an important promotional tactic.

With this program, you email your electronic database or send your manual database (registration cards) to a direct-mail service provider. Each month, it will update your list for accuracy, then send a postcard to those customers who are three months away from the anniversary of their last stay.

The mailer can be customized to feature color photos of your location and can even be printed to feature customers' names on a photo of your awning or marquee. The offer should communicate a welcome-back message and be accompanied by an added incentive, a gift certificate.

Materials   Registration cards or electronic database.

Timing

Four weeks prior:

Prepare photos of staff and property that will appear on the card. Prepare registration cards or electronic database for delivery to service provider.

Three weeks prior:

Email photos to service provider for design of piece.

One week prior:

Discuss program with staff.

Start:

Receive inbound calls and track response rate.

Ongoing:

Continue to send in new registrations each month to keep the database growing.

96. Bounce-Back Offer

Best For   Most retail businesses.

Objective   Increase awareness, increase frequency, promote activity during slow periods.

Target   Existing customers and potential new customers.

Have your staff distribute bounce-back coupons, designed to encourage repeat business within a short period of time, to all customers. In certain businesses, that time period could be the same day; in others, it might be within a week or even a month. Distribute the coupons during a two-week period and allow a four-week redemption period. For example, a bookstore could distribute coupons good for 50 percent off any purchase of a book, redeemable within 30 days.

Materials   Bounce-back coupons.

Timing

Two weeks prior:

Print coupons.

One week prior:

Describe activity to staff.

Start date:

Begin distribution and redemption of coupons at specified times.

Two weeks after:

Cease distribution of coupons.

Four weeks after:

Cease redemption of coupons.

97.   Gift Certificate/Coupon Tie-In

Best For   Most retailers and restaurants.

Objective   Increase frequency, generate traffic, keep staff busy, increase sales, promote activity during slow periods, stimulate trial.

Target   Existing customers and potential new customers.

Use the sale of gift certificates as a method of distributing four different bounce-back coupons that are valid during a typically slow four-week period. Offer all four coupons for free with the purchase of a gift certificate. Choose products that are high-profit and/or popular, to build on your existing strength.

Week 1 coupon: Buy one, get one free—any product of equal or lower value.

Week 2 coupon: Free add-on product with another larger purchase.

Week 3 coupon: Free add-on product (different from that in Week 2) with another larger purchase.

Week 4 coupon: Free add-on product (different from those in Weeks 2 and 3) with another larger purchase

Materials   In-store posters, gift certificates, bounce-back coupons.

Timing:

Three weeks prior:

Prepare gift certificates, posters, discount cards.

Two weeks prior:

Print gift certificates, posters, discount cards.
Discuss program with staff.

One week prior:

Set out posters.
Display gift certificates.

One day prior:

Review program with staff.

Start:

Sell gift certificates.

One week after:

Begin redeeming coupons.

Four weeks after:

Cease redemption of coupons.
Evaluate program.

98.   Contests and Sweepstakes—General Information

In the following pages you'll find two slightly different techniques for attracting people by giving them the opportunity to win desirable prizes. The difference between the two is that one requires skill and the other luck.

Contests involve some sort of ability—the best poem, a coloring contest, the best recipe, and so on. Sweepstakes are purely chance—participants have no influence over whether they win.

The difference is legally significant. The laws of most states say that lotteries are illegal, except when they are run by the states themselves. Under the law, the three main elements of a lottery are chance, consideration, and valuable prizes.

Contests are okay because they substitute skill for chance. Sweepstakes are okay as long as they eliminate consideration by allowing entry without proof of purchase. The most common sweepstakes rules say, "Send in proof of purchase seals from two packages of (name of product), or simply print your name and address on a 3" × 5" card, along with the name of the product, and send it to . . ." This "or" is the elimination of the consideration in the form of a purchase that makes the sweepstakes legal.

If you intend to run a contest or sweepstakes, you should consult an attorney or your local authorities to make sure you comply with all state and local laws. You may also want to include a formal release by participants that allows you to use their likeness in your marketing materials.

99. All Family Sweepstakes

Best For   Most retailers and restaurants.

Objective   Increase awareness, build mailing list, create excitement, increase frequency, generate traffic, increase sales, stimulate trial.

Target   Existing customers and potential new customers.

Giving customers a chance to win valuable prizes creates an exciting, traffic-building event.

Each time customers visit your business, they should be given a sweepstakes entry blank. This alone will build frequency. Customers complete the entry blank and deposit it in a drop box near the entrance.

It is illegal to require a purchase in order to enter a sweepstakes, but you can control ballot-box stuffing by keeping the entry blanks where customers cannot just pick them up. They should be distributed by your staff, one to each customer. To counteract stuffing, you should make use of a computerized database that will allow you to clear out any multiple entries.

The prize structure should depend on your budget. The rule of thumb is that no matter how valuable the prize is, the more prizes you have, the greater customers perceive their chances of winning as being. On the other hand, the grand prize should always have real value.

A sweepstakes of this type should be promoted via newspaper ads, in-store posters, and, if you can afford it, radio. Prizes and posters should be displayed attractively and should be visible at all times during the promotion.

Materials   Newspaper ad, posters, entry blanks, drop box, display items, prizes.

Timing

Four weeks prior:

Decide on type of sweepstakes and select prizes.
Contact radio station (optional).
Design posters, entry blanks, newspaper ad.
Design coupons (if applicable).

Three weeks prior:

Buy media.
Design prize display.
Purchase prizes.
Print posters, entry blanks, coupons (optional).

Two weeks prior:

Discuss program with staff. Explain responsibilities and operational
execution.
Place newspaper ad.
Begin radio campaign (optional).
Display posters in store.

One day prior:

Set out display.

Start:

Begin distribution of entry blanks and continue until one day before
the drawing.

End:

Award prizes and contact winners.
Photograph major prize winners and mail with press release to local
newspapers.

At the end of this promotion, you should be left with a huge database
of email addresses and postal addresses. Think about how you will put
it to use with some of the other promotions in this book.

100. Autograph Contest

Best For   Most retailers and restaurants.

Objective   Build mailing list, create excitement, generate PR, generate
traffic, increase sales, stimulate trial.

Target Existing customers and potential new customers.

Tap into the popularity of your region's major sports teams by providing families with pre-autographed photos of a popular team member. If possible, arrange special days when team members will be available to give autographs.

Give the photos only to customers who shop at your business or dine at your restaurant. Encourage customers to sign up for a chance to win a team-autographed football, basketball, or baseball at the end of the promotion by filling out their names and addresses on a card to be deposited in a drop box.

Winners should be notified by telephone and, if possible, should come in to be photographed with a popular team member and their prize. Give a copy of the photo to the winner, and send a copy, with a press release, to your local newspaper for publication.

Generate interest through newspaper ads announcing team members' appearances. Also, pass out flyers at participating team games. Begin the program at the start of a season and run it for at least two weeks.

Materials Flyers, newspaper ad, autographed photos, grand prize autographed ball.

Timing

Three weeks prior:

> Discuss program with teams to arrange participation and usage of player's likeness—research any licensing issues.
> Prepare newspaper ads, entry blanks, and flyers.
> Arrange for autographed photos and grand-prize ball.
> Arrange team member visits.
> Buy media.

Two weeks prior:

> Discuss program with staff.
> Print flyers.
> Distribute flyers at games.
> Place newspaper ad.
> Prepare entry blank drop box.

One week prior:

Rerun newspaper ad.

One day prior:

Display winning ball prominently at business.
Review program with staff.

Start:

Begin handing out pre-autographed photos to customers.
Begin handing out entry blanks for grand prize.

Two weeks after:

Draw name of grand-prize winner and notify.
Photograph prize winner with team member and prize and send the photograph, with press release, to local paper.

Be sure to have the winner sign a release form permitting you to use his or her image in your promotions. You can obtain a standard release form from a local ad agency or commercial photographer.

9

New Customers

101. New Resident Direct-Mail Program

Best For   All consumer-oriented businesses.

Objective   Stimulate trial.

Target   New residents.

As many as several hundred new residents a month move to within a three- to five-mile radius of your business, and most of them are anxious to learn about the businesses serving their new community. Sending these new neighbors a full-color mail piece for your business, along with an offer for a free product or service or some other special offer redeemable at your location, is an effective way to stimulate new trials.

The latest digital printing technology makes these programs affordable, and they can be highly personalized. Be sure to include some visuals in your mailer, such as photos of your personnel and your location and any other imagery that will help the recipient visualize why he should patronize you.

You can purchase the addresses on a regular basis from a list broker or other source.

Materials   Self-mailers.

Timing

Four weeks prior:

Prepare photos.

Three weeks prior:

Email photos to printer/mailer for design of piece.

One week prior:

Discuss program with staff.

Start:

Collect redemptions.

Ongoing:

Once established, this tactic can be easily repeated every month. Track your redemption rate, collect customer information, and build your database.

102. New Homeowners Program

Best For All consumer-oriented businesses.

Objective Increase awareness, build mailing list, increase frequency, stimulate trial.

Target New homeowners.

This is similar to the new resident program but is targeted to homeowners, whose interests may be more specific. You can obtain a mailing list for all new homeowners in your trading area from a list broker, or you can use a company like Smartleads, Inc., which not only will help with the list, but can also produce a customized, four-color direct-mail piece. The mailer should contain a specific offer good for a limited time (always less than a month). Make sure you have a method to track the success of this mailing, such as a "mention this mailer" discount or a coupon.

After their first visit, offer these new customers a bounce-back coupon, good for a return visit in a very short period of time. The bounce-back should be good for a buy-one-get-one-free offer or something else of real value.

Materials From Smartleads. Call 1-800-235-9647 for more information.

Timing

Four weeks prior:

Determine what your offer will be.

Three weeks prior:

> Send your offer and your business information (logo, background, and so on) to a vendor such as Smartleads.

One week prior:

> Discuss program with employees.

One day prior:

> Discuss program with employees and get them geared up.

Start:

> Redeem new homeowner mailing.

103.   Captain Hook

Best For   Most business types.

Objective   Generate traffic, stimulate trial, increase goodwill.

Target   Other local businesses.

A highly targeted way to promote yourself right in your neighborhood is to appoint or hire someone to be your Captain Hook, to go out into the community for an hour or so each day and hook prospective customers. Choose someone with outstanding people skills and a complete knowledge of your business and its products and services, and have that person spend an hour or so each day visiting neighborhood businesses, offering them free samples and/or literature. Remember to include a coupon or gift certificate good for a specific product to be used by a specific date, as soon as possible after the visit.

If you own a restaurant, call and offer free sandwiches or desserts to the employees of the business you're visiting that day, then deliver a platter of goodies. If you run a retail shop, deliver a sampling of what you sell or what you are currently promoting. If you operate a window-washing service, wash the business's front windows for free. If you own a spa, offer a five-minute shoulder massage on the spot. If you own an insurance agency, offer a free quote on car insurance. The possibilities are limited only by your creativity and initiative.

The recipients of these visits will be surprised and delighted. They'll remember you, and they'll tell their friends and coworkers.

104. Retail Partnership-Promotion

Best For Retailers and food service.

Objective Increase awareness, increase community goodwill, generate traffic, increase sales, stimulate trial.

Target Local retail outlets.

This tactic allows you to cross-market with another business in such a way that you both increase your sales and get new customers.

Contact the owners or managers of retail outlets within your local trading area (three to five miles) that cater to an audience or market segment similar to yours. If you are not in the restaurant business, consider a restaurant. If you are, find a nonfood business. Offer to provide the other business with gift certificates at a discount that it can give its customers as a thank-you for their patronage or as a thank-you for purchasing more than a certain amount.

You may wish to offer the other business five certificates for the price of four. Let the other business determine the face amount of the certificate, or it can tell you what it is willing to pay for the certificates, and you can come up with an offer that is appropriate to your product.

As an added incentive for participating in the program, the partnering merchant should be given a 10 percent discount card good for its staff, too. Be sure to place a two- week expiration date on both the certificates and the discount cards.

To promote this offer, display posters both at your location naming the participating merchants and at the participating merchants' locations advertising the program.

Materials Gift certificates, in-store posters, merchant posters, discount cards.

Timing

Three weeks prior:

Visit area merchants to recruit them for the program.

Prepare gift certificates, posters, and discount cards.

Two weeks prior:

Print gift certificates, posters, and discount cards.
Distribute merchant posters, gift certificates, and cards to merchants.

One week prior:

Discuss program with staff.

Start:

Display posters.
Begin certificate redemption.
Honor discount cards.

Two weeks after:

Discontinue redemption and evaluate results.

105. Commuter/Traveler Flyers

Best For   Most consumer businesses.

Objective   Increase awareness, generate traffic, increase sales, stimulate trial.

Target   Local railway stations, hotels and motels.

Several evenings a week, pass out flyers at the railroad and/or bus station to commuters and passengers. The flyers should have directional maps that pinpoint your business as well as other key buildings.

If your business is appropriate for travelers, flyers could also be given to local hotels and motels for distribution to their customers. Be sure to include a discount coupon at the bottom of the flyer. Although this program can be ongoing, make sure to print each batch of flyers with a four-week expiration date to deter unintentional coupon collection and usage by hotel/motel employees.

Materials   Flyers.

Timing

Three weeks prior:

Obtain a map of the area from the Chamber of Commerce.
Design coupon and flyers.

Two weeks prior:

Print flyers.

One week prior:

Begin flyer distribution.
Discuss program with your staff.

Start:

Begin redeeming coupons.

Four weeks after:

Evaluate results.

106. Home Team Support

Best For   All retailers and restaurants.

Objective   Generate traffic, increase sales, stimulate trial.

Target   Local sports teams, new and current customers.

If your local sports team hits a scoring level that you set, all fans who present a ticket stub get a free gift or product.

During each sports season, set attainable goals for the home team to achieve. You might want to get some basic stats for your teams so that you can make sure that the goal will be achieved at least once. For example, the offer is good when the basketball team scores 100 or more points or when the baseball team wins a game by three runs or more. Do the same for hockey, football, and any other locally popular sports. This can also be done successfully with college and high school teams when there is strong community support.

When a team achieves the goal, all fans, your potential customers, can redeem their game ticket stubs for a gift or, in a restaurant, a free dessert, for example. If your business doesn't have a product that lends itself to being given away, like a carpet store, purchase a reasonable gift with good perceived value to give away. Try to come up with something that ties in with your type of business, such as a bottle of "nonstaining" white wine for a carpet store. Or partner with another business, such as a restaurant, to give away a gift certificate and make it a cross-marketing opportunity. A good partner, depending on who your audience is, might be a sports bar.

Advertise in local newspapers, distribute flyers at games or other places where fans congregate, and put posters in your business. Include in any literature the set goals for each team to establish the integrity of this offer.

Materials   Flyers, posters, newspaper ad, reader board.

Timing

Three weeks prior:

Discuss program with staff and set goals for game scores.
Prepare ad, posters, and flyers.
Buy media.

Two weeks prior:

Print posters and flyers.

One week prior:

Put up posters.
Place ad.

Start:

Review program with staff.
Distribute flyers at games.

107.   Social Consciousness

Best For   All business types.

Objective   Increase goodwill, build customer loyalty.

Target   Local charities.

Consider offering and promoting one of the following programs. These should be carried out during specific times, typically when you are busy, to increase the impact on your customers:

1. Donate 5 percent of every sale to the homeless.
2. Offer customers the option of donating a percentage of their bill to their favorite charity.
3. For restaurants, arrange to take unserved leftover foods to city shelters.
4. For bars, offer free rides to patrons who have consumed too much alcohol. (This service should be more available anyway.)

There are a hundred variations on this theme. Use your creativity to figure out how it might work best for you.

108. Shopping Spree Sweepstakes

Best For   Retailers and restaurants.

Objective   Increase awareness, build mailing list, increase community goodwill, create excitement, generate PR, generate traffic, build your image, increase sales, stimulate trial.

Target   Existing customers, potential new customers, and high-quality retailers.

Join with several high-volume, high-quality retailers in your trading area and hold a drawing at your business for free merchandise at the shops of the other retailers.

In one example, the first-place winner gets a $200 shopping spree, two second-place winners each receive a $100 spree, and five third-place winners each get a $50 spree.

Each prize should be awarded by a different retailer, so it would be necessary in this example to get eight different area merchants to join in. If you get fewer merchants, award fewer prizes; if you get more merchants, award more prizes. The dollar value of the prizes will depend on the merchants' individual choices.

Your business contributes the advertising for the promotion, such as posters to display in your place and at the other retailers' locations. Customers are invited to visit any participating business to pick up an entry blank. Put a locked drop box in each participating merchant's store. Supply sweepstakes rules and odds on posters distributed to each participating retailer. Make sure the retailers actually put them up and support the promotion.

Materials   Posters, entry blanks, drop boxes.

Timing

Four weeks prior:

> Visit area merchants to discuss the program.
> Prepare posters, entry blanks, drop boxes.
> Show merchants a proof of the poster prior to printing.

Three weeks prior:

> Print posters and entry blanks.
> Distribute posters, entry blanks, and drop boxes to merchants.

Two weeks prior:

> Discuss program with staff.
> Display posters in your restaurant or place of business.
> Review program with participating merchants.

Start:

> Pick up completed entry blanks from merchants regularly so that they have room in their drop boxes.

Two weeks after:

> Announce prize winners.

109.   Art Drawing Contest

Best For   Retailers and restaurants.

Objective   Increase awareness, increase community goodwill, generate PR, generate traffic, build your image.

Target   Schools, children, and parents in your trade area.

Have a window-decoration contest for local schoolchildren, and make it a big deal.

An appliance store in Fort Wayne, Indiana, has a contest every year for a number of second-grade classes from area schools. The owner promotes the contest by handing out flyers to all the schools in the area. Each class that joins gets a large windowpane in the front of the store, where it creates a Christmas design and paints the window.

After about two weeks, the designs are judged by people such as the mayor, a city council member, and a local television anchor or DJ, and prizes are awarded. Generally, every entrant wins something. The contest involves a lot of people and generates a lot of traffic, especially by parents who come out to see their children's handiwork. The appliance store gets holiday decorations at very little cost and creates goodwill in the community at the same time.

This same appliance store also created a special event called "The Refrigerator Art Gallery." School kids submitted their artwork, and it was mounted with magnets on all the refrigerators in the store. That really brought in the parents.

A drawing or painting contest can be used in many different businesses, for example, menu cover designs for a restaurant and windshield painting for a car dealership. America West Airlines once featured a reproduction of a child's drawing on the side of one of its planes.

There's tremendous opportunity for media coverage as well.

Look at your business and figure out where you might take advantage of a drawing contest—on bags, invoices, windows, delivery trucks, uniforms, or T-shirts for your employees.

Materials   Flyers to hand out to local schools.

Timing

Four weeks prior:

Develop flyers to hand out to area schools.

Three weeks prior:

Print flyers.
Secure prizes and rewards.
Distribute flyers to area schools.

Two weeks prior:

Discuss program with staff.
Invite and secure judges for the contest.
Review program with area schools.

Start:

Have classes decorate your business or produce the item with the
drawings on it.

Two weeks after:

Have judges on hand to announce winner(s) of the contest.
Award prizes.

10

Promotions for Charities and Churches

110.   Houses of Worship Promotions

Best For   All business types.

Objective   Increase goodwill, increase awareness, build loyalty.

Target   Churches, synagogues, mosques, and so on.

The next few pages describe ways in which you can show that you value the spiritual life of your community and support it, regardless of creed.

Promotions designed around houses of worship have never been money-makers on their own. It is the involvement and goodwill that they evidence to congregations that make them worth doing.

Almost everyone in your community will have at least one member of their family who actively attends or is involved with a house of worship. That person's involvement in your promotion will bring other family members into your business.

Tactics in this category can be targeted toward almost all of the objectives outlined in this book: increasing goodwill, increasing awareness, stimulating trial, increasing frequency, building your image, increasing sales, promoting activity during slow periods, and improving the bottom line.

111. Church Social

Best For   Restaurants and some retailers.

Objective   Increase awareness, increase community goodwill, generate traffic, increase sales, stimulate trial.

Target   Local houses of worship.

This program is designed to acquaint the community with your business and create a good image for you.

Contact clergy by mail, then follow up with a phone call. The letter explains how a church social sponsored or catered by your business could be a fund-raiser. It would, at the same time, be a bonding social event for members of the congregation.

Provide the church or synagogue with two-part tickets. Tickets can be sold by the church's women's club, men's club, youth group, and so on, for $5 each. For each ticket redeemed, the church receives $2 (the other $3 helps defray part of your costs). You should determine the correct amount for your business. A ticket entitles the bearer to a full choice of meal and dessert. Attendees retain their ticket stubs to use them in a drawing for a free meal for two or some other gift at the end of the event.

Hand out bounce-back coupons for $1 off (or some other appropriate amount) on any return visit to everyone who attends, within a limited time. Since most people will bring a guest, the bounce-backs provide the potential for two return visits.

Materials   Letter, two-part tickets, bounce-back coupons.

Timing

Eight weeks prior:

Write to local house of worship to solicit participation.

Seven weeks prior:

Make follow-up phone calls.

Six weeks prior:

Prepare coupons and two-part tickets.

Five weeks prior:

Print coupons and tickets.
Deliver tickets to participating church or synagogue.

Four weeks prior:

House of worship announces program in its bulletin and begins sales.

One week prior:

Check on sales and review details of social.
Discuss program with staff.

One day prior:

Get final number of tickets sold from church.
Review program with staff.

Start:

Begin redeeming tickets.
Conduct drawing for gift or free dinner for two.
Pass out bounce-back coupons to attendees.

One week after:

Evaluate results.

112. Bingo and Carnival Prizes

Best For Retailers and restaurants.

Objective Increase awareness, increase community goodwill, generate traffic, increase sales, stimulate trial.

Target Local churches.

Most churches sponsor bake sales, carnivals, bingo games, and card parties. In most cases, tickets to these events are sold and the proceeds are used for the needs of the church or as a donation to a charity.

Provide local churches with coupons good for a gift at your business or free food at your restaurant (such as free dessert with dinner) when people make donations to the church by purchasing tickets. You can also provide coupons good for a more valuable gift that can be used as prizes for parishioners at carnivals and bingo games.

Materials   Coupons, flyers announcing the program.

Timing   This can be an ongoing program if it works well. Distribute flyers and coupons to different churches in your community and repeat as often as you wish.

113.   The 10 Percent Solution

Best For   Most business types.

Objective   Generate traffic, increase sales, stimulate trial.

Target   Local churches.

Parishioners are always looking for ways to help their church. Make it easy for them by offering to return 10 percent of the proceeds of the sale when they patronize your business. Ask church leaders to distribute coupons that, when redeemed, give 10 percent of the sale proceeds to the church. You can tailor these coupons to fit your prices and your products or services.

To increase traffic during your usually slower periods, you may wish to make the coupons valid for slower days or hours.

Provide a space on the coupon to identify the church, and ask customers to present the coupon with their payment. Consider using a preprinted form designed to fit credit card imprinter machines. The cashier will write in the church's name and imprint 10 percent of the total sale. This will act as the customer's receipt and will be returned to her with her change. However you choose to do it, it is very important that you make sure that each customer has proof of the transaction.

Instruct the customers to turn the receipts in to the church. At the end of the promotion, the church leader returns all the receipts to you for a cash redemption.

Materials   Coupons, preprinted receipts.

Timing

Six weeks prior:

Contact church and club leaders by mail, by phone, or in person.

Three weeks prior:

Confirm participation.
Prepare coupons and receipts.

Two weeks prior:

Print coupons and receipts.

One week prior:

Present coupons to churches.
Explain program to staff.

Four weeks after:

Present check to church.
Evaluate results.

114. Sample Letter to Clergy

(On your letterhead)

Dear Reverend/Father/Rabbi (Name):

As a member of our community who appreciates the important role you play, I would like to offer you a simple, cost-free way to raise money for your building fund, your youth group, your foreign ministry, or some other program you need money for.

Here's how it works:

We'll furnish you with coupons that can be given to your congregation. The coupons state that XX percent of any purchase made with the coupon at our store/business/restaurant will be donated to your church for your unrestricted use.

It's that simple. There's nothing else for you to do. We will tabulate and distribute funds to you on a weekly basis for four weeks, beginning as soon as you like.

After you've had a chance to think about the idea, I'll call you to answer any questions and to discuss the program in more detail.

I look forward to working with you and helping you meet your fund-raising goals.

Cordially,

(Your Name)

115.   Charity/Fund-Raising Tactics

Best For   Most business types.

Objective   Increase goodwill, increase awareness, increase community involvement.

Target   Local charities and nonprofits.

In the following pages you will find a number of tactics similar to those you use with churches, but directed at creating warm and caring feelings between your neighbors and your business by creating bonds with non-profit institutions—charities. This is more than just raising awareness about you.

You can do this in any number of ways: involvement in helping younger children or seniors, direct involvement with the community in promotions designed to aid the community, and fund-raising promotions. You will be limited only by your creativity. Donald Trump, who owned the Trump Shuttle airline in New York, once offered Thanksgiving Day travelers a bargain price on flights that day if they brought with them a can of food to donate to the poor.

Target your promotions to those causes that are most popular or of most particular interest to your community. Avoid choosing causes that are political or that otherwise tend to divide your neighbors.

116.   Discounts to Organization Members

Best For   Most retailers and restaurants.

Objective   Increase awareness, increase sales.

Target   Local civic groups, associations, and clubs.

Contact your local Chamber of Commerce to obtain a list of all civic groups, associations, and clubs in your local trading area.

Send letters to group leaders making the same basic offer that you made to churches (see previous tactics). Wait one week and make follow-up phone calls. Offer special incentives to select groups that have a large enrollment. Always put a time limit on every offer, up to a month. Here are some suggestions:

1. A 10 percent discount to members who present your ad from their club newsletter or bulletin. You may also want to consider creating this ad so that it looks like an I.D. card that customers present at your business.
2. Start a birthday club for organization members.
3. Offer discounts for group events that use your services, facilities, or products.
4. Offer to donate to their charity 10 percent of every transaction that is larger than a set amount (choose the amount so that it is attainable and suits your products and services).

Materials   Letters, ads.

Timing:

Four weeks prior:

   Contact Chamber of Commerce and obtain mailing lists.
   Send letters to heads of civic and charity groups.

Three weeks prior:

   Follow up with phone calls.
   Begin visiting interested organizations.

Two weeks prior:

   Place ads in organizations' newsletters and bulletins.
   Discuss program with staff.

One week prior:

   Follow up and confirm any special elements (such as catering, music, or entertainment).

Start:

   Begin accepting I.D. discounts.

End:

   Discontinue discounts.
   Send thank-you letters to participating organizations.
   Evaluate results.

117.   Big Bucks

Best For   Most business types.

Objective   Increase awareness, increase community goodwill, generate traffic, increase sales, stimulate trial.

Target   Local civic organizations.

Print "Big Bucks" and distribute them to local charities and civic organizations (i.e., Boy Scouts, Lions Club, and other such organizations) for resale to the public. Each "Buck" is worth $1 toward any purchase at your store.

The organization or charity sells the Bucks for their face value of $1 (or higher, as appropriate) and gets to keep a portion of each Buck redeemed at your business. This allows the charity to make a profit and you to cover your cost while building overall traffic and sales.

At the end of the promotion, be sure the charity returns all unsold Bucks to you. The promotion should run for six weeks, allowing a four-week selling period and two additional weeks for redemption.

Depending on your product or service, you could print $5, $10, or $20 bucks for this promotion.

Materials   Letters to organizations, "Big Bucks" coupons.

Timing

Six weeks prior:

Set program goals and determine costs.
Begin contacting charities/organizations by letter to explain program.

Five weeks prior:

Follow up letters with phone calls.

Three weeks prior:

Design and print "Big Bucks."

Two weeks prior:

Confirm organization/charity participation and prepare promotional materials.

One week prior:

Distribute "Big Bucks" to participants.
Explain program to staff.

Start:

Begin redemption of Big Bucks.
Record redemption count daily for reimbursement.

Six weeks after:

Unsold Big Bucks are returned.
Participants reimburse you for coupons redeemed.

End:

Discontinue discounts.
Send thank-you letters to participating organizations.

118. Community Car Wash

Best For Most business types.

Objective Increase community goodwill, generate traffic, increase awareness.

Target Local civic organizations.

Offer to host a car wash for groups that are willing to raise funds this way. You supply the location and the water and take care of advertising the event through flyers placed under windshields in local parking lots.

Make sure you have enough personnel on hand during the event to handle the crowd. Ask the group that is sponsoring the car wash to be responsible for supplies—hoses, buckets, towels, and so on—and make sure it supplies the people to wash the cars!

Have bounce-back coupons on hand to give to the people who get their cars washed.

Materials Flyers, bounce-back coupons.

Timing

Six weeks prior:

Contact charity groups to arrange event.

Four weeks prior:

Confirm arrangements and meet to discuss details.
Prepare flyers and bounce-back coupons.

Three weeks prior:

Print flyers and bounce-back coupons.

Two weeks prior:

Discuss program with staff and determine area to be used.

One week prior:

Distribute flyers.
Reconfirm with participating charity.

One day prior:

Prepare car-wash area.
Review program with staff.

Start:

Begin car wash.
Distribute bounce-backs to car-wash patrons.

Evaluate the results after the coupon expiration date. This could be an ongoing event–say, the first Sunday of every month.

119.   Benefit Mini-thons

Best For   Most business types.

Objective   Increase community goodwill, generate PR, increase sales, stimulate trial.

Target   Local nonprofit organizations.

For most businesses, it's become increasingly difficult to deal with the steady flow of requests for donations to every charity in the community. You want to help them all, but you can't.

Instead, consider adopting your favorite charity and putting all your energy into helping it. You'll make a bigger impact, and you can say with honesty to all the others that your charity plate is full.

Mini-marathons are a great way to target a particular cause. The following pages contain some examples that you can flesh out to suit your particular business type and community.

120. Score a Hole-in-One

Dirk Todd, the golf pro at Raccoon International in Granville, Ohio, knew someone who needed a lifesaving kidney transplant. While much of the cost of the operation was covered by insurance and grants, the antirejection medication that was needed to make the operation succeed was not covered. With the help of the family and their friends, Dirk coordinated a benefit day. The goal for this benefit was to raise a great deal of money for the family.

Many area businesses donated food. One of the biggest money-makers came from a local microbrewery that donated kegs of its own beer for the event.

Eighteen local businesses sponsored individual holes, and a local sign company donated the signs. One very creative fund-raising element was the sale of "gimmies" and "pro shots."

Gimmies were sold by the foot. Prior to the event, players could buy string for a buck a foot that they could cash in on a given green. If a player's ball landed within the length of the string, that counted as the final shot on that hole. On a particularly rough hole with a water hazard, players could make a donation to have the pro drive the ball. These little games raised money and made the event fun.

The event raised over $5,000 and introduced many new golfers to the course.

121. Life and Breath

Twelve-year-old Valerie Yearicks suffered from cystic fibrosis and needed a double lung transplant. The general manager of an area restaurant offered to help by setting aside one day when he would donate half his sales over and above the average or usual sales for that day.

Valerie's father, Robert, led the effort to promote the event with an army of volunteers. The restaurant's general manager arranged for karate demonstrations and an appearance by a boxing champ. Volunteers raffled off door prizes and football tickets to help the cause.

The volunteers, including some servers from the restaurant, passed out flyers and put up posters that were donated by the local printer. They handed out announcements door to door and placed them under windshield wipers. They got mentions in the local newspaper and on the radio. The event was also promoted for a week inside the restaurant and on the marquee.

A total of $2,500 was donated, and the restaurant got all the credit. The manager was interviewed on two Philadelphia TV newscasts. The restaurant received an estimated $20,000 of free publicity. Customer counts were up 30 percent, and many of those were new faces.

This program took some moderate effort on the part of the manager, but volunteers did most of the promoting. There was no risk to the business, as the manager had taken in enough money to cover his costs after the donation.

Many new customers visited the restaurant and paid full price for their meals. Since the restaurant didn't use a discount or coupon to motivate those new customers to visit, it had a much better chance of getting them to come back and pay the regular price.

122. Pulpit Power

A grocery store owner set up a register tape promotion to help area churches raise money. The participating church did all of the promoting to its congregation, and congregants would then shop at this store and deposit their register tape receipts in a special collection bin at the church. The store then made a monthly donation to the church based on a percentage of the tapes' totals.

Each participating church was motivated to get as many of its congregants as possible to do the bulk of their shopping at this store. As the community had three grocery stores that offered the same products at competitive prices, this promotion helped give the store an edge over the competition.

123. You Sew, and the Charity Reaps

Bob Kramer of Kramer's Sew & Vac in Cincinnati ran a promotion with a well-known residence and training center for the visually impaired that was located around the corner from one of his stores. Bob offered a 10 percent cash donation on sales generated, based on the following four rules:

1. All receipts for purchases and services made during a specific three-month period would qualify.
2. Receipts would be turned in to the center.
3. Kramer's would issue a check to the center for 10 percent of the total net sales before tax.
4. Donations on individual transactions would be limited to a maximum of $200.

The store gained exposure for the promotion through the center's mailings, including its newsletter, and payroll stuffers offered to other area businesses. It also got publicity. The organization did the work, so there was little distraction for the sewing store.

124. Healthy Gums for a Healthy Community

Instead of receiving a plaque for his community contribution, Dr. Steve Oppenheimer of Atlanta helped to remove it. Dr. Oppenheimer organized a teeth-cleaning event that brought awareness and financial help to victims of a hurricane in the neighboring state. He opened his office on Sunday and cleaned teeth, with the fees for each procedure going to the cause. The event was promoted primarily to his existing patients, who were encouraged to bring their friends.

In addition to new patients, Dr. Oppenheimer received a ton of positive publicity.

125. Fund-raising Big Top

Stubby's Food Marts, a six-store chain based in Lake Livingston, Texas, does a fund- raising program for its local Muscular Dystrophy Association chapter. It generates impressive returns on a small investment through the sponsorship of car washes, shamrock sales, and other drives throughout the year. Its summer fund-raising finale always gets the attention of the Houston TV stations.

A carnival of activity under a large circus tent, Stubby's big fund-raiser features magicians and fortune-tellers, a bake sale, a garage sale, and games and activities for kids. Customers can dunk local business leaders. One year, a Houston radio station broadcast from the event and one of the city's most popular newscasters attended as a guest.

The event raises more than $10,000 each year, and the Stubby's Food Marts chain generates more free publicity, goodwill, and top-of-mind awareness than you could imagine.

126. The Trade-in Donation

This is a clever and appreciated way to generate donations of used items that are needed by the less fortunate, and it creates tremendous goodwill for participating businesses.

Kuppenheimer, a chain of discount, factory-direct men's clothing stores, turns a sale into a charity event by inviting customers to bring in any suit and get a credit for the purchase of a new one. Store employees make minor repairs as necessary to the old suits, have them cleaned, and then donate them to a local homeless shelter. The effort required to take care of repairs is moderate, and a dry-cleaning cosponsor provides the cleaning free of charge.

Advertising must be done at the stores' expense. What makes this promotion work is that the store is giving the same discount when customers bring in a used suit as it would normally extend with a coupon, which wouldn't have nearly the same credibility or appeal.

In Columbus, Ohio, a local grocery store chain partnered with a local dry-cleaning chain to serve as collection points for used winter coats. Though the stores didn't offer any savings on purchases when people made a donation, it was still an effective promotion that benefits the needy with minimal cost to the businesses.

Trade-in promotions have also been used for collecting shoes at a shoe store, eyeglasses at an optical center, books at a bookstore, canned goods at a grocery or convenience store, and toys at a toy store. There are many more possibilities. If you don't have a product that lends itself to a trade-in approach, then it makes sense to volunteer your store as a collection point for those items. It costs you nothing, and you're likely to get a little exposure and foot traffic that you otherwise would not have gotten.

11
Civic Tactics

Best For Most business types.

Objective Increase goodwill, increase awareness, generate media attention, increase traffic.

Target Communitywide civic and public agencies.

Political and civic promotions are designed around events and concerns that deal with government or quasi-government agencies and the community at large.

They are less personal and specific than, for instance, promotions designed around religious organizations and holidays. Instead, they attempt to reach all areas and all members of the community.

127. Operation Cleanup

Objective Increase awareness, increase community goodwill, generate PR, generate traffic.

Target Local youth groups.

Contact your local youth service groups (such as 4H Club, Scouts, and so on) and sponsor a cleanup of the neighborhood. Provide participants with trash bags and T-shirts with your business's logo. Contact the local press for media coverage, and be sure to contact city officials to get them to participate in the program.

This program can also be used as a fund-raiser if you donate a fixed amount of money for each filled bag of trash or for each pound of trash collected.

Plan the program for a Saturday or Sunday. Be sure to give all participants free refreshments at the end of the day. If the program is handled as a fund-raiser, invite the local press when you count the bags or weigh the trash to present your donation.

Make sure to ask city officials to arrange a special pickup at your business to remove the collected trash bags.

Materials   Trash bags, T-shirts, press release.

Timing

Six weeks prior:

Contact youth service groups to arrange event.

Five weeks prior:

Confirm arrangements and meet to discuss details.
Purchase and imprint T-shirts, bags, and any other collateral materials.

Two weeks prior:

Send press release to media.
Contact city officials.

One week prior:

Discuss program with staff and determine area to be used to store filled trash bags.

Start:

Distribute trash bags and T-shirts.

End:

Present donation to charity.
Serve refreshments to participants.

128.   Library Amnesty Day

Best For   Most consumer-oriented businesses.

Objective Increase community goodwill, generate PR, improve your image.

Target Public libraries.

Contact local public libraries to arrange an amnesty day on which anyone holding an overdue library book can return it to your business without paying a fine. Libraries like this program because they get back books that normally would never be returned. Your business will benefit from the increased traffic.

Construct or purchase an attractive box to hold the returned books until the library picks them up. Promote the program via in-store posters and posters at the libraries for at least one week before the promotion. In addition, send press releases to the local papers, preferably written by the libraries on their stationery.

This promotion can bring heavy traffic into your business. If you can afford it, place an ad in the local newspaper for maximum exposure. See if the library will share the expense with you.

Materials Deposit box, posters, press release, ad.

Timing

Four weeks prior:

Contact area libraries to arrange promotion.

Three weeks prior:

Prepare ad.
Buy media.
Prepare posters.

Two weeks prior:

Print posters.
Purchase or construct deposit box.

One week prior:

Distribute posters to libraries.
Place ad.
Put up posters in your business.
Explain program to staff.

Start:

Begin accepting returned library books.

129.   Events Services

Best For   Food-service companies and some retailers.

Objective   Increase awareness, increase sales.

Target   Agents for community events.

Here you will use the kiosk or cart you learned about in Tactic 41. Contact those responsible for staging community events at least eight weeks in advance of a particular event. Arrange to place your cart or a stand containing your products, foods, or advertising specialties and coupons. If the event draws enough traffic, and if you can afford to do so, consider cosponsoring the event in order to get your name on any print or radio media on a cooperative basis.

Materials   Cart or movable kiosk, advertising specialties, coupons.

Timing

Eight to ten weeks prior:

Contact agents responsible for staging community events.

Six weeks prior:

Discuss program with staff and decide on items to be offered, type of cart necessary, and so on.

Five weeks prior:

Begin looking for appropriate advertising specialties.
Purchase, construct, rent, or prepare cart.

Three weeks prior:

Purchase advertising specialties.
Prepare coupons.

Two weeks prior:

Reconfirm participation and meet to discuss details.
Print coupons.

One day prior:

Review program with staff.

Start:

Set up cart.
Begin selling products and food and distributing coupons.

130.   Foil a Thief

Best For   Most business types.

Objective   Increase awareness, increase community goodwill, generate PR, generate traffic, stimulate trial.

Target   Local police departments.

To allow people to easily identify stolen items, the police department recommends that they put their names, or at least their initials, on the back of valuable items such as portable stereos, cell phones, or tools.

Offer free engraving services on a particular day and send press releases to all local media. Buy or rent a couple of electric engraving pens, and have one or two members of your staff do the engraving for customers.

Notify your local police department of the program and ask to have an officer (who may even help with the engraving) available to answer any questions patrons may have about keeping their valuables and their homes safe from thieves.

Flyers placed under windshields in busy parking lots and/or doorknobbers will give you maximum exposure for this program.

Materials   Flyers, doorknobbers, electric engraving pens.

Timing

Three weeks prior:

Prepare press releases.

Contact local police department to have an officer present.
Prepare flyers/doorknobbers.

Two weeks prior:

Print flyers/doorknobbers.
Purchase or rent electric engraving pens.
Discuss program with staff and designate at least two staff members
to do the engraving during the promotion.
Fax/email press releases.
Distribute flyers/doorknobbers.
Confirm police participation.

Start:

Review program with staff.
Begin engraving valuables.

131.   Community Events Coupons

Best For   Most retailers and restaurants.

Objective   Generate traffic, increase sales, stimulate trial.

Target   Local events management organizations.

If your business is unable to participate in large community events
through sponsorship, cosponsoring, or booths, position a few of your
staff members at key locations to hand out coupons good for merchandise, free food, or a sample of your services. Be sure the coupons give
directions to your business. To encourage repeat visits, hand out bounce-back coupons to customers who redeem the coupons.

Materials   Free food/product coupons, bounce-back coupons.

Timing

Four weeks prior:

Contact event management for permission to distribute coupons.

Three weeks prior:

Prepare coupons.

Two weeks prior:

Print coupons.

One week prior:

Meet with staff to discuss the program and schedule the staff members who will be handing out coupons at the event.

Start:

Distribute coupons.
Hand out bounce-backs to customers who redeem coupons.

132.   Blood Donation Tie-In

Best For   Retailers and restaurants.

Objective   Build mailing list, increase community goodwill, generate traffic, stimulate trial.

Target   Local blood banks.

During a local blood drive, offer a free item to anyone who brings a valid donor card to your business on the same day she gives blood. When the card is presented, have the donor fill out her name, her address, and the date of the visit, both to prevent reuse of the card and to add names to your mailing list.

Promote the event with posters in hospitals, doctors' offices, supermarkets, and any cooperative high-traffic neighborhood stores. Be sure to send press releases to local media. If you are in the food business, contact the Red Cross for information on high-iron foods to offer to donors.

Present customers with bounce-back thank-you coupons to generate repeat visits.

Materials   Posters, press releases, bounce-back coupons.

Timing

Six weeks prior:

Begin contacting hospitals, doctors' offices, supermarkets, and stores to get them to cooperate by displaying your posters.

Four weeks prior:

Prepare posters, bounce-back coupons.
Contact the Red Cross for high-iron-food information.

Three weeks prior:

Print posters and bounce-back coupons.

Two weeks prior:

Discuss special items with staff.

One week prior:

Distribute posters.
Discuss program with staff.

Start:

Begin serving donors.
Distribute bounce-back coupons.

133. Armed Forces Reserve Unit Discounts

Best For Restaurants and some retailers.

Objective Increase community goodwill, generate traffic, increase sales, stimulate trial.

Target Armed Forces Reserves.

If your business is near a reserve unit facility, take advantage of the daily, weekly, or monthly reserve member traffic. Contact the local unit to set up a program to supply the unit with one or more meals or special product offerings during the monthly active meetings.

If the unit has its own restaurant facility available, a catering program won't be a good fit. However, you can still offer a special discount to any reserve member going to or coming from meetings.

Materials Discount cards.

Timing

This is an ongoing program. If you cannot arrange catering or you aren't in the food-service business, print discount cards and distribute them to members through their reserve units.

134. We Support Our People in Uniform

Best For Restaurants and some retailers.

Objective Increase community goodwill, generate traffic, improve your image, stimulate trial.

Target Anyone who wears a uniform in his work or organization.

Offer a free item with a purchase to anyone who shows up in uniform—police officers, firefighters, Boy Scouts, Girl Scouts, auto mechanics, factory workers, security guards, members of the armed forces, members of sport teams, members of marching bands, nurses, doctors, waitresses, and so on.

Promote this program with posters in your business, as well as anyplace you will find people in uniform. For exposure to the general public, distribute flyers in shopping centers and parking lots. Occasional ads could also be placed in local newspapers for maximum exposure.

Materials Posters, flyers, ads.

Timing

Six weeks prior:

Begin contacting the working places of people in uniform to get management cooperation and permission to display your posters.

Four weeks prior:

Prepare posters, flyers, ad.

Three weeks prior:

Print posters and flyers.
Buy media.

Two weeks prior:

Distribute posters.

One week prior:

Distribute flyers.
Discuss program with staff.

Start:

Begin serving people in uniform.

12

Direct Mail and Ads

135. Cheap, Targeted Mailing Lists

Best For   All business types.

Objective   Generate traffic, increase sales, stimulate trial.

Target   New customers.

You can use an inexpensive technique that many big marketing companies employ to find the most likely audience for your product or service: public lists of things like real estate transfers and new business filings, trade association lists, and lists you swap or barter for with other businesses in your neighborhood.

A young man I know of had worked for several years for a unit of a national chain of sign shops. He finally had learned enough to feel competent at his trade, and he had grown tired enough of working for someone else to go into business for himself.

He knew from studying the store he worked in that the customers who needed signs most frequently were new businesses and, in this fast-growing suburb, the construction industry. He also knew that there were five other sign shops in the area that he would have to compete with, not including his previous employer.

He contacted the state Corporations Department and got a list of all the new incorporations that had been filed in the past year. He sorted the list to pull out those that were in his trading area and sent them all a mailing offering his services. New companies need new signs.

He also contacted the local building trades association, got its mailing list for a reasonable fee, and sent a different mailing, offering quick turnaround for the signage these firms use to mark and announce new projects. In a couple of months he had more business than he could handle.

111

If you are marketing to high-end customers, you can obtain lists of owners of large parcels of real estate from your county deeds office. The IRS maintains lists of nonprofit organizations. Every licensed physician is on a list. There are many services online that maintain corporate records that you can sort by state and zip code. Bar associations maintain lists of lawyers. Many states have professional regulatory agencies that keep lists of all practitioners in each field, from psychology to pest control.

If you want to target people who are politically motivated, you'll find complete lists of donors to specific political campaigns, often online. Join your Chamber of Commerce and you'll automatically get access to its mailing list. Membership can cost as little as $150.

Check out trade associations. Look in your Yellow Pages under "List Brokers" and "Mailing Services" to see what they have to offer that's within your budget. Your community newspapers and magazines also make their lists available for a fee.

Make sure you know your target market, which you researched by doing the customer survey. And think creatively. If you are a dentist, why not do a mailing to all your local doctors offering them special hours on Sunday when they aren't so busy at the hospital?

136.   Custom Newspaper

Best For   All business types.

Objective   Increase awareness, increase frequency.

Target   The entire community.

People put a high value on news and information about their own communities. Even when you can't get the local papers to write about you, you can write about yourself, both for your existing customers and for prospective customers.

This program consistently exceeds expectations. It's an "advertorial" presented in a newspaper format, four pages printed in color. With this tool, you can promote just about anything, including features about regular customers or key employees and useful information about your area of expertise. You can also include testimonials, publicity reprints, coupons, punch cards, and even sales copy about employment opportunities.

You may be able to cut the cost by getting a vendor or vendors to underwrite some of the expense in exchange for prominent sponsorship ads. Your custom newspaper can be sent out as a self-mailer, inserted in a local or suburban paper, or even hand-distributed by employees.

Businesses that have used this promotion tactic report sales increases of at least 10 to 12 percent, and some as high as 35 percent. It can be done two or three times a year. You may be surprised to learn that once you've done it a few times, your customers will complain if you stop.

Materials Custom newspaper.

Timing

Eight weeks prior:

Determine what you want to say, the offers you want included, and the distribution method—in the newspaper or in the mail.

Six weeks prior:

Prepare write-up and offers.

Four weeks prior:

Review first draft of custom newspaper.

Three weeks prior:

Approve custom newspaper.

Two weeks prior:

Print custom newspaper and deliver to newspapers or local direct mail service to be mailed.

One week prior:

Discuss program with staff.

One day prior:

Discuss program with staff again.

Start:

Redeem offers from custom newspaper.

Six weeks after:

Evaluate program.

137. The Power of the Stars: Horoscopes

Best For   Most business types.

Objective   Increase awareness, generate traffic.

Target   Everyone in the community.

The third-best-read feature in the newspaper (after the comics and the obituaries) is the daily horoscope. You can have some fun and generate some interest by creating a direct-mail piece or a newspaper or magazine ad that reads like a horoscope. Remember to make this a coupon or similar offer that is good for a limited time.

Decide what products or services you want to feature, then write some humorous or clever copy linked to each astrological sign. If you aren't comfortable writing it yourself, find someone to do it for you, or read some generic horoscopes and paraphrase them to suit your purpose. You want to make sure your copy is light, entertaining, and in good taste.

Here are some examples:

To sell more beer: Cancer—A relative's visit will be longer than expected. Treat yourself to a cold one. You deserve it.

To sell more clothing: Gemini—A change in your appearance will put new romance in your life. So will our new fall sweaters.

Materials   Direct mail or ad.

Timing

Six weeks prior:

Prepare direct mail or ad.

Four weeks prior:

Print direct mail.

One week prior:

Discuss program with staff. Send direct mail or place ad.

One day prior:

Discuss program with staff again.

After:

Evaluate results.

138. Speling Error Ad

Best For Consumer-oriented businesses.

Objective Increase awareness, generate traffic, stimulate trial.

Target Existing customers and potential new customers.

About 80 percent of newspaper readers look only at the headline on an ad. You need a headline that compels people to want to read more. Here's one that always works: *There's a spelling error in this ad. If you spot it, we'll give you $5.* You might consider a subheadline that says something like, *We're willing to pay you to try us out.*

Place the error deep in the ad copy so that the reader has to receive the message before he discovers how to claim the reward. Adjust the reward to an amount that is appropriate for your products or services. If your offer is $5, you should have a lot of $5 items available. If your product sells for hundreds, you may want to make your offer $50 or $100.

Make it clear that the reward is good toward a purchase, like a gift certificate. Don't make it look like a discount or a coupon!

Material Newspaper ad.

Timing

Four weeks prior:

Prepare newspaper ad.

One week prior:

Discuss program with employees.
Place newspaper ad.

One day prior:

Discuss program with employees.

Start:

Redeem newspaper ads.

Six weeks after:

Evaluate program.

139. The Gold in Customer Databases

Best For All businesses.

Objective Increase awareness, generate traffic, stimulate trial.

Target Existing customers and potential new customers.

Building and maintaining your customer database—address, email, birthdays, anniversaries, purchase history, and so on—is essential to successful marketing and helps you understand what traits and characteristics separate your customers from the general population. You can learn a lot about your market by studying, manipulating, and interpreting your data.

Your customer database should be kept clean—updated and accurate. It's more than just a list of your best customers; it's a compilation of their lifestyle traits and purchasing behavior. Once you have created the database, it provides ongoing marketing opportunities to increase frequency and gives you valuable insight into where future marketing dollars should be spent.

After several months of data capture (some methods for doing that appear in later chapters), your list can be profiled to show you the average age of your customers, their gender, how many children they have, their average income, their occupation, and even what type of magazines they subscribe to. All of this information can then be compared to the general population to see what sets your customers apart.

Once the information has been captured, it is up to you to ensure that you will get the greatest return on your efforts. A recent study showed direct-mail offers that are highly personalized and printed in full color increased the response rate by 37 percent. New digital printing technologies make color affordable and easy.

140. Customer Thank-You Program

Best For   Most business types.

Objective   Improve your image, build mailing list.

Target   All customers.

Each time a customer fills out a customer comment card or joins your loyalty program, you have an opportunity to increase your exposure to that customer for years to come. Depending on the size and activity of your business, this can be done by your staff, or you can easily farm it out to a provider. Data-capture companies will handle the painstaking task of manually entering data and keeping it valid—the rest is up to you.

Within days of the customer's visit, you or the data-capture company sends the customer a four-color personalized postcard thanking the customer and inviting her to come in again soon.

Materials   Comment cards and/or registration cards, envelopes to send the cards to the data capture company.

Timing

Four weeks prior:

> Prepare photos of staff, location, and merchandise or menu items.
> E-mail photos to service provider for design of piece.
> Prepare comment cards or registration cards.

Three weeks prior:

> Email photos to service provider for design of piece.
> Pre-address envelopes to send the filled-out cards to the service provider.

One week prior:

Discuss program with staff.

Start:

Collect registration information and mail it to the service provider.

Ongoing:

Continue to send in registration information on a regular basis.

13

Staff Incentives

141. Hire Sunshine

Best For All business types.

Objective Recruit and retain the best employees.

Target New employees.

Your marketing messages are conveyed one-to-one, first to your employees, then from your employees to your customers, and finally from your customers to their families, friends, neighbors, and coworkers. Face-time marketing is intimate and personal, the opposite of slick mass media advertising.

You start face-time marketing by hiring, training, motivating, and then leading your employees to go beyond the idea of service and embrace your own belief in hospitality. Service is mechanical. It's putting the right size tire on your car, installing carpet right side up, or writing your airline ticket to the correct destination. It's essential, but it's not hospitality.

Service is something you can teach. Hospitality comes from the heart. It's the personal gift of caring. It's me taking care of you because you're you, not because you're one of 75 people coming through my business this afternoon. You don't serve 75 people. You serve one person at a time, 75 times.

Whatever your business, you are in the business of creating customers. You do that by making them feel important, by showing them that you care.

But before a single person crosses your threshold or phones or emails you to make a purchase, your first customers are your employees. Too many businesses ignore this essential element of success, even the big ones that should know better.

119

How do you hire, train, motivate, and retain people who care about other people? It's a way of life, like the rest of marketing. If a smile is the way you greet your customers, it's the way you should greet your employees. If excitement is the goal of a promotion aimed at generating new customers, excitement is what you should offer your employees. Everything you do for customers to gain their loyalty, you should do for your staff.

Businesses complain that we have a recruiting problem in America, but they're dead wrong about that. What we have is a retention problem because our hiring processes and decisions are terrible, and then we don't take care of the people who we do employ.

Red Auerbach, the legendary coach of the Boston Celtics basketball team, once said, "If you hire the wrong people, all the fancy management tactics in the world won't help you out." You should develop a profile of the person whom you want to be a member of your staff. If you do that, the rest is relatively easy. Low-cost employees are not cheap if they quit in three months. And the person you have to fire is the most expensive of all.

Hire people who are sunshine, and keep them as long as possible. Some people radiate warmth. You see it in their smile, hear it in their voice, and sense it in the way they move. They're gifted in the art of relating.

You can't train people to be sunshine. You may find someone who seems awesome in every other respect, but doesn't smile. You may think to yourself, "I can teach her to smile." You're wrong. You must determine up front exactly what the qualities of the people you want are. You want people who are experienced, people who already have a job and are good at it. This is marketing at its most basic.

142. Recruit from Your Customers

Best For   All business types.

Objective   Recruit employees.

Target   Current customers.

Almost without exception, businesses complain about the avalanche of résumés and applications that they receive whenever they run a classified employment ad. It doesn't make much sense to attract 50 applicants when you need only 2 and then have to spend three days telling 48 of the applicants that they aren't needed.

Just as your marketing should be focused and efficient, so should your hiring.

Recruit through customers. When you or your managers spot a customer with great people skills, ask him or her, "You wouldn't have any friends or family members who need a job, would you?"

You will quickly find the people you need. Your customers will feel complimented because the manager had the judgment to identify them as people with good personal qualities who must know other people with those same qualities.

143. Recruiting Bonus

Best For All business types.

Objective Recruit employees.

Target Current employees.

This very simple idea saves you money on advertising and back-office staff when you need to hire. Recruit within your four walls by offering current employees a $100 bonus for recruiting someone else. Pay the bonus only when that new hire has been on the job at least three months.

The need to pay the bonus will force you to evaluate the new hire after three months to determine whether or not this was a good recommendation. You should think about this at three months because after that time it becomes exponentially more difficult to justify firing someone.

Paying the bonus will make the recommending employee feel that he or she has a say in what goes on in the workplace and will increase loyalty.

144. Send Them Shopping

Best For All business types.

Objective Research the competition to learn how you can improve your business.

Target Employees.

One of the things you should always be doing is checking out the competition. In the marketing wars, intelligence is crucial. One way you can simultaneously check out the competition and make your employees feel important is to send them out to shop the competition.

Encourage them to go with no expectations or agenda. It does you no good to have your employees think that their job is to prove how great you are and how bad the other guy is. Make sure they understand that they are to come back with a list of 10 things that your competitor is doing as well as or better than you, even if they seem trivial.

Are you in the carpet business? Send your salespeople to other showrooms to comparison-shop. Or have them call for an in-home estimate from all your competitors. Don't let them ask a friend or family member. Make sure your employees are learning firsthand what tricks the competition has up its sleeve.

Are you in the plumbing business? Have your plumbers call other plumbers to come in and give an estimate to replace a toilet, or whatever service is comparable. Be creative. Have your staff study every aspect of the other guy's business, from how he answers the telephone to how he prices his product or service.

Now your internal customers are your partners. You have given them respect and dignity, and you have recruited them in your efforts to grow your business and give better customer service. They've become your loyal internal customers.

Don't do this once and then forget about it. Make it a regular program. Send your staff out once a month or once a quarter, whichever is appropriate to your business.

145.   The Praise Department

Best For   All business types.

Objective   Increase retention of your best employees, motivate other employees.

Target   Staff.

Many businesses have a complaint department, but almost none have a praise department. Yet praise is the cheapest employee incentive you can offer.

Gerald Graham, dean of the business school at Wichita State University, found in one study that employees rated personal thanks from a manager for a job well done as the most motivating of a variety of incentives offered. Unfortunately, 58 percent of the workers in Graham's study said that their managers didn't typically give them such thanks.

Appoint someone in your business to be the manager of the Praise Department. Have business cards printed up, put up a sign or poster, or otherwise make it clear and obvious that you are in the business of caring about your employees.

Train your staff and your managers to direct happy customers to the manager of the Praise Department. Keep a public record of praise for employees; create a Wall of Fame for those who have been "caught" doing something right. Leave voicemails of praise for those who deserve it.

Recognize your employees' birthdays by sending them cards and gift certificates, or give them something special on their wedding anniversaries. Enclose inspirational messages or notes with their paychecks telling them that you appreciate them.

Give your staff members a "Get Out of Work Free" card with seven days advance notice for doing a high-quality job or consistently showing up for work on time. We pay people for being sick, and we should reward them for being well.

There is an endless supply of techniques for remembering to recognize employees. Consider buying a book on the subject, like Bob Nelson's *1,001 Ways to Reward Employees* (Workman Publishing).

146. Staff Marketing Committee

Best For   All business types.

Objective   Involve employees in your marketing plans.

Target   Staff.

Too often, business managers spend countless hours crafting and fine-tuning a spectacular marketing program, then dump the program into the laps of their employees and expect them to execute it. Instead, recruit employees to be part of your marketing efforts early on. It'll make them feel invested in the outcome, and you may be surprised to learn how well they actually know your business. They may even save you from disastrous mistakes.

Look around your business and see whom you can recruit for your marketing committee. Draw employees from all the different areas of your business. If you've got a promotion that starts in a month and lasts a month, each department needs to know what it is supposed to do. This helps employees take ownership of the process. If they take ownership, they're going to be able to sell the promotion to their peers better than management ever could.

Before you run your promotion, prepare a detailed description of how it's going to work, put the description on paper, and hand it out to all of your employees so that they know exactly what's expected of them. This also makes them better marketing partners and better able to answer questions from customers about what's going on.

Build employee incentives into each marketing program so that the members of your staff see some direct benefit to themselves from making the program a success.

147. Let Your Staff Decorate

Best For   Most business types.

Objective   Increase awareness, provide crew incentives, create excitement, generate traffic, keep staff busy.

Target   Existing customers and your staff.

You and your staff can decorate your business to suit the various holidays, especially during special holiday promotions. This can be done somewhat inexpensively with a little imagination.

Getting your staff members involved is very important—it serves to build enthusiasm and holiday spirit. You will inevitably discover a host of talents among them. Consider letting your staff members submit ideas and then vote on the most imaginative decorations for a particular holiday. Reward the winner with a real treat, such as letting her choose her own schedule for the following week.

Another great twist on decorating is to invite your staff's families to the business for a special decorating party, either after hours or on a day that you're closed. Provide free food and beverages if your staff will supply the decorations. The cost will be returned to you many times over in both the appearance of your business and the loyalty and goodwill of your staff.

Materials   Holiday decorations.

Timing

Six weeks prior:

Discuss the holiday with your staff members. If it is unusual, explain it to them in detail, so that they will understand how to decorate.

Two weeks prior:

Have staff bring in decorations. Buy anything else you will need.

One week prior:

Meet with staff to decide the grand prize for the winning decorator. Decide on decorating schedule with staff.

Day before:

Hold decorating party for staff and family (optional).

Start:

Decorate.

148.   MVP Rewards

Best For   Most retail businesses.

Objective   Increase awareness, increase community goodwill, provide crew incentives, create excitement, generate traffic

Target   Existing customers, potential new customers, and your employees.

Mail a promotion consisting of two gift certificates for an appropriate item of high perceived value to all residents in your trade area. If your average sale is $100, the value might be $50. Both gift certificates should be for the same amount. One is for the customer to use at your business, and the other is for the customer to give to an employee who has given him excellent service.

The customer's gift certificate should have an expiration date of 30 days. The employee's gift certificate is good toward purchases at other merchants or tickets to sporting events and/or concerts. Make sure the value to the employee is high. Otherwise it will be seen as an empty gesture.

Materials   Customer gift certificates, employee gift certificates, merchant gift certificates or sports/concert tickets

Timing

Eight weeks prior:

Determine what merchandise or event tickets you want to purchase.

Six weeks prior:

Prepare customer and employee gift certificates.

Four weeks prior:

Send gift certificates to printer.

One week prior:

Discuss program with employees.
Pick up merchant gift certificates and/or event tickets.
Mail out invitation to residents in trade area.

One day prior:

Discuss program with employees.

Start:

Redeem gift certificates.

Six weeks after:

Evaluate program.

149. Mystery Shopper

Best For Most retailers and restaurants.

Objective Increase awareness, provide crew incentives, create excitement, improve your image.

Target Your staff.

Three times a day, over a period of six weeks, have your personal friends or members of your family (and/or those of your owner or manager) visit your store posing as shoppers. Make sure they aren't known to your staff, or there is no mystery.

Do this at all your locations. Have shoppers grade each operation on speed of service, accuracy of the transaction, appearance of the product or service, suggestive selling by employees, cleanliness, friendliness, personality of employees, and overall impression.

Provide each mystery shopper with forms to turn in on a weekly basis. At the end of each week, discuss the evaluations with the manager of each location.

At the end of the promotion, schedule a wine and cheese or coffee and dessert party for the entire staff at a central location. Present prizes to the managers of the location scoring the highest and to employees who score high in individual performance.

Materials Checklist for mystery shoppers, prizes for manager and staff members.

Timing

Three weeks prior:

Contact mystery shoppers and explain program.

Two weeks prior:

Make up an evaluation checklist and have copies made.

One week prior:

Recontact mystery shoppers to verify the times of their visits and get them the checklists.
Decide on and purchase prizes.

Start:

> Mystery shoppers shop and turn in their sheets. Tabulate and evaluate results.

End:

> Hold surprise party for managers and staff and give out prizes.

Follow-up:

> Meet with staff regularly to give them feedback on the results of the program and give them recommendations.

150.   Employee of the Month

Best For   Most retailers and all restaurants.

Objective   Increase awareness, provide crew incentives, create excitement, improve your image.

Target   Your employees.

This tactic recognizes and rewards your finest employee each month based on overall performance or improvement.

The manager can select the employee of the month, or if staff members get along well, they can decide the winner themselves. Winners are selected on the basis of a set of criteria that you've predetermined, such as punctuality, appearance, attitude, job performance, cooperation with others, and so on.

For the benefit of your business, the criteria should include areas where you feel your staff needs improvement. If people are showing up late too often, punctuality should carry a lot of weight. The competition will motivate your staff members to improve.

The winning employee each month receives a cash bonus, tickets to a special event, or something else that you or other staff members know that employee would like. Also, display a plaque in a prominent spot with the year engraved on top and the new winner's name engraved each month. This is a constant reinforcement of each winner's accomplishment and will motivate the other members of your staff as well.

Materials Plaque with the year engraved on top and plates that can be engraved each month.

Timing This is a staff incentive tactic that should run regularly. It has no time constraints, but it works best when it begins with a new year so that the names can be engraved beginning in January.

151. First Impression

Best For Most retailers and restaurants.

Objective Increase awareness, provide crew incentives, create excitement, improve your image.

Target Your employees.

Whatever your business, your grand opening period is the first impression you make on the community. Your employees will have only that one chance to make a good first impression. Your success will depend on the proficiency of your staff.

To help motivate your staff during the two-week grand opening period, rate each staff member daily in the following areas: enthusiasm, punctuality, speed of service, courtesy, and appearance. Assign points to each area.

Let staff members know how important it is that they keep their motivation high, and explain the program to them thoroughly. Set cash awards and write them on the staff communications board as a reminder. Print a list of their names with the points they scored each day and their running total, so that they will be even more motivated to pull ahead and get the prizes.

At the end of the two-week period, tally the points for each staff member. Award cash prizes to the five staff members who scored the highest, with the highest cash prize, of course, going to the highest scorer and so on.

Materials Rating card.

Timing

Two weeks prior:

Explain the "first impression" idea to the staff.

One week prior:

Explain the importance of the customers' first impression to the staff.

Start:

Rate staff daily on predetermined areas. Each area has a point value, and staff members receive points daily, to be tallied at the end of two weeks.

End:

The five staff members with the highest number of points win cash awards.

152. Silver Service Dollars

Best For All restaurants and some retailers.

Objective Increase awareness, provide crew incentives, create excitement, improve your image.

Target Your employees.

Your employees should be thoroughly trained in quick, efficient service and suggestive selling. To determine whether each staff member is performing this way on a consistent basis, ask your friends and family to stop by on a regular basis—once every couple of days or as frequently as twice a day—to evaluate staff members.

When a high level of performance is noted, the mystery shopper or diner should notify the manager or owner by telephone just after leaving the establishment, and the staff member will almost instantaneously be rewarded with a silver "service" dollar, an actual silver dollar. Mystery customers should, of course, be reimbursed for their expenditures; the payment for their services is patronizing your establishment at no cost. In the case of nonfood businesses, shoppers should be reimbursed for any purchased items.

Run this program for four to six weeks, to be sure that all members of the staff have been evaluated under different conditions during that time.

Materials   Checklist for mystery diners and shoppers, silver dollars.

Timing:

Three weeks prior:

Contact mystery patrons and explain program.

Two weeks prior:

Make up an evaluation checklist and have copies made.

One week prior:

Recontact mystery diners or shoppers to verify the times of their visits and get them the checklists.
Obtain your supply of silver dollars.

Start:

Meet with employees regularly to give them feedback on the results of the program and give them recommendations.
Keep handing out silver dollars for great performance.

153.   Sample Evaluation Checklist

Evaluation Checklist

Name of staff member:
Date:
Time:
Please rate the above staff member on a scale of 1 to 4:
(1 = excellent, 2 = good, 3 = adequate, 4 = poor)
Immediate attention =
Greeting =
Appearance =
First service =
Attentive during meal/transaction =
Suggestive selling =
Received check quickly =
Comments:
Your name:
Signature:

154.   Family Album

Best For   Most business types.

Objective   Increase awareness, create excitement, improve your image.

Target   Your employees.

Meet with your staff and select a committee to compile an album containing photographs and other entries pertaining to your business and its staff. Suggestions include press releases with related photos about promotions you have done, staff picnics or parties, articles about individual staff accomplishments, employees of the month, individual photos of staff members, and special photos of staff during special occasions.

This program will build camaraderie among the members of your staff and result in greater teamwork. Make sure that the albums are accessible and that you have a camera and (if necessary) film on hand at all times. Be sure to take regular candid photos of your staff in action as your contribution to the albums.

Materials   Album, camera, film (if necessary).

Timing   This is a continuing program and can begin whenever you like.

155.   Score a Touchdown

Best For   Most business types.

Objective   Increase awareness, provide crew incentives, create excitement, improve your image.

Target   Your employees.

This is a month-long contest during which your entire staff tries to meet a goal you've set for it. This goal can be an overall sales increase or an increase in the unit sales of one or more particular products. Make sure the goal is reasonable and attainable. If the goal is a sales increase, make sure you set a percentage increase that is realistic based on past sales.

Once the goal has been set, convert each step along the way into a certain number of yards on a football field. For example, if the goal is to increase overall sales by $10,000, then each $1,000 would represent a gain of 10 yards. If the goal is achieved, a touchdown is scored, and the entire staff is rewarded.

Create a graduated prize scale to reward the staff members for their achievements even if they do not reach 100 percent of the set goal. For example:

Progress to:

50-yard line = $10 per staff member.
40-yard line = $20 per staff member.
30-yard line = $30 per staff member.
20-yard line = $40 per staff member.
10-yard line = $50 per staff member.
Touchdown = $100 per staff member.

These goals should suit the size of your staff and your budget. Promote this program by displaying a poster in the shape of a football field with a movable marker to record progress.

Materials   Staff "football field" poster.

Timing

Three weeks prior:

Determine goal and develop prize structure.

One week prior:

Set up staff meeting and explain goal and prize structure.
Produce football poster.
Display poster and record information.

Start:

Begin recording progress on football poster.

One week in:

Discuss progress with staff; congratulate or discuss performances.

End:

Award prizes based on progress.

156. Costume Day

Best For   Most retailers and restaurants.

Objective   Increase awareness, provide crew incentives, create excitement, improve your image.

Target   Your employees.

Anytime you run a promotion, introduce a new product, or celebrate a local or national holiday, explain the event to the staff and ask each person to dress up in whatever attire would best suit the event.

Be sure to decorate your business to match the event, to create an atmosphere of fun for both staff and customers.

On the first day of the event, have the staff vote for best costume, and allocate some cash or "time off with pay" prizes for the winner.

Materials   Decorations, prizes.

Timing   This is an ongoing event and requires no definite timing, except to be sure to give your staff enough notice to come up with creative attire.

157. Staff Auction

Best For   All business types.

Objective   Increase awareness, provide crew incentives, create excitement, improve your image.

Target   Your employees.

Every three months, run a serious auction specifically for your staff members, in which they have a chance to bid on valuable prizes. They pay, however, with play money that they earned when they performed specific duties and responsibilities during the previous three months.

Print play money with your business's name and logo, in $10 and $20 increments. Leave room for the signature of the store manager who is distributing the money, as well as the signature of the staff member who is receiving the money. This will prevent the staff members from pooling their dollars for the auction and give them a further incentive to earn the dollars individually.

Explain the program to your staff and let them decide on the auction prizes. A budget of about $250 is reasonable for a small to medium-size business, but you should determine the budget based on your own needs. Make sure to explain the criteria by which the dollars will be distributed. For example:

Helped train a new employee: $10

Changed shifts when needed: $10

Perfect weekly attendance: $10

Staff person of the month: $20

Materials　Play money, prizes for auction.

Timing

Four months prior:

Decide on criteria and budget.
Print play money.

Three months prior:

Explain program to staff and begin distributing play money.

Two months prior:

Contact an auctioneer and arrange three-month scheduling.
Purchase prizes.

Start:

Hold auction for staff.

158.　Staff Adopt-a-Street Marketing Campaign

Best For　Most retailers and all restaurants.

Objective　Increase awareness, provide crew incentives, create excitement, generate traffic, improve your image, increase sales, stimulate trial.

Target   Existing customers, potential new customers, and your staff.

Choose a particular number of streets in your business's trading area to receive doorknobbers containing a coupon or flyer for products. Make sure the number of streets you assign is evenly divisible by the number of people on your staff.

Color-code each group of streets and assign that color to a staff member. For example, thirty streets and six staff members equals five streets per staff member. Select six colors and assign each color to a staff member.

Prepare color-coded flyers or coupons and have staff members distribute the flyers in their color code on the doorknobs of the streets they have been assigned. Prepare a chart for the staff bulletin board giving the staff members' names and their color codes. As coupons are redeemed, check their color code and record the redemption next to the staff member's name on the chart.

This program works best when it's run for a six-week period, with weekly prizes awarded to the staff member with the highest coupon redemption rate. Awarding prizes on a weekly basis will keep momentum going among the staff. At the end of the six-week period, tally the totals and award a grand prize.

Materials   Color-coded flyers, chart, weekly prizes, and grand prize.

Timing

Four weeks prior:

Obtain street map and decide on streets to be canvassed.

Three weeks prior:

Prepare and print color-coded flyers.

One week prior:

Make up chart.
Explain program to staff.

Start:

Have staff distribute flyers.
Begin coupon redemption and award weekly prizes.

Six weeks after:

Tally color-coded redemptions and award grand prize.

159. Bring the Family Incentive

Best For Entertainment and food-service businesses.

Objective Increase awareness, provide staff incentives, create excitement, improve your image.

Target Your staff.

After employees reach their 90-day anniversary of working for your business, they earn the benefit of bringing their family any time, 365 days a year, and getting half off the cost on each and every visit. The employee must be present for the family to get this benefit. This builds loyalty and shows family members that your staff considers your business a good place to visit or eat, and each family member is likely to tell someone that she or he knows about you.

160. Knock-Knock

Best For Most retailers, restaurants, and food-service companies.

Objective Increase awareness, provide staff incentives, create excitement, improve your image, increase sales.

Target Existing customers and your staff.

Promote the use of suggestive selling to increase sales of selected items through the game of Knock-Knock, played between staff and customers. This is a simple icebreaker, and although your staff may initially feel a little foolish, you'll be surprised how well it works.

Staff members should wear a button that says "Knock-Knock." Customers will be curious and ask what the button means. For example:

CUSTOMER: "What's with the button?"
EMPLOYEE: "Do you want to play Knock-Knock?"
CUSTOMER: "O.K."
EMPLOYEE: "Knock-Knock."
CUSTOMER: "Who's there?"
EMPLOYEE: "Dewey."

CUSTOMER: "Dewey who?"

EMPLOYEE: "Dewey care to order an appetizer?"

Or,

EMPLOYEE: "Knock-Knock."

CUSTOMER: "Who's there?"

EMPLOYEE: "Ida."

CUSTOMER: "Ida who?"

EMPLOYEE: "Ida like to recommend a tie to go with that shirt you're buying."

Track the item sales of each employee on a tally board each day. At the end of each week, the employee with the highest sales wins a $10 to $20 bonus. Run the promotion for four weeks. At the end of that period, the employee with the most sales for the month wins an extra day's pay. The employee who comes in second wins an extra half-day's pay. Make sure you set minimum sales necessary to cover the cost of the promotion, including the bonuses and grand prize.

Materials   Tally board, Knock-Knock buttons.

Timing

Three weeks prior:

Set minimum sales goals and determine bonuses.
Order Knock-Knock buttons.

One week prior:

Make up tally board.
Explain program to staff.

Start:

Keep daily running totals on scoreboard.

One week after:

Tally scores and award bonuses.

One month after:

Award grand prize and second prize.

161.   Weekly Add-on Bonuses

Best For   Most retailers, restaurants, food-service companies.

Objective   Increase awareness, provide staff incentives, create excitement, improve your image, increase sales.

Target   Existing customers and your staff.

Increase your average transaction by asking your staff to promote add-on items. Reward them with a weekly bonus added to their paychecks.

For every extra item ordered, set a point scale. For simplification, use the price of the item as its point. For example, if you own a kitchen appliance store and a corkscrew sells for $5.25, then a corkscrew is worth 525 points. If you own a restaurant and onion rings are $1.50, then onion rings are worth 150 points, and so on. Keep track of the points earned on a tally board near the staff bulletin board.

At the end of each week, tally the points of each employee, and award an appropriate modest bonus to the employee with the most points. Make sure you set a minimum sales goal that employees must reach in order to be eligible, based on the amount you need to make the program profitable.

Materials   Tally board.

Timing

Two weeks prior:

   Set minimum sales goals and determine bonuses for add-on sales.

One week prior:

   Make up tally board.
   Explain program to staff.

Start:

   Review program with staff.
   Keep daily running totals on tally board.

One week after:

   Tally scores and award bonuses.

162. Temperature Pricing

Best For   Restaurants, food-service companies, some retailers.

Objective   Increase awareness, provide crew incentives, create excitement, increase sales.

Target   Existing customers and your staff.

Put a large outdoor thermometer outside your front door and encourage members of your staff to chat with customers about the weather. The employee announces that certain items are being offered for that price. For example, if it's 45 degrees out, all soups by the cup that are on the menu are offered for 45 cents. If the items you're offering are higher-priced, just add a zero if that seems appropriate: All best-selling books on the *New York Times* list that week are $4.50.

Each item sold by the employee or server wins her a bonus point. Points are noted daily on a tally board. At the end of each week, the employee with the most points gets a bonus. The employee with the second most points gets half that.

Run this promotion during high-traffic periods only, to make sure that the cost of the discounted items is covered by other sales.

You will find that customers have a tendency to try as many of the category items as possible at one time. If they find one or more that they like, they will come back for those items at another time.

Materials   Tally board, large outdoor thermometer.

Timing

One week prior:

> Purchase thermometer and install it where it's visible to the staff.
> Make up tally board.
> Explain program to staff/servers.

Start:

> Review program with staff/servers.
> Keep daily running totals on tally board.

One week after:

Tally scores and award bonuses.

163. 90-Day Anniversary

Best For   All business types.

Objective   Provide crew incentives, create excitement, improve your image.

Target   Your staff.

When new employees reach their 90-day anniversary, reward them with their own business card. This is an inexpensive way of recognizing employees' contributions and their commitment to the business and their jobs.

Business cards can be used in several ways that empower the employee. They can be given to customers with the instruction "ask for Kevin, the next time you visit." During a particular promotion, employees can stamp their cards with a free offer and give them to customers, or you can reward employees with extra stamps for their cards when they "wow" a customer with outstanding service.

Materials   Business cards, stamps, ink pad.

Timing

Two weeks prior:

Order employee business cards.

Start:

Have 90-day anniversary meeting with employee.
Give employee her or his business cards.

164. Restroom Sign

Best For   Restaurants, some service and entertainment businesses.

Objective   Provide staff incentive.

Target   Your staff, current customers.

Hang a sign in the restroom that says, "This restroom is proudly maintained by (employee's name)." Not only will team members feel more accountable for the restroom's cleanliness, but they will be recognized for their work as well. Your customers will appreciate it and may even thank, or ask you to thank, the team member for a job well done.

Make sure the restroom is kept clean, and be prepared if it isn't, because customers will ask for your employee by name to complain.

165. Exercise: Flow-through

Best For   All business types.

Objective   Increase staff loyalty.

Target   Your staff.

If employees are to feel invested in the success of the business, you need to give them information on how you're doing. It often surprises business owners and managers to discover that staff members often have distorted ideas about how much things cost and how much profit a business generates.

Have a flow-through discussion at a staff or team meeting. Take a dollar's worth of change and lay it on the table. Ask team members to write down their answers to the following questions:

1. How much of this sales dollar paid for the cost of labor last period?
2. How much of this sales dollar paid for the cost of sales last period?
3. How much of this sales dollar paid for semivariables last period?

Explain what expenses go into each category and tell team members what the correct amount is for each question, removing the correct amount of coins each time. Explain that the money left over is what we call flow-through, or controllable profit. Make sure you tell them what your flow-through goal is and what your actual results were for last period.

If a team member writes down the correct answers, give that person a dollar and write "Flow-Through Scholar" on it. Post the winning team member's correct answers on the bulletin board. Repeat this exercise periodically to keep your team's financial knowledge fresh.

166. Suggestive Sell Surprise

Best For Some retailers, restaurants, food-service companies.

Objective Provide staff selling incentive.

Target Your staff.

Put a stack of soft drink cups by each cashier and instruct the cashier to remove a cup every time he sells an item you want him to suggest. In one of the cups near the bottom, hide a $5 bill in an envelope. Write on the envelope, "This is for selling so many (items). Thanks for the great job!" When the cashier sells enough to reach the $5 bill, he keeps it. You can also have the cashier manually keep track of how many items are suggestively sold and reward the top seller.

167. Tip Time

Best For Restaurants, service businesses.

Objective Provide staff incentive.

Target Your staff.

In businesses where tipping is customary, organize a "Tip Time" meeting with your staff. Ask each employee to share a story about when she received a great tip and explain why she deserved it. Record the stories on colored index cards and post them on a bulletin board for all to see. Provide your own tip to the team member who offered the best service tip.

168. Adopt a Wall

Best For Most consumer-oriented businesses.

Objective Provide staff incentive.

Target Your staff.

Have each team member adopt a section or wall of the business. That person is responsible for the upkeep and care of that wall or section for one month. At the end of the month, the team members will vote on who's the proud parent of the cleanest, best-kept section. The winner gets to make his own schedule for a week.

169. Priceless Rewards

Best For All business types.

Objective Provide staff incentive.

Target Your staff.

Here are a few simple things that you can offer employees as an incentive or reward for a job well done, a good attendance record, going the extra mile, and so on.

Create their own schedule for a week.
No cleaning bathrooms for a week.
No doing dishes for a week.
Parking space for a week with "Champion" sign on the space.
Owner or manager washes a team member's car.
Team member of the week/month–place photo at counter or on wall.
Manager for a day.
Team member gets a weekend off.
Owner or manager works employee's shift.
Employee becomes coach or trainer of others for the day.
The choice of delivery route for the week
Attend the area or regional general manager's meeting as a guest.

170. Losing Your Marbles?

Best For Most business types.

Objective Provide staff incentive.

Target Your staff.

Place a jar full of marbles in the employee break area and another empty jar next to it labeled "Great Service Jar." Decide what value to give each marble—25 cents, 50 cents, or $1. Each time a team member does something extra to help a customer or another team member, that team member takes a marble and puts it in the Great Service Jar. At the end of the week, count the marbles in the Great Service Jar and ask team members how they want to spend this money—whether they want to save it for the next week or spend it immediately on a group lunch, movie passes, or a reward of their choice.

171. Fun with Candy

Best For   Most business types.

Objective   Provide staff incentive.

Target   Your staff.

Candy is a great recognition tool. Everyone loves it, it's a high-energy sugar boost, and it breaks the rhythm of a normal day or meeting.

Passing out assorted candy or offering a grab bag raises the fun level at a meeting. Certain candy bars also make great rewards.

Mars Bar—For a far-out idea.

Milky Way—Your way is smooth sailing.

Three Musketeers—For the three individuals who made a difference in your business this week.

Kudos—Congratulations!

PayDay—To commemorate a paycheck well deserved.

Snickers—For having a great sense of humor and making us laugh.

Starburst—You are a STAR and a burst of energy!

M&Ms—For Magnificent and Marvelous work.

Gold Coins Made of Chocolate—You're worth your weight in gold!

Junior Mints—For your junior management team.

Whatchamacallit—For indescribable performance.

Sweet Tarts or Sweeties—For being so sweet to a customer.

Nestlé's Crunch—You came through in a crunch.

Other foods:

Fortune cookies—You have a bright future with us.

Klondike bar—For being COOL under pressure.

Dr. Pepper—You're just what the doctor ordered.

Doughnut holes—For a hole-in-one performance.

Grandma's Cookies—You're one tough cookie.

Bunch of bananas—Thanks a bunch!

172.   16 Ways *not* to Treat Your Employees

Never say "Hello" or "Goodbye."

Never ask, "How are you?"

Never say "Thank you."

Never take the time to listen.

Never acknowledge a team member's strengths.

Never have team member meetings.

Never have one-on-one meetings, except to give criticism.

Never acknowledge a job well done.

Never be flexible with schedules.

Never emphasize people skills, only technical skills.

Never ask your management team for input when decisions are being made.

Never make a person feel important.

Never get your team's commitment.

Never show empathy.

Never acknowledge the need to cross-train and grow in the job.

Never give a team member credit when credit is due.

—Adopted from *101 Recognition Secrets: Tools for Motivating and Recognizing Today's Workforce*, by Rosalind Jeffries.

14

Miscellaneous Tactics for Retailers

Many tactics in this section will work well for any business, but they are geared toward retailers of all types, from clothing to cars. Use this as a guide, but also consult other sections of this book to stimulate your creativity.

173. Sample This!

Best For Retailers, many service businesses.

Objective Increase awareness, increase community goodwill, increase sales.

Target Businesses in your trading area.

Sampling is a very effective way to introduce your business to potential customers. However, sometimes you have to take your samples to customers in order to get them to give you a try. This program is designed to introduce you and your business to people working at other businesses in your trading area. If you sell a type of product or service that is easily delivered outside of your own location, you have the ability to reach nearly 200 such businesses and countless new customers in the course of one year.

Although this tactic is tailor-made for food businesses, you can easily adapt it to the retailing environment and certain services, especially by using coupons or gift certificates. Determine a product or service that you offer that is easily sampled and in some way is a good representation of your business. A car wash can't move its equipment, but it could offer an inexpensive item like an air freshener with an attached certificate good for a free basic car wash.

The key to the success of this promotion is that potential customers get something immediately that introduces them to your business without cost or obligation.

A hair salon could give out free samples of shampoo and conditioner with a special certificate inviting the potential customers back to the salon.

A bookstore can give away bookmarks along with a coupon.

A dry cleaner can give away lint rollers and a coupon for a free suit cleaning.

A dentist can distribute toothbrushes and toothpaste samples along with a coupon for a discount on teeth-whitening.

Assign one person to do this, and have this person visit three or four businesses per week. You will definitely see an increase in sales.

When using a product give-away for your outreach program, ask suppliers to provide you the samples for free or at a reduced rate. It's to their advantage to help you.

Materials   Bounce-back coupons, flyers, samples.

Timing

Four weeks prior:

Prepare list of businesses.

Three weeks prior:

Prepare bounce-back coupons.
Prepare flyers.

Two weeks prior:

Print bounce-back coupons.
Print flyers.

One week prior:

Contact businesses to set up appointments to deliver samples.
Discuss program with staff.

One day prior:

Confirm appointments with businesses.

Start:

Prepare samples.
Visit businesses.

Six weeks after:

Evaluate results.

174. Roll the Dice

Best For Retailers, some service businesses.

Objective Create excitement, build customer loyalty.

Target Current customers.

In general, I don't recommend discounting your product or service in any mass-marketing program. Instead, I suggest gift certificates and cross-promotions. But if you want to run a special offer, be creative about it and aim it at your target customers.

One of my favorite promotional tactics is called Roll the Dice. When customers come into your establishment, invite them to roll a die to see how much of a discount they will receive. A one gets 10 percent off; a six gets 60 percent. This will build an air of excitement and unpredictability within your store, creating a memorable experience for both your employees and your customers.

Do this without announcing it, just often enough to tantalize people to keep coming back. It's easy, cheaper than advertising, and a lot more effective.

175. Incremental Punch Card

Objective Increase awareness, generate traffic, increase frequency.

Target Existing customers.

Incremental punch cards are much more effective at increasing frequency than standard frequency cards, which most people lose, leave at home, or throw away.

Your customers get instant gratification, and they have a strong incentive to keep coming back, as the discounts grow with each transaction. You can set the increasing value in percentages or in dollar amounts. See Tactic 183 for additional details about these cards.

Cards can be given to customers or mailed.

Materials   Punch cards, punch.

Timing

Three weeks prior:

Prepare punch cards.

Two weeks prior:

Print punch cards.

One week prior:

Discuss program with staff. Mail punch cards (if applicable).

One day prior:

Discuss program with staff.

Start:

Hand out punch cards to all guests.

176.   Smile Button

Best For   Retailers, service businesses.

Objective   Increase customer service, increase satisfaction.

Target   Your staff.

It's sometimes hard to get your sales staff to smile, but here's a way to make it worth their while. It's the $2 smile button. In order to create hospitality and get people to smile, buy some cheap smile buttons and attach to them a $2 bill (it's unusual and has interest by itself) with a little sign that says, "If I don't smile, you get this $2 bill."

Give each staff member five $2 bills and tell them they can keep the ones they don't have to give away. That'll have them grinning! Do this often enough to keep up the momentum.

177. Bookstore Sandwich Service

Best For Retailers, some service businesses.

Objective Increase customer goodwill.

Target Current customers.

Independent bookstores have been battered in recent years by huge bookstore chains and online booksellers like Amazon.com. Yet they can survive and even thrive by aggressively marketing to their neighbor-hoods. Do what the big stores do. Put in some comfortable couches. Have an information counter right at the front door, and keep it staffed at all times. Bookstore customers get frustrated very quickly when they can't find what they're looking for.

Have a hostess or server go around to people who are sitting and reading and offer to bring them a cup of coffee or to go get them a sand-wich from a nearby sandwich shop. You will surprise and delight your customers, even if they decline, and they'll tell their friends.

178. Customers Phone Home

Best For All business types.

Objective Increase customer service, improve complaint resolution, provide staff incentive.

Target Current customers.

I once wandered into an ice-cream store in the Bronx in New York that was like any other ice-cream shop you'd find anywhere except for a cou-ple of obvious differences. It was sparkling clean, and it was a lot better run. The employees were helpful, smiling, and eager to please.

Sitting prominently on the counter was a stack of business cards, the owner's business cards. In addition to all the usual information the card said, "If you have any comments at all about the store, please call me at home." Then it gave the owner's home phone number. You couldn't help but notice the cards.

The owner's internal customers, his employees, couldn't help noticing the walk-in customers eyeballing those cards and sticking them in their pockets. It's all about accountability. The rest is human nature.

179.   Car Dealer Tie-In

Best For   Most retailers, restaurants, service businesses.

Objective   Increase awareness, increase frequency.

Target   Car dealerships in your trade area.

Car dealers spend a small fortune on advertising and are always looking for something special to bring in the buyers. So why not make your product or service the incentive for customers to go to that car dealer and test-drive one of its cars? Provide the dealer with gift certificates that can be redeemed at your business. Ideally, you want to sell these certificates to the dealer so that you at least cover your out-of-pocket costs. However, if the dealer plans to really promote this event and to put your company name in his other advertising, consider giving the certificates for free.

If you want to get reimbursed for your costs but still make the promotion attractive to the dealer, charge only for the certificates that get redeemed. In any certificate promotion, there will be a certain amount of slippage. The dealer may distribute 200 of your certificates during the course of that promotion. But perhaps only 125 customers actually come into your business to redeem them. You charge the dealership only for the 125 redemptions. Your cost is covered, and the dealership gets a break on the cost of the promotion as well. Everyone wins.

Materials   Gift certificates.

Timing

  Six weeks prior:

    Contact local auto dealer to partner with.

Three weeks prior:

Prepare gift certificates.

Two weeks prior:

Print gift certificates.
Discuss program with staff.

One week prior:

Discuss program with staff.
Give gift certificates to auto dealer.

One day prior:

Discuss program with staff again.

Start:

Redeem gift certificates.

Six weeks after:

Evaluate program.

180.   Picket Your Own Business

Best For   Retailers in high-traffic locations.

Objective   Increase awareness, create excitement, increase frequency, generate PR.

Target   Existing customers and potential new customers.

Designed to build awareness of your business, this promotion is done right outside your restaurant or business. Picket signs will promote your business in a positive way. Have either off-shift employees or, if you have more than one location, employees from another location do the picketing at your business.

Meet with employees and come up with fun things to put on the picket signs. Make sure to keep your slogans to five words or so, and the message should be tasteful: Best Linens In Town! Choose a day of the week when traffic will be heavy to get the most exposure.

Materials   Picket signs.

Timing

Six weeks prior:

Meet with employees and determine what will be written on picket signs.

Four weeks prior:

Prepare picket signs.

Two weeks prior:

Print picket signs.

One week prior:

Discuss program with employees.
Line up employees who will be doing the picketing.

One day prior:

Confirm who will be doing the picketing and give them their signs.

Start:

Picket the business.

Two weeks after:

Evaluate program.

181.   Fortune Cookie Coupon

Best For   All business types.

Objective   Increase awareness, increase frequency, stimulate trial.

Target   Existing customers.

This is one of the most effective, cheap, and fun promotions there is, and it's been used by every kind of business from a local clothing shop to a global pharmaceutical corporation.

To reward existing customers, give them special fortune cookies customized for your needs. The "fortune" is a percentage off their purchase during that visit. The discount should be significant enough to make it attractive. There is a company whose name is listed in the "Materials" section that provides the cookies and will print anything you want on the slip of paper that goes inside.

You should mix the percentage discounts, having a certain number of cookies that offer 5 percent, 10 percent, 15 percent, 20 percent, and so on, as appropriate to your goals and business.

You can design this promotion in two ways, whichever makes sense for your business. Customers can pick their fortune cookie out of a jarful either after they've selected their purchase or before, depending on the desired effect. After is a thank you; before is an incentive to customers to buy more.

A clothing store, for example, can keep a jar of cookies at the front desk with a sign (or a sales clerk) inviting customers to pick one, break it open, and find out how large a discount they'll get.

This promotion has been done numerous times, and one of the effects is that customers who get 20 percent off that day decide to buy more than they had intended to take advantage of the offer. As a result, it may make sense to have the majority of the cookies give shoppers 20 percent off. This is a much more effective way to run a sale than to simply advertise a 20 percent off sale. Always include a few big discounts. Those people will become your ambassadors.

You can even use these fortune cookies as part of a direct-mail campaign. You can ship your cookies in a Chinese food carryout container, which is then placed in a white corrugated shipping box. One such campaign for a pharmaceutical company resulted in an average response rate of 24.9 percent. It did a series of three mailings, one week apart, to promote a new drug to doctors. The drug's key information was provided as an insert in the shipping box.

Materials Fortune cookies. For information contact Fancy Fortune Cookies at (317) 299-8900; fax (317) 298-3690, visit www.fancyfortunecookies.com.

Timing

Six weeks prior:

Determine what your offer will be.

Four weeks prior:

Order fortune cookies.

One week prior:

Discuss program with employees.

One day prior:

Discuss program with employees and get them geared up.

Start:

Hand out fortune cookies.

Four weeks after:

Evaluate program.

182. Mystery Night

Best For Retailers, some service businesses.

Objective Increase awareness, create excitement, keep staff busy, promote activity during slow periods, generate traffic, stimulate trial.

Target Existing customers and potential new customers.

Choose a traditionally slow night of the week, such as a Monday or Tuesday, and establish a specific time period, such as between 6:00 and 8:00 p.m. For those two hours, purchases (excluding those items you want to exclude) are free. But don't announce it ahead of time! Do it randomly, and without notice.

The first time you do this, you'll find that the word-of-mouth exposure will be unreal. The key to this promotion's success is that it is unadvertised (except through word of mouth), so nobody knows when it's going to happen. But when it does, everyone will be talking about it.

All of a sudden your slowest nights become some of your strongest nights. This works best for businesses offering lower-ticket services, such as small cafes, movie rental shops, car washes, and ice-cream shops.

Materials None required.

Timing

One week prior:

Discuss program with employees.

One day prior:

Discuss program with employees.

Start:

Offer free items on designated day during designated time period.

Four weeks after:

Evaluate program.

15

Cards, Coupons, Tear-Outs

183. Incremental Punch Card

Best For   Retailers, some service businesses.

Objective   Increase awareness, generate traffic, increase frequency.

Target   Existing customers.

Many businesses use the traditional punch card to gain repeat guests. This innovative version is an incremental punch card and is much more effective. Most punch cards require a series of purchases, with customers getting something free once they complete all the punches. The incremental punch card gives the customers something of value every time they visit. And, the value increases with each purchase.

On a customer's first visit, the customer gets the card. When the card is punched on the second visit, the customer saves 10 percent. On the third visit, the discount is 15 percent. On the fourth visit, it's a whopping 25 percent, and it's 50 percent on the fifth visit.

What makes this approach work so well is that it gives your customers instant gratification. They don't have to wait to get value, and therefore they are more likely to come back repeatedly. The traditional punch card takes too long for the customer to get any value, so generally the only ones who redeem them are your die-hard loyal customers.

Another variation is to use dollar amounts instead of percentages. Adjust the amounts so that they are appropriate for your situation. You can go up by the same dollar increment: $1, $2, $3, $4, $5. Or, for some real excitement, you can double the offer with each visit, if your margins allow for it: $1, $2, $4, $8, $16, and so on.

The punch card can also be mailed to your database or handed out within the four walls of your business.

Materials   Punch cards, punch.

Timing

Three weeks prior:

Prepare punch cards.

Two weeks prior:

Print punch cards.

One week prior:

Discuss program with staff.
Mail punch cards (if applicable).

One day prior:

Discuss program with staff.

Start:

Hand out punch cards to all customers.

184. Bingo

Best For   Retailers, some service businesses.

Objective   Increase awareness, increase sales, increase frequency.

Target   Existing customers.

The bingo card promotion encourages existing customers to patronize your business more often and sample a greater variety of your offerings.

When customers pay for a purchase or transaction, they're given a bingo card displaying 16 items (4 per row). Each time a customer tries one of the featured items, the cashier stamps it out on the card. Every "bingo" horizontally, vertically, or diagonally is awarded a gift certificate for a predetermined freebie. Be sure to promote the most profitable as well as the most popular items.

This program should carry an expiration date of 30 days, printed clearly on each bingo card.

Materials   Bingo cards, stamp, inkpad, promotional posters.

Timing

Four weeks prior:

> Prepare bingo cards.
> Prepare posters.

Two weeks prior:

> Print bingo cards.
> Print posters.
> Purchase stamp and inkpad.

One week prior:

> Discuss program with staff.

One day prior:

> Discuss program with staff again.
> Hang posters.

Start:

> Hand out bingo cards.

Six weeks after

> Evaluate program.

185.   Passport Promos

Best For   Retailers, restaurants, service businesses.

Objective   Increase awareness, increase frequency, build mailing list.

Target   Existing customers and local retailers.

This promotion works well if you have a number of locations; if you don't, it works equally well as a partnership promotion with other businesses.

Customers are given a promotional "passport." Employees stamp the passport each time the customer patronizes one of your locations or one of the partnering businesses. When the customer has purchased something in each of the locations, the passport can be redeemed for a prize. The more locations you require, the bigger the prize.

Chart House Restaurants, with 61 locations throughout the world, made its offer that a customer who ate at all 61 locations would win a trip around the world. The passport can be mailed to your database and/or promoted within the four walls of your business.

If you only have one or two locations, you can do a variation of this promotion by teaming up with several noncompetitive businesses. When customers visit you and your promotional partners, they can win the prize. The cost of the prize is shared among the partners.

For example, if you run a photo-processing store, you might also tie into other area merchants, such as a pizza restaurant, a dry cleaner, a convenience store, an ice-cream shop, and a car wash. Once customers have bought at all six of these businesses, they can redeem their passport for the prize.

In this case, the prize could be a booklet containing certificates for one free pizza, one free ice-cream cone, one free roll of film, a free car wash, and a free large coffee or fountain drink at the convenience store. The total value of the prize is perhaps $20 to $30. In this way, all six merchants are helping to promote one another. The cost is very low.

Be sure to provide each of the merchants with counter cards, posters, and other in-store promotional material to help them market the passport program. Also, you want to be very selective about the promotional partners you choose. You may not want to choose a partner that is right next door to your location, since you're likely to get those customers anyway. So, go farther down the street. Find a pizza place near one of your competitors. The customers you generate from that exposure are much more likely to be new customers for you.

Also you want to make sure that your partners will honor all the certificates and help promote the event as much as you will. For that reason, deal only with merchants that you know and trust and that have a good reputation in the community.

Materials Passport, stamp, inkpad, booklet (if applicable), counter cards, posters.

Timing

Six weeks prior:

  Contact local retailers to partner with.

Four weeks prior:

  Prepare passport, booklet (if applicable), counter cards, poster.

Two weeks prior:

  Print passport, booklet (if applicable), counter cards, poster.
  Discuss program with staff.

One week prior:

  Discuss program with staff.
  Mail passport or booklet.

One day prior:

  Discuss program with staff.

Start:

  Stamp passports.
  Redeem coupons in booklet.

Six weeks after:

  Evaluate program.

186.   Lottery Ticket Giveaway

Best For   Most business types.

Objective   Increase awareness, increase frequency, increase sales.

Target   All customers.

If your business is located in a state that has a lottery, giving away tickets can be a productive way to increase visit frequency and interest, especially when the jackpot reaches a sizable amount.

  At that point, purchase $100 worth of lottery tickets and hand one out to each customer who purchases a featured product or service. Instruct your employees to call attention to the potential for a major payday. Hang promotional posters in highly visible areas to further cement customers' involvement.

Once the posters have been developed, you can execute the promotion every time the lottery swells.

Materials Posters, lottery tickets.

Timing

Four weeks prior:

Prepare posters.

Two weeks prior:

Print posters.
Discuss program with staff.

One day prior:

Purchase lottery tickets.
Hang posters.
Discuss program with staff again.

Start:

Hand out lottery tickets.

187. V.I.P. Card

Best For Retailers, restaurants, some service businesses.

Objective Increase awareness, build mailing list, increase frequency, generate traffic.

Target Existing loyal customers.

Invite regular customers to join your V.I.P. Club. Membership will have rewards such as a V.I.P. card, priority service, invitations to members-only events, and other such benefits.

In order to build awareness of the club and its many rewards, conduct the initial membership drive within your four walls with posters and handouts. Employees will ask customers if they are members of the

V.I.P. Club. If not, they will be encouraged to join. To join, guests fill out a data capture card including birthday and other information for follow-up. There are no costs for joining the club.

Materials   Data capture form, handout, V.I.P. card.

Timing

Four weeks prior:

Determine the rewards of membership.

Three weeks prior:

Prepare card.

Two weeks prior:

Print card.

One week prior:

Discuss program with employees.

One day prior:

Discuss program with employees.

Start:

Membership drive begins.
Hand out data capture piece.
Give guests V.I.P. cards.

Four weeks after:

Evaluate program.

188.   Yellow Pages Rip-Off

Best For   Retailers, restaurants, most service businesses.

Objective   Increase awareness, increase frequency, stimulate trial.

Target   Existing customers and potential new customers.

This is a clever, in-your-face promotion that literally saved a small pizza chain in Denver, Colorado. The stores specialized in delivery, living and dying by their Yellow Pages advertising. They had a small ad on page three of the pizza section, and it worked fine for years.

Then Domino's Pizza started a major expansion, opening up a lot of franchises in Denver. It spent a lot of money on advertising, including a full-page Yellow Pages ad. As a result, Domino's got page one of the pizza section. Four major competitors were on the back of the ad. This small chain's ad was shoved deeper into the section.

This meant that when the new Yellow Pages book was released that year, customers had to turn more pages to find the chain's ad. Sales dropped. Then the owner got an idea. He ran a campaign that said, "Bring the Domino's Yellow Page out of the phone book into my locations, and you'll get a discount." People started ripping the ads out. It got so you couldn't find a Domino's Yellow Pages ad anywhere in Denver.

To build your business or stay one step ahead of the competition, place an ad in your local newspaper asking people to bring in *any* ad for one of your competitors from the Yellow Pages in a phone book for a discount. You can also display a poster in your restaurant and have employees wearing buttons that say "Ask me about the Yellow Pages."

Materials   Ad, poster, employee buttons.

Timing

Four weeks prior:

Determine what your ad will be.
Develop poster.
Order buttons.

Two weeks prior:

Place ad.
Print poster.

One week prior:

Discuss program with employees.

One day prior:

Discuss program with employees and get them geared up.
Hang poster.

Hand out buttons to employees.

Start:

Redeem competitors' ads.

Six weeks after:

Evaluate program.

189.   Dash Back and Save Cash Coupon

Best For   Retailers, restaurants, most service businesses.

Objective   Increase awareness, increase frequency.

Target   Existing customers.

Distribute a bounce-back coupon good for 50 percent off to all customers, who return within a very short period of time, generally 24 hours. The bounce-back can also be used to get customers to return at a generally slower time. For example, if you are busy during the day, hand out the bounce-back during the day and have it good for 50 percent off when used within 24 hours.

Materials   Bounce-back coupons.

Timing

Four weeks prior:

Prepare bounce-back coupons.

Two weeks prior:

Print bounce-back coupons.

One week prior:

Discuss program with employees.

One day prior:

Discuss program with employees.

Start:

   Hand out bounce-back coupons.

Four weeks after:

   Evaluate program.

190.   Preferred Patron Bounce-Back

Best For   Retailers, restaurants, service businesses.

Objective   Increase awareness, increase frequency, generate traffic.

Target   Existing customers and potential new customers

Produce "funny money" bills or certificates that customers can use on their next visit. Use denominations of ones, fives, and tens, depending on your average transaction. If a customer spends $20, give her $2 in bounce-back bills or certificates.

   This promotion is not advertised, so it surprises and delights customers and creates word-of-mouth exposure. To ensure the return business, make the expiration date for the coupons in 30 days.

Materials   Funny money or gift certificates.

Timing

   Six weeks prior:

      Prepare funny money or gift certificates.

   Four weeks prior:

      Print funny money or gift certificates.

   One week prior:

      Discuss program with staff.

   One day prior:

      Discuss program with staff again.

Start:

Distribute and redeem funny money or gift certificates.

Six weeks after:

Evaluate program.

191. Parking Ticket Summons

Best For   Retailers, restaurants, some service businesses.

Objective   Increase awareness, generate PR, generate traffic, increase sales, stimulate trial.

Target   Potential customers in your trade area.

Follow the lead of a lawn and garden shop in San Antonio, Texas. The owners put a promotional piece under the windshield wipers of cars parked at downtown meters. Designed to look like a parking ticket, the piece read: "RELAX! This is NOT a parking ticket. We just happened to be going by your car and noticed that the meter was ready to run out, or had already done so. To save you the hassle and cost of a fine, we've taken the liberty of putting a little bit of money in the meter for you. Compliments of The Lawn & Garden Shop."

The shop got a lot of attention—and a lot of word-of-mouth business, too! It also got phone calls, including one from the San Antonio Police Department. As it turned out, because of a policy of not ticketing the same car twice, true violations were going unnoticed. Eventually, the color of the promotional piece was changed from yellow to blue.

A simple gesture like this makes a big impression.

Materials   Tickets.

Timing

Six weeks prior:

Prepare tickets.

Four weeks prior:

Send tickets to printer.

One week prior:

Discuss program with staff.
Pick up tickets from printer.

One day prior:

Discuss program with staff again.

Start:

Distribute tickets.

Six weeks after:

Evaluate program.

192. Scratch-Off Mailer

Best For Retailers, restaurants, some service businesses.

Objective Increase awareness, create excitement, generate traffic, increase sales, stimulate trial.

Target Existing customers and potential new customers.

This tactic works particularly well if you have multiple locations and/or concepts, or as a partnering opportunity with other businesses. It's a flyer containing mystery gift certificates, with the offer hidden under a scratch-off box. Contact a local advertising agency, direct-mail specialist, or commercial printer to find out how to go about producing these.

Mail the flyers to your database. If you don't have a database, purchase a mailing list, or, if mailing is too costly, you can hand out the flyers. Customers bring the flyer into one of your locations, where an employee scratches off the offer to see what the customer has won.

Make sure your flyer explains what the prizes are, and make sure the prizes are of sufficient value to get people to come in.

If you don't have multiple locations, you can work a similar program by partnering with a dozen or so other businesses in your trade area. They could be stores in a shopping center located nearby, stores in a mall, or any stores that share your target customer base. For example, you can team up with other noncompetitive businesses, such as a gas station, a quick oil change facility, a car wash, a tire store, a muffler shop, or an auto repair shop.

If you're handing out the flyers, once the customer gets the flyer at the first store, that customers has an incentive to visit all of the other stores on the flyer. Each of the participating stores shares in the cost of printing the flyers. They are distributed to each of the participants based on the expected weekly customer count during the week of the promotion. Support the flyer with a point-of-purchase display and other in-store marketing to make customers aware of the promotion.

Materials   Customer gift certificate with scratch-off offers, merchant gift certificates or sporting/concert tickets

Timing

Six weeks prior:

> Make a list of merchants you want to partner with. Contact each of the merchants to explain the promotion and get a commitment.
> Explain that the printing costs will be split by all participating merchants.

Four weeks prior:

> Develop flyer with scratch-offs.

Three weeks prior:

> Send flyers with scratch-offs to printer.

One week prior:

> Discuss program with employees.
> Pick up flyers from printer.
> Mail out flyers to database or purchased mail list.

One day prior:

> Discuss program with employees.

Start:

> Hand out flyers (if you opt not to incur mailing costs).

Six weeks after:

> Evaluate program.

16
Community Tactics

193. Parks and Recreation Tactics

Best For   Some retailers, restaurants, some service businesses.

Objective   Stimulate trial, increase goodwill, generate PR.

Target   Prospective customers, community.

Promotions focused on public parks and recreation events are a good way to make friends—both within the community and on a larger scale.

Local civic organizations plan many community events, such as fairs, arts and crafts festivals, boat shows, and home shows. These are usually held outdoors during warm weather, frequently run for long hours, and are a prime opportunity to set up promotions to sell your specialties.

Many types of businesses sell products or offer services that would fit well with many of these events. You should look at these events less as profit opportunities than as a chance to introduce yourself to the community during a community event.

In many locales, food festivals are regular summertime events. These, of course, are a perfect time for you to display any food-related product to the public to create awareness, promote trial visits, and encourage more frequent visits by existing customers.

The following pages offer a number of specific tactics that have proved successful. Tailor them to what makes the most sense to your situation.

194. Beach Activities

Best For   Most business types.

Objective   Increase awareness, increase community goodwill, improve your image, stimulate trial.

Target   Potential new customers.

This is a year-round promotion for businesses located in warm-weather climates and a spring-through-fall project for temperate zones. It's a bit more ambitious than some other tactics, but it's very effective for introducing yourself to a new audience.

Contact local sporting-goods retailers to arrange sponsorship of community beach or other public outdoor activities as a partnership promotion. Activities like volleyball, Frisbee, or tug-of-war tournaments on the beach work great—the participating retailer supplies the sporting goods, and you follow that up with a luau, barbecue, or clambake sponsored by your business. As the event ends, present trophies to the participants as prizes.

Consider partnering with a caterer or local restaurant for the food portion and/or a local beverage supplier for the drinks. Be sure to contact the proper authorities when you plan on sponsoring such an event, as different rules and regulations apply in different counties and states.

Promote the activity through the use of newspaper advertising, radio advertising, and posters in your business and the sporting-goods store. On the day of the event, if you can afford it, hire a banner tow plane to fly over the beach for a couple of hours.

Contestants must sign up for the sporting event, either at your business or at the sporting-goods retailer. When they sign up, they also make a reservation and prepay for the food portion of the event.

Suggestion: Give separate tickets for event participation and food. Reservations and prepayment are a must.

Be sure to prepare signs and have a kiosk where you can either sell your products or give out brochures. Make sure you have plenty of coupons to distribute to beach traffic not participating in the event. Make sure the coupon offer is valid for no more than 30 days.

Materials   Newspaper ad(s), radio script, sporting goods, banners, banner tow plane, posters, food reservation list, sporting participant list, food tickets, sports entry tickets, coupons.

Timing:

Eight weeks prior:

Contact proper authorities for rules and regulations.
Get any necessary licenses.
Begin contacting sporting-goods retailers and food and beverage providers.

Six weeks prior:

Put together a calendar of events with participating retailers and schedule employee work hours for the promotion.

Five weeks prior:

Prepare newspaper ad(s), radio script, banners, posters, lists, tickets, and coupons.

Four weeks prior:

Buy media.
Arrange for and schedule tow plane.
Print banners, posters, lists, tickets, and coupons.

Three weeks prior:

Reconfirm promotion with partners.
Discuss program with staff and hand out work assignments.
Distribute posters, lists, and tickets to promotion partners.
Display posters.
Meet with staff and caterer/beverage supplier to discuss food preparation at beach.

Two weeks prior:

Reconfirm tow plane.
Place media.
Begin taking reservations.

One week prior:

Meet with partners, their staffs, and your staff to finalize details.

One day prior:

Meet with partners, their staffs, and your staff to review procedures.

Start:

> Begin events.
> Redeem food tickets.
> Present prizes.

One week after:

> Begin redeeming coupons at your business.

Four weeks after:

> Evaluate results.

195.   Team Sign-Ups

Best For   Most retailers, restaurants, some service businesses.

Objective   Increase community goodwill, generate traffic, improve your image, increase sales, stimulate trial.

Target   Existing customers and potential new customers.

Offer your business's parking lot as a sign-up area for youngsters in Little Leagues and other recreational programs. Contact parks and recreation administrators to make the arrangement and volunteer the assistance of your staff.

During the sign-ups, pass out coupons for free products or gifts redeemable at the next visit to your business, with a one-month expiration date.

This is also a good opportunity to form relationships with coaches and park administrators, who might be more willing to cooperate with you for other future promotions as a result.

Materials   Coupons, communications board.

Timing

Six weeks prior:

> Contact parks and recreation administrators to arrange participation.

Three weeks prior:

Meet with staff to discuss participation and scheduling of shifts. Prepare coupons.

One week prior:

Display location and date of sign-up on communications board.

Start:

Distribute coupons to families of youngsters who sign up.

One to four weeks after:

Redeem coupons.

196. Tape It and They Will Come

Best For   Most retailers, restaurants, some service businesses.

Objective   Increase awareness, increase community goodwill, generate traffic, improve your image, increase sales, stimulate trial.

Target   Existing customers and potential new customers.

Building foot traffic is always a challenge. One way to do it is to videotape a Little League game or junior soccer match.

Distribute flyers to all the parents and other spectators at the game explaining that you'll be showing the video at your business after the game. When people arrive to see the video, give them a bounce-back for a future visit.

You can even expand this concept to include school concerts and plays.

Materials   Flyers, bounce-backs.

Timing

Four weeks prior:

Get schedule of games for the season from the sports association.

Three weeks prior:

Prepare flyers.
Prepare bounce-backs.

One week prior:

Explain program to the staff.
Print flyers.
Print bounce-backs.

Start:

Distribute flyers at the game.
Distribute bounce-backs in business after the game.

Four weeks after:

Evaluate program.

197.   Parking Lot/Sidewalk Tactics

Best For   Most retailers, restaurants, some service businesses.

Objective: Increase awareness, create excitement, generate PR, generate traffic, improve your image, increase sales, stimulate trial.

Target   Existing customers and potential new customers.

Your parking lot and the sidewalk in front of your business are additional sources of promotions, especially those aimed at getting yourself noticed and creating trial visits. If you are lucky enough to have a large outdoor area available to you, you can try tactics that would be unthinkable inside.

Sidewalk sales held on a cooperative basis with other retailers are great places to sell products and food to shoppers. They may be customers of neighboring retailers who have never even noticed that you are there, let alone tried your business.

Promotions with very large groups, promotions involving the use of water, civic fund-raising promotions that generate a large amount of traffic—these are the perfect candidates for your parking lot and sidewalk.

You can be as creative as you want. Involve your staff members—they may have some great ideas. But whatever you do, don't overlook this important promotional location.

Some specific tactics will be found on the following pages.

198. Live Entertainment

Best For Most retailers, restaurants, some service businesses.

Objective Increase awareness, create excitement, generate PR, generate traffic, improve your image, increase sales, stimulate trial.

Target Existing customers and potential new customers.

Live entertainment always draws a crowd. If your business caters to a younger crowd, invite the high school band to play on a particular weekend day and set up a booth for your products or to serve simple foods and beverages. Promote the booth by posting a sign near the outdoor activities. In addition to the band, you could host a talent show from the local high school, where students bring their outside bands or single instruments for entertainment and exposure. Provide the participants with free food.

If your business does not have an outdoor facility, similar activities can be held inside, run as a talent contest. Try this on any day of the week that normally needs a sales boost, as it will surely draw the families, neighbors, and friends of the contestants. To get the best response, offer cash as your first-place prize. Second-place winners receive gift certificates, and third-place winners receive a two-for-one or other appropriate discount.

Advertise these events in your local paper, and be sure to place attractive banners announcing the events outside your business.

Materials Newspaper ad, banners, booth, prizes.

Timing

Five weeks prior:

Contact local authorities for rules and regulations on holding an outside event.

Four weeks prior:

Meet with local high school principal to arrange participation of band or talent contestants.

Three weeks prior:

Prepare newspaper ad and banners.
Order banners.
Buy media.
Discuss booth program with staff.

Two weeks prior:

Begin preparing booth.
Confirm band and other participation.

One week prior:

Place ad.
Discuss program with your staff.

One day prior:

Set up special area for the event.
Display banners.
Set up booths.

Start:

Enjoy entertainment.
Award prizes.

199. Sidewalk Sale

Best For Most retailers, restaurants, some service businesses.

Objective Increase awareness, create excitement, generate PR, generate traffic, improve your image, increase sales, stimulate trial.

Target Charities and nonprofit organizations.

A sidewalk sale can be a great way to draw crowds to your business, while at the same time creating community goodwill and raising funds for several different charities and not-for-profit organizations.

Involve the humane society—it can set up a puppy and kitten adoption event.

Involve several local churches—their membership can set up a bakery and/or craft sale.

Involve disabled citizen groups—they can sell their own wares.

Participants keep the profits from their own sales. You keep your business open, perhaps offering snacks or beverages, and display posters outside the door stating that a set percentage of the profits will be shared among the participating charities.

Be sure to distribute bounce-back coupons to customers, as they will remember your goodwill. Also, be sure to have members of your staff on hand to assist with selling and/or crowd control.

Distribute flyers announcing the event throughout the community. Church groups and professional societies will probably be making announcements in their local publications.

Materials   Coupons, posters, flyers.

Timing

Twelve weeks prior:

> Contact churches, charities, and other groups to arrange participation.
> Contact local authorities about the rules and regulations for this type of event.

Six weeks prior:

> Confirm participation of groups.
> Discuss program with your staff and decide on setup and decorating.

Four weeks prior:

> Prepare coupons, posters, and flyers.

Three weeks prior:

> Print coupons, posters, and flyers.

Two weeks prior:

> Display posters in your location and distribute them to participants.
> Discuss program with staff and decide on possible snacks and beverages, if appropriate.

One week prior:

> Reconfirm with participants.
> Review program with staff.

Distribute flyers as doorknobbers and in parking lots.
Purchase items necessary for setup and decorating.

One day prior:

Set up and decorate.

Start:

Begin sidewalk sale.
Distribute coupons.

One week later:

Distribute the stated percentage of your profits among participants.

200.   National Pet Week Dog Wash

Best For   Most retailers, restaurants, some service businesses.

Objective   Increase awareness, create excitement, generate PR, generate traffic, improve your image, increase sales, stimulate trial.

Target   Existing customers and potential new customers.

This event is fun, creates a lot of excitement, and should get you some great publicity.

The first week in May is National Pet Week. On the Saturday on either side of the holiday, schedule a dog wash in your parking lot. You will generate a tremendous amount of enthusiasm from pet owners, and the event will provide a great fund-raising opportunity for the local Humane Society.

Offer your local Humane Society a healthy percentage of your profit from purchases during the day of the event. During the promotion, as well as in your ad, specify what percentage of the day's profits will be donated to the Humane Society. In return, ask the Humane Society to provide volunteers and materials necessary for the dog wash.

Set aside a specific area and time frame. Make sure there are hoses and accessible water and that the area has good drainage. Also, be sure the area is completely clear of car traffic. Set prices for small, medium, and large dogs. Donations over and above the set prices are acceptable and appreciated, with all proceeds going to the Humane Society.

Be sure to give bounce-back coupons, good for two weeks following the event (not the day of the event), to all people having their dogs washed. This event will bring in a considerable amount of traffic, especially of owners of large dogs, so be sure to advertise well in advance.

Materials   Newspaper ad, bounce-back coupons, flyers and posters.

Timing

Six weeks prior:

Contact local Humane Society and arrange promotion.

Five weeks prior:

Prepare newspaper ad, flyers, bounce-back coupons, posters.

Four weeks prior:

Buy media.
Print enough flyers for double distribution (so that Humane Society can hand them out, too).
Print posters and bounce-back coupons.

Three weeks prior:

Discuss program with staff.

Two weeks prior:

Place ad.
Reconfirm promotion with Humane Society.
Give half of flyers to Humane Society to distribute.
Determine area and items you will provide for dog wash.
Display posters.

One week prior:

Distribute half of flyers (parking lots, etc.).
Purchase necessary items for dog wash.

One day prior:

Review program with your staff.
Finalize details with Humane Society.
Prepare dog wash area.

Start:

> Set posters outside in dog wash area.
> Hand out bounce-back coupons to participants.

One day after:

> Begin to figure day's profits for presentation of check to Humane
> Society.

17

Students and Their Families

201. School/College Tactics

Best For Most businesses catering to students and their families.

Objective Increase awareness, increase community goodwill, generate traffic, improve your image, increase sales, stimulate trial.

Target Students of all ages and their families.

Even though your business may not cater directly to young people, you should consider how you can get their attention because young people often form lifelong loyalties based on experiences that they have as children. Some years ago Texaco did some unique market research that uncovered the fact that children whose parents bought gas at Texaco stations had a tendency to buy gas from Texaco as adults. So Texaco looked for ways to cater to the children of customers as well as the customers themselves.

   The tactics outlined in this chapter are designed specifically to appeal to the different age groups that will be found at each school level: ages 6 to 12 in elementary school, ages 12 to 18 in junior high and high school, and ages 18 to 21 in college.

   For the younger group, tactics are targeted to create goodwill toward your business on the part of parents, schools, and the community at large. For the junior high and high school group, the tactics are designed to create excitement—to bring the students, with their parents or by themselves, into your business. At the college level, promotions should be designed to bring students in for a trial visit. The warm, friendly atmosphere of your business and staff, combined with continuing promotions to regenerate interest and excitement, will bring you a steady flow of both new and repeat customers.

You will find in this chapter a number of specific promotional ideas that can be tailored to your needs.

202. Elementary School Report Card Incentives

Best For Most businesses catering to students and their families.

Objective Increase awareness, increase community goodwill, generate traffic, improve your image, increase sales, stimulate trial.

Target Local elementary schools.

Contact the local elementary school principals to offer incentives of free products, gifts, services, or food and beverages to students who achieve high grades. Any child who, at the end of a marking period, receives at least two As or three Bs (and no grades lower than a C) may show the report card at your business and receive the reward.

Ask the school to send notices announcing the program to all teachers at the beginning of the school year. The teachers, in turn, should send notices home with the students to inform the parents of the program.

Print posters for display in the classrooms as a reminder to students and for display in your business as a reminder to customers with children.

To prevent resubmission of the same report card, have a small punch on hand to validate report cards when they are redeemed for free food or other items.

Materials Posters, punch.

Timing

Three weeks prior:

Contact school principals to arrange program.
Prepare posters.

Two weeks prior:

Print posters.
Buy punch.

One week prior:

Discuss program with staff.

Start:

Distribute posters to schools for display in classrooms.
Display posters in your business.

After first marking period:

Begin validating report cards with punch and distributing rewards.

203.   Sample Letter to School Principals

(On your letterhead)
Dear (Principal's Name):
(Your business's name) has an incentive program for students to earn high grades. We'd like to share the program with your school.
This is how it works: At the end of each marking period, any children who receive at least two As or three Bs (and no grades lower than a C) may bring their report card to (name of your business) for (a reward).
We ask that you inform your faculty of the program and that you lend your support. Please have your faculty send notification of the program home to parents, as well as explain the program to the students.
We will provide attractive incentive posters for the classrooms, to remind students of the program.
We at (your business's name) enjoy advocating the virtues of getting good grades, and we appreciate your support and cooperation.
Sincerely,
(Your name or manager's name)
(Your business's name)

204.   Elementary School As Program

Best For   Most businesses catering to students and their families.

Objective   Increase awareness, increase community goodwill, generate traffic, improve your image, increase sales, stimulate trial.

Target   Local elementary schools.

Very similar to the previous program (Report Card), the "As Program" gives students rewards that are solely dependent upon the number of As they receive on their report cards. One A gets the lowest-value reward, and five or more As gets the highest-value reward.

Materials Coupons, posters, flyers.

Timing See Tactic 202, "Elementary School Report Card Incentives."

205. Elementary School Coloring Contest

Best For Most businesses catering to students and their families.

Objective Increase awareness, increase community goodwill, generate traffic, improve your image, increase sales, stimulate trial.

Target Local elementary schools.

Promote this program, which is open to children under 12, through the use of local newspaper advertising, doorknobbers, mailings, and flyers. Make both the entry blank and the coloring area part of the ad and flyer space.

Children must draw and color a picture that depicts how they spent their summer vacation. No purchase should be necessary to enter, and you should be sure to have additional entry blanks available at your business.

When entries are submitted, give each participant and/or the accompanying adult coupons. Display all entries as soon as they are received.

Contact your local schools and ask the school principals and art teachers to act as judges. Have a small party on a weekend day for the judging. After the judging, notify the winners and let them know when prizes will be awarded. The prizes should be awarded in different age categories: Under 6, 6 to 8, and 9 to 12. Award first-, second-, and third-place prizes.

Contact your newspaper to announce the presentation of the awards. Take photos of the winners and post copies next to the winning entries in your business for several weeks after the end of the promotion. Also, send the winning entries and the winners' photos to the newspapers with a short press release about the winners and their prizes.

Materials Newspaper ad, mailers, doorknobbers, flyers, counter cards, posters, coupons, entry blanks, prizes.

Timing

Four weeks prior:

Prepare ad and other printed materials.

Three weeks prior:

Discuss program with your staff and get suggestions for prizes.
Purchase prizes.
Buy media.
Contact school officials and art teachers to act as judges.
Set up area for small party for the day of the judging.
Print flyers, coupons, and entry blanks.

Two weeks prior:

Display posters and counter cards.
Distribute flyers and other materials.
Place ad.

One week prior:

Contact newspapers about awards ceremony and arrange a photographer from the newspaper to attend.
Confirm judging with school officials and art teachers.

Start:

Begin accepting entries and handing out coupons.
Begin displaying entries.

Two weeks after:

Hold awards ceremony.
Present prizes.
Display winning entries next to winners' pictures.
Send pictures of winners and their entries, along with press releases, to local newspapers.

Three weeks after:

Evaluate results.

206. Elementary School Tour

Best For   Many business types.

Objective   Increase awareness, increase community goodwill, generate traffic, improve your image, increase sales, stimulate trial.

Target   Local elementary schools.

Contact your local elementary schools and youth organizations, such as the Cub Scouts, Brownies, and Little League, and offer them tours of your business as field trips. Select a slow time of day for the tour, and, if possible, arrange to serve refreshments.

During the tour, explain the operation of your business. Show the areas where you carry out the different aspects of your business, and have several staff members ready to assist. With older children, let them assist, if possible.

When the group leaves, give each child a goodie bag containing fun things from your store, some candy or gum, and bounce-back coupons. In addition to a coupon geared toward the children, also include one geared toward their parents.

Materials   Bounce-back coupons, goodie bags.

Timing   This can be an ongoing program. Simply contact as many organizations as you wish and arrange the group tours.

207. Elementary School Book Reports

Best For   Most businesses catering to young students and their families.

Objective   Increase awareness, increase community goodwill, generate traffic, improve your image, increase sales, stimulate trial.

Target   Local elementary schools.

Choose a particular month during the school year to offer a free item or gift to any child who reads a complete book during that month.

Contact local school principals and ask them to cooperate by having teachers and/or school librarians give coupons good for a gift or a treat, such as ice cream, to children who have read a book and answered a short quiz or handed in a book report.

Ask school officials to announce the program over the school P.A. system and/or in flyers sent home to parents.

Materials Coupons for gift or free ice-cream sundae.

Timing

Six weeks prior:

Contact the local elementary school principals and ask for their co-operation.

Four weeks prior

Confirm program with schools.

Three weeks prior:

Prepare and print coupons.

One week prior:

Discuss program with staff.

Start:

Begin redeeming coupons for gifts or treats.

End:

Evaluate results.

208. Elementary School Window-Decorating Contest

Best For Most retailers catering to young students and their families.

Objective Increase awareness, increase community goodwill, generate traffic, improve your image, increase sales, stimulate trial.

Target Local elementary schools.

During either Halloween or Christmas, schools often look for merchants who will give up their store windows to display students' artistic talents.

The schools set up a school contest with competition between classes to create excitement and student enthusiasm.

Choose your nearest local elementary school and contact the administration to arrange the contest. Let each class choose a theme and elect a class representative to paint a mural on a window. Use poster paints for easy cleanup, and be sure the students know that they're responsible for all materials and cleanup.

Have school officials and art teachers act as judges. Reward the grand prize winner with a gift or a free party at your business for the entire class.

Materials   None.

Timing

Six weeks prior:

Contact a local school official to arrange this promotion.

Four weeks prior:

Determine number of entrants and decide what windows or sections of windows will be painted.

Three weeks prior:

Arrange one class representative per day for painting, so as not to interfere with regular business.

Two weeks prior:

Discuss program with staff.

One week prior:

Arrange reward, party, or other prize.

Start:

Begin contest.

End:

Announce winner.
Schedule reward event or party on a slow evening.

209.   Junior High/High School Talent Show

Best For   Most retailers catering to young students and their families.

Objective   Increase awareness, increase community goodwill, generate traffic, improve your image, increase sales, stimulate trial.

Target   Local junior high and high school students.

Contact your local junior high and high school for dance, music, or voice students who would be interested in competing in a talent competition at your business. Arrange for each entrant to perform for no longer than five minutes. Present two entrants in a row, and then allow 20 minutes for your customers to relax, enjoy themselves, and talk to others. Repeat each half hour during the evening. If you hold the show between the hours of 5 and 9 p.m., this will allow for 16 students per evening.

Try to arrange to have a prominent member of the community, such as someone in the music industry, available during the entire evening to act as judge. Offer this person a free gift certificate for his or her cooperation.

If you have more than one junior high and high school in the area, you may wish to arrange the competition over more than one evening, with semifinal winners during each evening and then a finals competition on the final day.

Semifinal prizes could be gift certificates for the students. The grand prize could be a small scholarship.

Materials   Stage area, microphone, sign-up sheets, prizes.

Timing

Eight weeks prior:

Contact local school officials to arrange promotion.

Seven weeks prior:

Determine number of entrants and decide on number of nights for contest and number of judges necessary.

Six weeks prior:

Contact prominent musicians and artists to act as judges.

Five weeks prior:

Discuss program with staff and arrange stage area.

Four weeks prior:

Arrange grand prize scholarship.

Three weeks prior:

Prepare sign-up sheets.

Two weeks prior:

Meet with contestants at schools and prepare schedule of dates and times of contestants' appearances.

One week prior:

Arrange microphone rental.
Prepare materials for stage area.
Confirm participation of judges.

Start:

Have talent contest.
Award semifinal prizes.

End:

Have final competition.
Award grand prize.

210.   High School Sporting Events

Best For   Retailers catering to teenagers.

Objective   Increase awareness, increase frequency, generate traffic, increase sales, stimulate trial.

Target   Local high schools.

These programs should start at the beginning of the winter semester and run throughout the sports seasons. Penetrate student sporting events with discount and premium coupons to promote visits after games, as well as general visits to your business. Offer the following:

Get a discount on any transaction or check over a minimal amount per person.

Buy one–get a second one at half price (or free).

Get a free item for any winning score correctly guessed.

Distribute coupons with event tickets purchased at the school box office. For the Winning Score promotion, set up an attractive drop box at the school box office that explains the promotion. Provide "Winning Score" forms at the box office that list the event and its date, with room for students to fill in their names, addresses, phone numbers, and score predictions.

Pick up the drop box from the school box office right after the start of the game. Invite students who guessed correctly to come in for their free item after the game and verify their winning eligibility by finding their original score form.

Materials   Discount coupons, drop box, winning-score forms.

Timing

Six weeks prior:

Contact local school officials to arrange promotion.

Four weeks prior:

Prepare drop box, coupons, and forms.

Three weeks prior:

Print coupons and forms.

Two weeks prior:

Discuss program with staff.

One week prior:

Begin coupon distribution.
Take drop box and forms to school box office.

Start:

> Begin redemption of coupons.
> Pick up drop box and give winners who come in free items.

211. High School/College Student Discount Cards

Best For Businesses catering to teenagers.

Objective Increase awareness, increase frequency, generate traffic, increase sales, stimulate trial.

Target Local high schools.

Distribute 20 percent discount cards to all high school and college students in your trading area. You can hand out the discount cards in a variety of ways:

> As students visit your business.
> During registration through college registrars.
> By hiring local students to pass them out at school and on campus. Make sure this is permitted.
> By giving them to your staff for distribution to friends and relatives.

Students establish their social habits early in the school year and are likely to be loyal to their chosen establishments throughout their school years and after. Therefore, start the program at the very beginning of the school year, and be sure to make students feel welcome on each visit.

Materials Student discount cards.

Timing

Three weeks prior:

> Prepare student discount cards.
> Print cards.

Two weeks prior:

> Discuss program with staff.
> Begin hiring students to pass out cards.

One week prior:

> Distribute cards to college registrars, students you've hired, and your staff. Keep cards on hand for in-business distribution.

Start:

> Begin offering discounts to students.

212. College Goodie Bag

Best For Businesses catering to college students.

Objective Increase awareness, increase community goodwill, increase frequency, generate traffic, increase sales, stimulate trial.

Target Local college students.

Contact university authorities to gain approval to present incoming freshmen with a goodie bag filled with useful products such as soap, toothpaste and toothbrush, disposable razors, and so on. The box should, of course, also contain multiple discount coupons good at your business. These products will be appreciated by students and will make quite an impression. Suggestions include:

> September coupon—half price on everything to get acquainted
>
> October coupon—50 percent discount on a specific item
>
> November coupon—buy one, get one free!

The combination of the goodie bag and the coupons will draw students to your business. Students tend to stay loyal to one business during their college career, so you will probably keep these customers until they graduate.

Materials Goodie bags, goodies, coupons.

Timing

Four weeks prior:

> Contact university officials for program approval.

Three weeks prior:

Prepare coupons and goodie bags.

Two weeks prior:

Print coupons and goodie bags.

One week prior:

Buy goodies and fill bags with goodies and coupons.

Start:

Begin redeeming coupons and getting acquainted with your new customers.

213.   College after the Game

Best For   Businesses catering to college students.

Objective   Increase awareness, increase community goodwill, increase frequency, generate traffic, increase sales, stimulate trial.

Target   Local college students.

Make sports enthusiasts at all grade levels aware of your business by purchasing inexpensive full-page ads in football and basketball programs. Always incorporate a "buy one, get one free" coupon that is good on the day of the game only.

Check with university athletic departments for a schedule of sporting events and to inquire about purchasing advertising space in the programs.

Materials   Coupon ads.

Timing

Late August:

Contact university athletic departments for sports schedule.
Contact administration for information on purchasing ad space.

Three weeks prior:

Prepare ads and buy media.

Start:

Begin coupon redemption.

214.   College Find-Your-Face Contest

Best For   Businesses catering to college students.

Objective   Increase awareness, increase community goodwill, increase frequency, generate traffic, increase sales, stimulate trial.

Target   Local college students.

Throughout the school year, you or a manager should frequent the college campus and take candid photos of students, either individually or in groups. In addition, attend campus sporting events and social events to get more candid pictures. Display selected photos in your business, changing them every couple of weeks as new photos are developed.

Distribute flyers on campus and place an ad in the campus newspaper inviting students to come into your business and "Find Their Faces" in the displayed photos. Offer any student who finds his or her face a free item of your choice or a 50 percent discount on any item.

Run the program throughout the school year, and don't place a limit on how many times a student can find his or her face. Be sure, however, to mark the found face with a marker to prevent students from coming in repeatedly to identify themselves in the same photo.

Materials   Photographs, flyers, ad.

Timing

Four weeks prior:

Begin taking candid photographs.

Three weeks prior:

Prepare flyers and ad.
Buy ad space in campus paper.

Two weeks prior:

Print flyers.

One week prior:

> Explain program to staff.
> Distribute flyers on campus and under car windshields.

Start:

> Run ad.
> Display photographs.
> Begin offering free or discounted items.

215.   College Defend Your Honor Contest

Best For   Businesses catering to college students.

Objective   Increase awareness, increase community goodwill, increase frequency, generate traffic, increase sales, stimulate trial.

Target   Local college students.

Give campus organizations the opportunity to win prizes by voting for their own organization each time they make a purchase at your business. Select a prize with broad student appeal, and announce the competition in the campus newspaper, through flyers, and on the radio.

Try to arrange a cross-promotion in which a local retailer or restaurant that caters to student traffic will supply the prize in exchange for cooperative mention. Or, the retailer may be willing to exchange the prize for an equivalent amount of coupons good for free food items at a restaurant to distribute to student customers.

Run the contest for at least eight weeks. It takes several weeks for school organizations to rally their members to get them to come in and vote. Suggested prizes include a stereo, a CD player, or a color TV.

When your student customers pay for their purchases, they should also be handed a voting ballot. Students check off the organization they wish to vote for and drop the voting ballot into the ballot box.

Materials   Ad, radio script, flyers, prize, voting ballots, ballot box.

Timing

Six weeks prior:

Contact local retailers/restaurants to try to arrange their cooperation with the program.

Discuss program with staff and decide on prize.

Five weeks prior:

Contact campus authorities to get the names of all student organizations on campus and prepare voting ballots.

Four weeks prior:

Prepare radio script, flyers, ad, and ballot box.

Three weeks prior:

Print flyers.
Buy media.

Two weeks prior:

Begin distributing flyers on campus.

One week prior:

Place ad in campus paper.
Begin radio advertising.

Start:

Display ballot box.
Begin distributing voting ballots with checks.
Display prize.

Eight weeks after:

Announce prize winner.

18
Leisure-Time Tie-Ins

216. Entertainment-Center Tactics

Best For   Retailers, restaurants, entertainment, leisure-time businesses.

Objective   Increase awareness, generate traffic, increase sales, stimulate trial.

Target   Existing customers and potential new customers.

Tactics designed around places of entertainment are especially easy to create and usually get great results. The people you are targeting are already out, so the hardest part is done!

These people are already in the process of entertaining themselves—at shows, movies, bowling alleys, and other such places—so they can be easily persuaded to add the additional entertainment of your business. This chapter offers some specific tactics that may suit your business.

217. After the Show

Best For   Most retail businesses.

Objective   Increase awareness, generate traffic, increase sales, stimulate trial.

Target   Current and potential new customers.

Offer customers a discount on a particular item when they bring in their ticket stubs from a movie or theater within four weeks of attending the show. Be sure to collect the stubs to authenticate your offer.

Place your promotional cards at participating local theaters to maximize reach, try to get mentions of your offer on theater and concert programs, and place posters and other materials in your business to make certain that the offer is well communicated.

Materials Counter cards, posters, newspaper ad.

Timing

Six weeks prior:

Set program goals and determine costs.

Five weeks prior:

Begin contacting movie and other theaters to arrange for their cooperation.

Four weeks prior:

Prepare ad, counter cards, and posters.

Three weeks prior:

Buy media.
Print counter cards and posters.

One week prior:

Distribute counter cards to participating theaters.
Place ad.
Put up posters and make other announcements.
Discuss program with staff.

Start:

Begin redeeming ticket stubs.

Four weeks after:

Evaluate results.

218.   Movie Discount Coupons

Best For   Most retail businesses.

Objective   Increase awareness, generate traffic, increase sales, stimulate trial.

Target   Existing customers and potential new customers, movie theaters.

Purchase and distribute discount movie tickets to customers. Any customer who makes a purchase above a minimum amount can receive a discount ticket good only at the local participating theater. This is a great way to generate midweek traffic for both you and the theater.

The cost is minimal. You can announce the program on your communications board and through flyers printed up by the theater. To give this effort a boost, place a newspaper ad and share the cost with the participating theater.

Materials   Discount movie tickets, flyers, newspaper ad.

Timing

Six weeks prior:

Contact theaters to arrange promotion.

Four weeks prior:

Meet with participating theaters to prepare ad and flyers.

Three weeks prior:

Buy media.

Two weeks prior:

Explain program to staff.

One week prior:

Place ad.
Pick up discount movie tickets from theater.

Start:

Distribute discount tickets.

219. After-Theater Special

Best For   Retail and food-service businesses that are open late.

Objective   Increase awareness, generate traffic, increase sales, stimulate trial.

Target   Current customers and potential new customers.

Ask local theaters to distribute a price-capped coupon good for items, services, food, or beverage from your business. In return, you hand out two-for-one coupons good at the participating theater.

You'll need to know how many seats are available at each location, so that you can date-stamp the coupons and deliver the exact number to each theater. Do this on a weekly basis. The coupons should be valid on the night of the performance or showing only.

Split the promotional costs with the participating theaters and agree that each party is responsible for its own discounts. You can announce the promotion in the theater section of your local newspapers.

Materials   Coupons, posters, newspaper ad.

Timing

Six weeks prior:

Contact theaters to arrange promotion.

Four weeks prior:

Prepare newspaper ad, posters, coupons.

Three weeks prior:

Buy media.

One week prior:

Place ad.
Distribute posters to theater.
Explain program to staff.

Start:

Begin coupon redemption.

220. Bowling Alley Tie-In

Best For   Retailers, restaurants, some service businesses.

Objective   Generate traffic, increase sales, stimulate trial.

Target   Local bowling alleys.

Distribute coupons that are good for a certain percentage off items, service, or food at your business to local bowling alleys. Design the coupons to expire in four weeks, and ask bowling alley managers to distribute the coupons at their discretion for high series/high game players or league tournaments.

In addition, suggest to managers that they use the coupons to get league sign-ups during registration periods. Usually, the inside billboard of the bowling alley will announce the program. Ask the manager to announce coupon winners' names over the loudspeaker periodically. Of course, you should offer a free item to the bowling alley managers for their cooperation.

Materials   Coupons.

Timing

Four weeks prior:

Contact bowling alleys to arrange cooperation.

Three weeks prior:

Prepare coupons.

Two weeks prior:

Print coupons.

One week prior:

Explain program to staff.

Deliver coupons to participating bowling alleys.

Start:

Begin coupon redemption.

Four weeks after:

Evaluate results.

19

Service and Professional Businesses

The tactics in this chapter are aimed at service providers and professionals, from dry cleaners to banks and everything in between. These tactics range from the simple to the quite elaborate. As with all the tactics in this book, some of these will fit perfectly with your activity, and others may stimulate your creativity to come up with variations.

Although this chapter is aimed at a specific group, if you're part of that group, don't forget to surf some of the other chapters in this book, especially those having to do with civic and community groups and the general tactics at the beginning. Throughout every chapter of this book you will find bits and pieces of useful information and ideas to help you craft a winning marketing plan for any sort of enterprise.

If you want to make a thorough study of promotional tactics, there are many other resources in the form of books, web sites, and professional associations that offer tips for practitioners in every field. As with all marketing and promotional efforts, spend some time developing a plan, a budget, and a calendar, and assemble your historical data so that you can measure your results against past performance.

221. Banks—Reach Out and Touch

Objective Increase customer frequency and service use.

Target Existing customers.

Banks are among the worst businesses at neighborhood marketing, and this makes no sense at all, since they do most of their business in their neighborhoods. They spend millions on advertising, and I have rarely seen a bank ad that didn't use the same tired wording and concept: "Your Friendly Neighborhood Bank." And they don't work very hard to distinguish themselves by name, either.

The two banks that I do business with have never once asked me what I need. You'd think that a bank would come and visit with me and say, "Look, you're a really great customer. Here are the five services you use. Here are twenty more that we would like to tell you about. We would like to develop a further relationship. We know you have money set aside in a money-market account. Why don't you let us set up a trust account for your kids through our trust department?"

They've got all these products, and they know just about everything about me—where I live, what I spend, what I save. They've got a built-in market to sell the other products. They could so easily mine the gold that they already have inside their four walls. Most customers are worth so much more to a bank.

There is no excuse for a bank not to have outreach officers whose sole job it is to call customers with potential and offer to discuss their needs, or just say, "Thanks for banking with us. By the way, we are running a special on CD rates this month."

Banks can also take advantage of some of the other marketing tools in this book: running promotions with other businesses, offering gifts and coupons good at client businesses to loyal customers, sending out a periodic newsletter, offering Internet service in the lobby, and serving fresh coffee to waiting customers. It's all Marketing 101.

One of the best bank-customer stories that ever made the rounds appeared many years ago in *USA Today*. It began when John Barrier, a building refurbisher, tried to get his parking slip validated at his bank in Spokane, Washington, to save 60 cents. Barrier was wearing his work clothes, and he hadn't conducted a transaction. The teller gave him a skeptical looking over and refused. Barrier demanded to see the manager, who also refused to stamp his ticket.

Barrier promptly announced that he was closing his accounts and withdrew more than $2 million, taking his business to another bank down the street.

It's the little things that count.

222. The Bank Courtesy Call

One of the most embarrassing moments in any banking customer's experience is having misjudged his bank balance and accidentally overdrawing his account. In any banking operation's customer list, there are many who do enough business with the institution to justify its having a clerk who is responsible for monitoring overdrafts and notifying customers before they have incurred a fee and an embarrassing overdraft.

Which is more profitable: a one-time $35 fee for a bounced check, or the appreciation and loyalty generated when a customer has been treated with the utmost dignity and been assisted in avoiding embarrassment? How many banking customers have been chased away by thoughtlessness?

223. Open When They Are Closed

Whatever business you may be in, consider being open when the other guys are closed. Why shouldn't banks be open on Sundays, when we aren't preoccupied with work, school, errands, and the ordinary rhythm of the rest of the week?

If you can't justify hiring extra hands to do this, look at your business and see if there aren't predictably slow times of the week when you could cut back your hours and move them to Sunday.

A perfect example of this is hair care. It is traditional for salons and barbershops to be closed on Mondays. That means that Tuesday through Saturday, you are fishing in the same pond at the same time as everyone else.

224. Ideas for Health Care Professionals

In certain areas of health care, such as dentistry and dermatology, there are elective services that can easily be marketed if you think creatively. As the baby boomers age, they become increasingly interested in cosmetic services such as teeth whitening and removal of skin blemishes, services that are typically offered in an office setting and therefore not subject to hospital schedules.

Here is an example that is specific to dentistry, but that could be applied to a number of other services in this field.

My dentist once complained to me that because tooth decay has been almost eliminated thanks to better dental products, education, and gum care, he has to rely more and more on elective cosmetic dentistry for his profits. Elective dental work is harder to sell in a down economy, and he was feeling the effects of a soft market in the wake of the bursting of the stock market bubble.

I asked him who his best patients were. He said doctors, because they are high earners and are less susceptible to economic ebbs and flows. So we put together a marketing plan aimed at local doctors in his trading area. It offered them something brand new—Sunday hours. After all, doctors are busiest when dentists are busiest. It stood to reason that a dentist who made himself available when doctors weren't busy would win new customers.

He bought a mailing list from the local hospital that had about a thousand doctors' names on it. Then he looked at his services and decided that the most popular would be veneers, which is the usual method of whitening teeth when a patient is older. He developed a postcard that had before and after photos of a client who had had her teeth veneered. The picture said it all.

As with all direct-mail campaigns, one mailing wouldn't do the trick. Customers hardly even notice you until you've reached them four or five times. So he started a program of seven monthly mailings. After the fifth mailing, he got his first customer—for $22,000 worth of dentistry.

Here are some other ideas:

- A dentist, doctor, or other health-care professional should never make patients push a button to get the receptionist to open the window. It's like being in prison. Your receptionist should be out front, visible, available, and smiling. Every patient should be acknowledged the instant she walks in, even if it's just to say, "Please be seated and we'll be right with you."

- The atmosphere in waiting rooms in health-care settings is important to creating customer loyalty. Be sure that the quality, the colors, the music, and everything else create a sense of well-being and hominess. Colors need to be soothing, chairs comfortable, magazines updated and not three years old. Most professionals stopped noticing their waiting rooms years ago. Consider asking some friends or relations who don't know your staff to mystery-shop your practice: Call for an appointment, come in and wait, and then report on what they liked and what they think needs improvement.

- Dentists should always sit when they are talking to patients so that they are on the same level as the patient instead of talking down to him.

- Health-care professionals are not exempt from marketing concerns. If you are wondering how to stand out from the other 15 dentists or dermatologists in your trading area, try this: Have your staff ask all your patients what newspapers and magazines they read. Contact the publications that are most often mentioned (that's your target audience) and buy the local addresses on their mailing list. Then do a seven-month mailing campaign offering a specific service.

225.   House Calls

There is a growing nostalgia for some of the services that we remember from our childhood, and smart marketers are finding ways to tap into that nostalgia. One of these is the professional house call.

There's no reason why a service or professional business can't offer at-home services, and in the process delight and surprise customers, garner positive public relations, and build its customer base. If you are a lawyer, an accountant, a banker, someone involved in certain alternative health-care services such as massage therapy, a hair care provider, a dry cleaner, or the provider of some other service, you have the opportunity to stand out from your competitors by offering customers the convenience of at-home consultations and actual services.

In addition to winning customers you ordinarily would not see, you will be creating marketing ambassadors who will tell their friends if they are satisfied with the experience.

226.   Create a Child-Friendly Office

If your customer base includes a large percentage of parents with children, consider setting aside a room or a corner of a room and keeping toys, drawing materials, and children's books there, so that kids can play and their parents won't be distracted while they are doing business with you. This tactic may not be appropriate in every setting, but if you can provide supervision, or it's comfortable to have such a corner in your office, you will find that your customers will be appreciative and will tell their friends who also have children.

227.   Customer Wall of Fame

This tactic, which works well in certain retail settings or for restaurant and food-service businesses, can also be applied in certain professional and service settings. If you are a lawyer, accountant, or financial services adviser, or if you are in any other service or professional business that caters to regular clients, consider putting the names of your significant customers on plaques on the wall of your office. You will want to get permission from your clients first, but you may be surprised at how many are honored and delighted to be recognized and therefore are more likely to recommend you to their friends and business associates.

228. Tax Freedom Day

If you are a tax professional of any kind, such as an accountant, a book-keeper, or a tax attorney, look for opportunities to take advantage of Tax Freedom Day, which is the day of the year when most people have earned enough money to pay their taxes for the year. This usually occurs in May.

Consider partnering with a local restaurant, bar, or other food-service or entertainment business to throw a Tax Freedom Day party. You can cross-promote this event, create positive public relations by notifying your local media, and cross-market by offering the restaurant or bar the use of your mailing list in return for providing the space and the food and beverage at a reduced price. Another possibility is to barter for your services with the restaurant or bar.

A twist on this would be to create an event that is tied to the fact that the average American worker spends almost half of his or her day working to pay local, state, and federal taxes before earning any money for living expenses. There are any number of opportunities to use this information to create an event—and, of course, there is always April 15.

229. Waiting-Room Tactics

Too many professionals and service businesses ignore the atmosphere that customers encounter in their lobbies and other waiting areas. Decoration is key. This is the first impression of your business that clients have, and you should spend some time and money creating an environment that is welcoming, warm, useful, and memorable.

Auto repair waiting areas are places where people typically spend an hour or two—enough time to check their e-mail on a computer that you provide, watch a movie on videotape, or browse a library of used books.

Encourage your customers to donate used books, both for swapping in the waiting room and for donation to local charities. Host a blood bank drive or a cholesterol screening. Waiting areas frequented by parents should always have a corner where children can sit at a small table and draw, read a book, or play with toys that you provide.

Consider running a holiday toy drive or some other community service and offer a discount for customers who bring in items for collection.

230. Rapid Responses Sell

When a potential customer calls your business or professional office, that customer is most likely ready to make a spending decision. If you don't have a receptionist to answer all calls, you should make sure that you are getting your messages as quickly as possible and, most importantly, responding immediately. More business is lost because of slow response than for any other reason.

Consider that many potential customers are finding you among a long list of your competitors. If they are calling you as a result of finding your listing or advertisement in the Yellow Pages, you can be sure that within minutes of having called you, they have already spoken to someone else. Consider including in your automated voice message a direction to another telephone number, which may be a mobile phone that you or someone else is able to answer almost all the time. Or retain a telephone answering service that you can trust to notify you of important calls.

231. Name Recognition Sells

The director of a very successful summer camp made it his business to recognize by name every single one of the 400 or so children that attended each summer. During the winter months, he spent hours studying photographs of each child and his or her camp record or application, memorizing every name and one fact about each child, such as his or her hometown or favorite sport.

When he attended the many camp reunions held around the country, and when the children arrived at camp on the first day, parents were stunned and children delighted by the fact that he instantly knew their names and something about them. He created a fiercely loyal customer base. Often a simple gesture like that can make all the difference between creating a customer and losing a sale.

232. Twenty-Four-Hour Marketing

People often need a plumber, an electrician, medical or veterinary advice, and sometimes even a lawyer after hours or on weekends. An effective marketing tactic would be to do a mailing or other promotional effort to let your customers know that you are available to them 24 hours a day. Give them either your home telephone number or a special mobile telephone number that you or someone on your staff agrees to answer 24 hours a day. Send them a magnet card that they can post on equipment, inside a medicine chest, or anywhere where they will be likely to see it when they need you.

The inconvenience of the occasional after-hours telephone call will be small compared with the word of mouth you will create and the customer loyalty you will earn just by making such an offer. Consider that some of your competitors may be offering the same service, and if you fail to do so, you risk losing a potential customer.

233. Volunteering

Giving your time and your expertise to charities, nonprofits, and other community groups is a powerful opportunity to meet potential customers in your neighborhood and strengthen your community ties. Depending on your expertise, look around your community for groups and organizations that are involved in activities that matter to you or that in some way intersect with your personal interests.

Most nonprofits and charities are always looking for legal, bookkeeping, accounting, maintenance, and other services that they would ordinarily have to raise the money to pay for.

If you feel you have the qualifications, consider volunteering to sit on a board of directors or participate in a fund-raising campaign. Even if you don't have special expertise that a particular group needs, consider volunteering to help with office tasks, make deliveries, drive members who don't have cars, or provide any other assistance that may be necessary.

234. The Unexpected Thank-You

When business gets slow, consider buying bags of fruits, a box of fancy cookies, flowers, or some other small gift for your best clients and dropping them off in person. Thank your clients for their business without overtly prospecting for new business. This will encourage customers to remember you when they need your service, it will be unexpected and therefore memorable, and it will make you feel more connected to your customers.

235. Getting to Know Them

According to most studies, 80 percent of your business comes from 20 percent of your customers. Take the time to create a list of your best customers. Post that list where you can see it at all times, and think about how you can create a stronger bond with each of these customers.

One simple method is to go out of your way to learn about your customers' businesses. Just as retail customers and restaurant patrons want to be made to feel important, so do clients of service and professional businesses. Imagine how important your clients will feel when you call up to make an appointment to come in and talk with them—not about what services you can sell them, but about what you can learn about their business.

Learn what obstacles they are struggling with, and consider whether you may know of other service providers in other business categories to whom you can recommend them. You may not make a sale that time, but they will remember you later.

236. Read a Newspaper with Scissors

As you read the newspaper or cruise the Internet, look for articles that would be of interest to your clients and customers. If you are an accountant, look for articles on changes in the tax laws. If you are a lawyer, look for articles about court decisions that may affect some of your clients' businesses. If you own a decorating service, consider sending articles about trends in design and color.

When you find news in your area of expertise or related to the service you provide, photocopy it and fax or mail it to your client list, or, if your list is large, send it to your best clients. Include a handwritten note suggesting that the information may be valuable to them.

237. Partnering

There are endless opportunities to cross-market with noncompetitive businesses that your customers will have an interest in knowing about. For example, in any home or building trades service, your clients and customers are frequently in need of services that you do not provide. However, you may know a competent business to which you can refer them. If you don't, you should develop a referral list based on research that you've done and cross-marketing agreements.

If you own a pool-service company, your customers may need a roofer, a driveway repaver, a lawn-service company, or any of a dozen other services. Determine which providers of these other services have the best reputations, and make an agreement with them to market each other's services. You can do this by offering to distribute each other's brochures, swapping mailing lists, and running special promotions.

Your business does not exist in a vacuum. You are part of a network of service and professional providers who, by combining forces, can help one another grow.

238. Publish Your Book

You are an expert in your business, and much of the information that you have in your head and in your organization could be brought together in a book or pamphlet that you can give away to current and potential customers. This is an activity that you will certainly want to hire a professional to execute. Find a competent ghostwriter with a track record, and be prepared to pay as much as $100 an hour and to be available for interviews and provide research and other materials.

Publishing has become very affordable and can be done in very small quantities at reasonable prices. You don't need a publishing company to publish your book. Expect to pay between $10,000 and $20,000 to have a ghostwriter create a full-length book for you, and expect to pay between $5 and $10 a copy to have it designed and printed in small quantities.

This may be a major expense, and you will be giving these books away rather than trying to make back your investment through book sales. But consider the impact that a book will have on your potential customers, the credibility it will give you, and the opportunity to get publicity and media attention that it will provide. If you are in a high- value, high-ticket business, such as financial consulting, law, or another similar profession, the cost of producing a book may be recovered from a single new client.

If you can't justify a full-length book, consider producing a long pamphlet or a booklet, which can be printed for a smaller investment but will still have a strong impact.

239. Small Gestures Leave Big Impressions

There are a number of inexpensive ways to let your customers know that you are thinking of them even when they aren't paying you for your services, and some ways that remind them on a regular basis that you appreciate their business. One of these is to give your clients a gift subscription to an industry or business publication.

Another is to simply remember their anniversary—on the anniversary of your first transaction with a client or customer, send a card thanking her for her business. If you stay in touch when you have nothing to sell, they will remember you when they need to buy.

240. Close to Home

If you are in any business that caters to homeowners, you have many opportunities to make yourself stand out from your competitors, and to please potential new customers.

If you do house painting, lawn maintenance, pool service, roofing, plumbing, septic service, and so on, during the off months you can go around your target neighborhoods offering to paint or repaint house numbers on curbs. Fire departments are always urging people to do this in case of an emergency, but many people never quite get around to it.

Make sure to get permission first, and to leave your literature and a coupon or gift certificate good toward your service during the slow weeks at the start of your season.

20

Restaurant, Food-Service, and Beverage Companies—Within Your Four Walls

In every business that customers patronize, what they see and experience has an enormous impact on their purchasing decisions. Nowhere is this more true than in all aspects of the food and beverage service business. Food is a commodity. You can live for a long time eating dandelions out of your lawn and drinking water from a stream. The restaurant, bar, and most food-service businesses are about presentation and theater.

Ask yourself what your customers' experiences will be—what will they see, smell, taste, hear, and feel? Killing your best efforts with a bad first impression is much easier than you would imagine.

Start outside your four walls, at your property line. If you haven't done it recently, get the parking lot lines restriped. Fix the potholes. Have the landscaping updated. Make sure that every scrap of litter is picked up. Cut out the dead parts of your hedges.

Ray Kroc, the founder of McDonald's, was a big proponent of lush landscaping and mounds of potted plants that were changed every season. At a recent marketing conference, Ed Rensi, the former McDonald's CEO, told an audience about his experiences with the company's philosophy:

> In the early days we had red and white tiled buildings, and we took glass wax and waxed our buildings once a week. I can't tell you how many Tuesday nights I waxed that building.

217

> I was a store manager in Jamestown, New York, and in the summer we had bugs galore up there. So we decided to put yellow fluorescent fixtures and yellow bulbs in all the incandescent fixtures. We had yellow bulbs everywhere, hoping the bugs would not be attracted. But the bugs turned out to like all kinds of light. I used fly swatters and bug spray. But the restaurant looked dirty when I did that.
>
> So I got rid of all the yellow lightbulbs, and I got some bright white bulbs. The bugs still came, but I cleaned them up every day. It was more work, but the restaurant looked better.

Although waxing the outside of a restaurant each week may seem like an extreme measure, for McDonald's it was an essential marketing tactic. It doesn't matter whether you own the most exclusive restaurant in the world or a sandwich shop in a bus station; you should always be looking at your physical property and thinking of ways to make it more enticing. It's easy to forget this as you rush about day to day just keeping the place running. But that's exactly when you should be paying attention, because when you're distracted, you no longer notice when things break, get dirty, and turn off your customers.

The next pages contain some specific tactics that all food- and beverage-service businesses should consider essential, ongoing, and part of the marketing way of life.

241. Toilet Marketing

Objective   Improve customer service, build loyalty.

Target   All customers.

One of the most egregious crimes committed by food- and beverage-service businesses is allowing bathrooms to remain dirty and in disrepair. This was once considered such an essential element of marketing that former McDonald's CEO Ed Rensi devoted an entire afternoon to discussing it in a speech to 8,000 franchisees.

> I discovered that clean bathrooms make food taste better. If you don't have a clean bathroom and you don't keep it clean and odor free, your customer thinks, 'How can the kitchen be clean?' If you don't have time to clean the bathrooms, you probably don't have time to clean the kitchen.
>
> I call this toilet marketing. If your customers walk into your restaurant and they can smell it before they see it, you have a problem. You should put ice in the urinals, to keep the waste from fermenting and the

smell from proliferating. You should install perfume spritzers that activate themselves every couple of minutes.

If I wanted to build a restaurant today, I would put nothing but white tile and white walls in the bathroom. I would put four four-bulb fluorescent fixtures in that bathroom. I would make it as bright and white and light as I possibly could to prove that it is sanitary. And when I got done scrubbing it, I would use some chlorine-based solution to sanitize it and make it smell clean. I guarantee your customers are going to think your food tastes better.

In the restaurants I managed, we had two thousand people a day using our restrooms. We used fourteen rolls of toilet paper a day. If you can measure it, you can manage it. We understood by keeping track of such things that our customers were spending a lot of time in there. This is so simplistic it's almost embarrassing to explain it.

242.   Bathroom Merchandising

Objective   Increase awareness, increase sales.

Target   All customers.

You may not have thought of promoting your business in the bathrooms, but this can be an effective way to capture customers' attention.

You can use posters displayed prominently in both the men's and the women's rooms to market special events, current promotions, and signature menu and bar items. If, for instance, your goal is to boost beverage and alcohol sales, consider featuring items with high profit margins, such as specialty drinks and bottles of wine. You could also communicate happy-hour value.

Be sure to update these posters as necessary to keep the marketing message fresh. It's equally wise to designate an employee or manager to monitor bathroom merchandising.

Materials   Posters.

Timing

Four weeks prior:

Prepare posters.

Three weeks prior:

Print posters.

One week prior:

Discuss program with staff.

Start:

Hang posters.

Ongoing:

Update posters for current events.

243. Sample This!

Objective Increase awareness, increase community goodwill, increase lunch sales.

Target Businesses in your trading area.

Sampling is a very effective way to introduce your business to potential customers. However, sometimes you have to take your samples to customers in order to get them to give you a try. This program is designed to introduce you and your restaurant to businesses in your trading area. If you sell a type of food or beverage that is easily delivered outside of your own location, you have the ability to reach nearly 200 such businesses and countless new customers in the course of one year.

One restaurant's version of this promotion was called "The Platters Program," because every day at noon, representatives would take a platter of subs to a business. First, they called the business to find out how many employees it had, so that they would be sure to bring enough food. Within the first three weeks of this promotion, the business saw a 30 percent increase in sales volume.

To adapt this promotion to your business, first determine what product you offer that is easily sampled or is in some way a good representation of your menu.

Materials Bounce-back coupons, menu flyers, samples.

Timing

Four weeks prior:

Prepare list of businesses.

Three weeks prior:

Prepare bounce-back coupons.
Prepare menu flyers.

Two weeks prior:

Print bounce-back coupons.
Print menu flyers.

One week prior:

Contact businesses to set up appointments to deliver samples.
Discuss program with staff.

One day prior:

Confirm appointment with businesses.

Start:

Prepare samples.
Visit businesses.

Six weeks after:

Evaluate results.

244. Food Booths

Objective Increase awareness, increase community goodwill, generate traffic, build your image, increase sales, stimulate trial.

Target Existing customers and potential new customers.

If you have a restaurant, set up food booths at county fairs, community arts and crafts shows, boat shows, and even flea markets.

Staff the food booth with kitchen staff and front-of-the-house personnel, and sell your restaurant's specialties along with general favorites. Make sure your restaurant's name is displayed prominently on the booth, as well as on paper napkins, paper plates, bags, and any other walk-away items. Print mini-menus and distribute them as bag stuffers.

Materials Equipped food booth, signage, imprinted walk-away items, mini-menus.

Timing

This is an ongoing event and requires no special timetable. It is especially useful for new restaurants or restaurants opening in a new area. Prepare your booth, signage, menus, and imprinted items so that you have them on hand whenever a community event warrants your participation.

245. Eat at the Competition

Check out your competition. Many restaurateurs neglect to do this. How in the world will you know where you stand in your market and your category if you don't keep a weather eye on the other guy?

Eat at your competitors' establishments, and go with an open mind. We all have a tendency to do this looking for everything our competitors are doing wrong. It makes us feel better and feel superior, and it helps us confirm that what we are doing is right.

Send your employees to do this as well, and reimburse them for their expenses. Have them come back with a list of things that the competition is doing well. You might suggest that they find one good thing in each of ten categories, such as outside appearance, signage, greeting, wait time, condition of the table, noise, smell, service, food quality, and price.

246. Worst Table in the House

Objective   Increase awareness, generate traffic, create excitement, generate PR.

Target   Existing customers and potential new customers.

Almost all restaurants have a table that is less than an ideal place to sit. This program will put sitting at the "worst table in the house" in an entirely different light. You won't believe how many people will choose to sit there and the publicity that can come from this one promotion. Just ask Dave Anderson, founder of Famous Dave's, about the promotion and how successful it was for him.

The host or hostess should ask guests if they've ever dined at the worst table in the house. If they haven't, this will be a lead-in to offer to seat them at this "choice" seating to enjoy the atmosphere and "special" offerings. Those guests dining at the worst table in the house will receive 50 percent off their entire check (excluding alcohol). Have guests sign the "worst table" guest book and provide their name and address so that you can further build your mailing list.

This tactic will be promoted within the four walls using posters and your most valuable asset—your staff.

There are some fun things can be done to promote this tactic:

Display a poster that asks, "Have you seen our worst table in the house?" Decorate the table totally different from the rest of the dining area, and point out its unique features when guests are seated.

Make sure the servers make the experience fun. For example, when greeting the guests, they could say, "Hi there! I'm told you've never sat at the worst table in the house," and when taking their order, "Boy are you in for a treat today!"

At the end of the meal, be sure to bring the guests a "special treat" dessert on-the house.

Materials Posters, decorations.

Timing

Four weeks prior:

Prepare posters.

Three weeks prior:

Print posters.

Two weeks prior:

Purchase decorations.

One week prior:

Discuss program with staff.

One day prior:

Discuss program with staff.
Put up posters.

Start:

Promote the "worst table in the house."

Six weeks after:

Evaluate program.

247. Events Catering

Objective   Increase awareness, increase sales.

Target   Agents for community events.

Contact the agents responsible for staging community events at least eight weeks in advance of a particular event. Arrange to place a cart or stand containing snack foods and advertising specialties and coupons. If the event draws enough traffic and you can afford to do so, consider cosponsoring the event in order to get your name into any mention of the event in the print or radio media on a cooperative basis.

Materials   Food carts, advertising specialties, coupons.

Timing

Eight to ten weeks prior:

Contact agents responsible for staging community events.

Six weeks prior:

Discuss program with kitchen staff and decide on food items to be served, type of cart necessary, and servers.

Five weeks prior:

Begin looking for appropriate advertising specialties.
Purchase, construct, or rent food cart.

Three weeks prior:

Purchase advertising specialties.
Prepare coupons.

Two weeks prior:

Reconfirm participation and meet to discuss details.
Print coupons.

One day prior:

Review program with kitchen and serving staff.

Start:

Set up food cart.
Begin selling food and distributing coupons.

248. Bar Bingo

Objective Increase awareness, increase sales, increase frequency.

Target Existing customers

The bingo card promotion encourages existing customers to patronize the bar more often and sample a greater variety of its offerings.

When customers pay their bar tab, they're given a bingo card displaying 16 items (4 per row) ranging from draft beer and specialty martinis to top-shelf margaritas, wines by the glass, and exotic cordials. Each time customers try one of the featured drinks, the bartender stamps it out on the card. Every "bingo" horizontally, vertically, or diagonally is rewarded with a gift certificate or a coupon for a predetermined freebie. Be sure to promote the most profitable as well as the most popular items.

Promoted within the four walls, this program should carry an expiration date of 30 days, printed clearly on each bingo card.

Materials Bingo cards, stamp, inkpad, promotional posters.

Timing

Four weeks prior:

Prepare bingo card.
Prepare posters.

Two weeks prior: Print bingo cards and posters.

Purchase stamp and inkpad.

One week prior:

Discuss program with staff.

One day prior:

> Discuss program with staff again.
> Hang posters.

Start:

> Hand out bingo cards.

Six weeks after:

> Evaluate program.

249. Points and Passports

Objective   Increase awareness, increase frequency, build mailing list.

Target   Existing customers and local retailers

A successful loyalty program at the TGI Friday's restaurant chain, owned by Dallas-based Carlson Restaurants, used a point-based system. Awards ranged from a free appetizer after spending $125 to a Seven Seas cruise after spending $25,000. Membership cards were issued at the restaurant. Customers could obtain points updates in the stores or via a toll-free 800 number. The program was also promoted on a web site.

Friday's increased its membership database from 500,000 to 3 million.

Charthouse Restaurants, owned by Houston-based Landry's, introduced a clever Passport program coupled with a point-based system, with awards ranging from a $25 gift certificate after spending $250 to a vacation cruise. Customers received a promotional passport that got stamped each time they visited a Charthouse location. The more locations they visited, the greater the prize value. This allowed Charthouse to collect data on each customer. Members received regular communications through newsletters and point statements.

Materials   Passport, stamp, inkpad, booklet (if applicable), counter cards, posters.

Timing

Six weeks prior:

> Contact local retailers as potential partners.

Four weeks prior:

Prepare passport, booklet (if applicable), counter cards, poster.

Two weeks prior:

Print passport, booklet (if applicable), counter cards, poster.
Discuss program with staff.

One week prior:

Discuss program with staff.
Mail passport or booklet.

One day prior:

Discuss program with staff.

Start:

Stamp passports.
Redeem coupons in booklet.

Six weeks after:

Evaluate program.

250. Live Entertainment

Best For Restaurants catering to a young crowd.

Objective Increase awareness, create excitement, generate PR, generate traffic.

Target Existing and potential customers.

Live entertainment always draws a crowd. If your restaurant caters to a younger crowd, invite the high school band to play on a weekend day and set up a food booth to serve simple dishes and beverages. Promote the food booth by posting a sign near the activity. Provide free food to participants.

If you cannot do this outdoors, do what you can fit indoors, such as a talent contest. Try this on a slow day, to draw families, neighbors, and friends of the participants. Offer cash for the first prize. Second-place winners receive gift certificates, and third-place winners get a two-for-one discount.

Advertise these events in your local paper and use banners outside to draw attention.

Materials   Newspaper ad, banners, food booth prizes.

Timing

Five weeks prior:

Contact local authorities for rules on holding an outside event.

Four weeks prior:

Meet with high school principal to arrange participation of band or talent contestants and select judges

Three weeks prior:

Prepare newspaper ad and banners
Order banners.
Buy media.
Discuss food booth program with kitchen staff.

Two weeks prior:

Begin preparing food booth(s).
Confirm band and other participation.

One week prior:

Place ad.
Discuss program with staff.

One day prior:

Set up area for event.
Display banners.
Set up food booth(s).

Start:

Enjoy entertainment.
Award prizes.

251. Catering to the Community

Objective   Increase awareness, increase sales.

Target   Local civic groups, associations, and clubs

By networking with community-based organizations, you can develop catering opportunities while also creating goodwill.

For this tactic, contact your local Chamber of Commerce to obtain a list of all the civic groups, associations, and clubs in your local trading area. Send letters to the organizations' leaders describing your ability and desire to cater banquets, parties, fund-raisers, and other such events. Wait one week and make follow-up phone calls. Offer special incentives to select groups that have a large enrollment. Suggestions:

- Offer a 10 percent discount to members who present your ad from their club newsletter or bulletin. You may also want to consider creating this ad so that it looks like an I.D. card that customers present at your restaurant.
- Offer meals at a discount for catered affairs, parties, and so on.
- Allow 10 percent of every catering check over a determined amount to be returned to the organization at the end of the month.

Materials   Letters, ads.

Timing

Four weeks prior:

> Contact Chamber of Commerce and obtain mailing lists.
> Send letters to presidents and authorities.

Three weeks prior:

> Follow up with phone calls.
> Begin visiting interested organizations.

Two weeks prior:

> Place ads in organizations' newsletters and bulletins.
> Discuss program with kitchen staff and other staff.

One week prior:

Follow up and confirm any catering assignments.

Start:

Begin catering assignments.
Begin accepting I.D. discounts.

End:

Discontinue discounts.
Send thank-you letters to participating organizations.
Evaluate results.

252. Wine and Add-On Sales

Objective   Increase awareness, provide crew incentives, create excitement, build your image, increase sales.

Target   Your employees.

The object of this promotion is to increase the total of the average check through the sale of bottled wine and other add-ons. Servers are often reluctant to promote add-ons, especially wines, because of their lack of confidence in their own product knowledge. This is a teaching program that, in the short term, rewards servers for their add-on sales. In the long term, however, it will continue to increase the average check as servers gain self-confidence in making suggestions.

Hold periodic seminars on specialty foods and wine. It is important to have the seminars conducted by the servers themselves, as they will react better to their peers than to an expert lecturing at them. Assign servers a particular food or wine that they must become knowledgeable about at an expert level.

Let's begin with wine. Divide your wine list into segments (Loire Valley, Chardonnay, Sauvignon Blanc, and so on). Subdivide any segment containing more than four wines. Once a month, assign one segment to a different server. Give that server a bottle of each wine to take home and taste, as well as all the literature you can find about the history of the wines and their wineries. Make sure the literature describes the food groups that are complemented by each wine, and allow the server two weeks to study the material. At the end of the two weeks, let that server teach the other staff members about the wine by holding an informal wine tasting/seminar for the entire serving staff. Keep this up on a monthly basis until all segments of your wine list have been studied and presented.

You can teach food product knowledge the same way with the help of your head chef. This, however, can be done on a weekly rather than a monthly basis. Allow one server per week time in the kitchen with the head chef while a particular specialty appetizer, soup, or dessert is being prepared. Have the chef prepare that food in sufficient quantity for every staff member who's there that day. Hold a "tasting" seminar for that food, where the server describes its attributes. Continue this practice until all add-on foods have been studied and learned, and continue it whenever your head chef adds a new food to the menu.

This program can go hand-in-hand with bonuses given for add-on sales. Members of your wait staff will begin to look forward to learning about the different foods and wines. As they feel more confident of their understanding, they will be more comfortable with suggestively selling the items. They'll also learn quickly to look forward to earning their bonuses!

Materials   Written materials to educate servers about wines and add-ons, wines for staff to take home for tastings.

Timing

Four weeks prior:

Set goals and determine bonuses for add-on sales.
Determine program costs.

Three weeks prior:

Contact purveyors and explain program. Purveyors, as a resource, could provide free bottles of wine and information.

Two weeks prior:

Explain program to kitchen staff and servers. Give one server literature on wine and a bottle of wine to take home and taste. Have server spend time in kitchen with head chef to learn of specialty items to pair with wine.

One week prior:

Go over program with kitchen staff and servers again.

Start:

Have servers teach wine class. Conduct "tasting" seminar.

Three weeks after:

Review program.

253. Wine "Sommelier in Training"

Objective Increase awareness, provide crew incentives, create excitement, build your image.

Target Your employees.

Each month, select a particular bottle of wine and place it on all tables. Also place a table tent on each table, explaining the wine's attributes, qualities, and origin.

At the beginning of each month, teach all servers the attributes of that month's wine. Suggest that each of them try to sell as much of the wine as possible.

Post a tally board near your employee bulletin board to keep track of each server's wine sales. At the end of each month, reward the server with the most wine sales with a $25 bonus and a "Sommelier in Training" certificate. To keep other staff members interested, keep this certificate posted during the entire next month of the promotion.

Continue the program, using a new wine and table tent, as long as add-on sales of wine continue and the program remains profitable.

Materials Wine, table tents, tally board, "Sommelier in Training" certificates.

Timing

Four weeks prior:

Set goals and determine bonuses for add-on sales.
Contact purveyors and explain program.

Three weeks prior:

Prepare "Sommelier in Training" certificates and table tents.

Two weeks prior: Print certificates and table tents.

Prepare tally-board.

One week prior:

Explain program to servers and distribute literature about the coming month's wine.

Start:

Begin tallying wine add-on sales.

Four weeks after:

Present bonus and certificate to server with most sales.
Display certificate and begin the following month's program.

254. Elementary/Junior High P.T.A./Home and School Meetings

Objective   Increase awareness, increase community goodwill, generate traffic, build your image, increase sales, stimulate trial.

Target   Local elementary and junior high schools' Parent-Teacher Organizations (PTO) and Home and School Associations (HSA).

Contact the heads of your local parent-teacher organizations to arrange your participation in sponsorship of their school events. Make your business or restaurant the place to go for support of any PTO/HSA-sponsored events, including regular meetings.

Contribute cups, paper products, catered food, and, of course, bounceback coupons. The exposure can lead to your participation in numerous school activities.

Materials   None, other than donated items.

Timing
This is an ongoing program that can grow until you are catering most of the activities of your local school organizations. If you have children in the local schools, be sure to join the PTO or HSA before attempting any contact.

255. Elementary/Junior High Field Trip Discounts

Objective   Increase awareness, increase community goodwill, generate traffic, build your image, increase sales, stimulate trial.

Target   Local elementary and junior high schools, elementary and junior high school administrators.

Students and teachers can make special arrangements ahead of time to get a special lunch rate for groups during field trips. This eliminates the inevitable lunch problem and is an inexpensive way for the children to be assured of a good meal when they're not in the school cafeteria.

Allow students to choose between a burger, fries, and a soft drink or milk and a tuna sandwich, potato salad or coleslaw, and a soft drink or milk; for dessert, give the choice of chocolate chip cookies or ice cream. Set the same price structure for either meal, both of which can be prepared easily for a large group.

Contact local school administrators to present the program and arrange their cooperation. Present them with flyers describing the program, the discount lunches, the pricing, and the amount of specific advance notice you will need in order to prepare for the group.

Materials   Flyers.

Timing
This is an ongoing program and can be started at any time, preferably at the beginning of a school year.

256. Après Ville

Objective   Generate traffic, increase sales, stimulate trial.

Target   Existing customers and potential new customers.

Après Ville is French for "after the city" and refers to any cultural event (opera, ballet, theater, symphony, art or museum showing) held in the city. For this promotion, prepare an Après Ville menu that offers postevent suppers, coffee, drinks, and desserts.

Place a newspaper ad in the theater or entertainment section of the local paper. Use the headline of the ad to focus on a particular event, and create an incentive for readers to make your restaurant the postevent stop.

Most newspapers produce a special section for the upcoming cultural season, designed as a pullout for readers to keep throughout the year. In general, the rates in these sections are very cost-effective. In addition, try to obtain a list of ticket holders and send invitations to them by direct mail, adjusting the invitation to focus on particular events.

Materials Après Ville menu, mailing list, invitations, newspaper ad.

Timing

Six weeks prior:

Set program goals and determine costs.
Discuss Après Ville menu with your kitchen staff.

Four weeks prior:

Obtain mailing list.
Prepare invitation and ads.

Three weeks prior:

Print menu and invitations.
Buy media.

One week prior:

Explain program to staff.
Mail invitations to names on mailing list.

One day prior:

Review program with kitchen and wait staff.

Start:

Set out Après Ville menus and begin program.

Four weeks after:

Evaluate results.

Chapter Twenty

257. Early Bird Tactics

"Early bird specials" have become a household term, especially among older members of the community and families with young children. It has become expected that almost all restaurants will offer an early bird special, and diners frequently rush to those that do to take advantage of the savings.

In addition, getting diners in at an early hour, before the usual lunch or dinner rush, is an excellent method of keeping your staff busy and gaining better control of your traffic flow. For these two reasons, restaurants have gone into keen competition with one another to keep the early birds flocking in.

The following tactics have been designed to make your restaurant's early bird offers stand out among the crowd.

258. New Luncheon Menu

Objective Increase awareness, generate traffic, build your image, increase sales, stimulate trial.

Target Existing customers and potential new customers.

If your restaurant is medium- or higher-priced, develop a new luncheon menu of six to eight items plus a daily special, served with a non-alcoholic beverage, for under $6. This will greatly improve customers' price-to-value perception.

This program can be promoted simply by the addition of a menu insert into the regular menu, and perhaps a mention on your communications board. If you wish, flyers announcing the new menu can be distributed to local area businesses.

Materials Menu insert, flyers (optional).

Timing

Three weeks prior:

Discuss new menu items with kitchen staff.
Prepare new menu inserts.
Prepare flyers (optional).

Two weeks prior:

Discuss program with staff.
Print new menu inserts.
Print flyers (optional).

One week prior:

Distribute flyers (optional).

Start:

Review program with staff.
Begin serving special menu items.

Two weeks after:

Evaluate program.

259. Seniors Early Dinner Club

Objective   Increase awareness, generate traffic, increase sales, stimulate trial.

Target   Seniors, church groups, retirement housing establishments.

Use "club cards" to entice area seniors to have dinner at your establishment between 4:00 and 6:00 p.m. on any day of the week.

Offer a 15 percent discount on the entire check to seniors presenting the card during the specified hours. Ask seniors to fill out a short-form application in order to receive their membership card. This way, you will have their names and addresses for your mailing list as well as proof of membership should they lose their cards. Make sure you ask for proof of age, as this will be flattering and promote goodwill. Generally, an age of 55 or over is required for membership.

Materials   Flyers, table tents, posters, short-form applications, "club cards."

Timing

Six weeks prior:

Set program goals and determine costs.
Write copy for flyers, short forms, and cards.

Determine the groups you wish to contact.

Four weeks prior:

Begin contacting and visiting groups.
Print table tents, posters, applications, flyers, cards.

One week prior:

Distribute flyers.

Start:

Set out table tents and posters.
Take applications and present cards.

Two weeks after:

Evaluate results.
Modify the program, if necessary.

260. One Dollar Off

Objective   Generate traffic, increase sales, stimulate trial.

Target   Existing customers and potential new customers.

Give every person who comes into your restaurant for dinner $1 off the order. Allow each member of a party to receive the discount. If there are four people paying on one check, take $4 off the total.

You may vary the hours for the special to suit your own needs, but generally 5:00 to 6:30 p.m. is recommended. Senior citizens generally dine early, so if there is a large senior citizen population in your area, you might want to consider backing up the start hour to as early as 4:00 or 4:30 p.m.

This program will also appeal to movie-goers and people who have commitments to meetings and sporting events, such as bowling team members.

Support the program with newspaper ads, direct mail, table tents or posters, and a menu insert.

Materials   Newspaper ad, flyers, table tents or posters, menu inserts.

Timing   This tactic requires no special timing or lead time and can be run throughout the year.

261. Dining at Dusk

Objective   Generate traffic, increase sales, keep staff busy, promote activity during slow periods, stimulate trial.

Target   Existing customers and potential new customers

This program is designed to give an upscale establishment an "early bird special" without the feel of an early bird special. Take extra care to emphasize dining in style early in the evening. Menu clip-ons and inserts should not be used. Instead, print a special "Dining at Dusk" menu to keep the upscale feeling.

On the special menu, offer a set price for soup or salad (or both) and a choice of entree at about the normal price of the entree alone. This allows room for add-on sales of beverages and desserts.

Present those who are dining at dusk with both your regular menu and the early dinner menu, as they may be tempted to order items that are not available on the early dinner menu. Make sure the hours you set for this program do not interfere with the times you begin to get busy with later evening diners.

When discussing the program with your staff, be clear about cutoff times, but be sure that your staff honors the dining at dusk offer for customers who ask for it within a reasonable amount of time after the cutoff. You must allow for traffic, slow watches, and so on.

This program is especially attractive to seniors and can be easily promoted to them. One great way to get this group's attention is to have your chef make a presentation on diet and/or nutrition at a local senior organization's regular meeting. Ask for their input in preparing the "Dining at Dusk" menu. For their help, hand out a bounce-back offer good for an additional $1 off their first visit during the early hours.

Materials   Newspaper ad, table tents, "Dining at Dusk" menu, bounce-back coupons.

Timing

Six weeks prior:

Discuss program with your chef.
Contact local seniors groups to arrange a presentation.
Plan and print bounce-back coupons.

Five weeks prior:

Make presentation at senior organizations.
Distribute bounce-back coupons.
Plan new menu.

Four weeks prior:

Print new menus.
Plan newspaper ad, table tents.

Three weeks prior:

Buy media.
Print table tents.

One week prior:

Discuss program with staff, explaining policies carefully.
Place ad.
Set out table tents.

Start:

Hand out both "Dining at Dusk" and regular menus.
Honor seniors' bounce-back coupons.

Two weeks after:

Evaluate results.
Modify the program, if necessary.

21
Coupons and Other Come-Ons

There is a nearly unlimited number of promotional tactics that involve certificates, coupons, and promotions aimed at certain population subgroups, such as military personnel or blood donors. Scan your local newspaper for fairs, street festivals, flea markets, sporting events, community events, and so on. All of these are great opportunities for you to hand out coupons good toward a visit to your establishment. Here are a couple of ideas to get you thinking.

262. Community Events Coupons

Objective Generate traffic, increase sales, stimulate trial.

Target Local events management organizations.

If your restaurant is unable to participate in large community events through sponsorship, cosponsoring, or food booths, position a few of your staff members at key locations to hand out coupons good for free food items. Be sure the coupons give directions to your restaurant. To encourage repeat visits, hand out bounce-back coupons to customers who redeem the coupons.

Materials Free food coupons, bounce-back coupons.

Timing

Four weeks prior:

Contact event management for permission to distribute coupons.

Three weeks prior:

241

Prepare coupons.

Two weeks prior:

Print coupons.

One week prior:

Meet with staff to discuss program and arrange schedule of staff who will be handing out coupons at event.

Start:

Distribute coupons.
Hand out bounce-backs to customers who redeem coupons.

263.   Blood Drive Tie-In

Objective   Build mailing list, increase community goodwill, generate traffic, stimulate trial.

Target   Local blood banks.

During a local blood drive, offer a free menu item to anyone bringing a valid donor card to your business on the same day he or she gives blood. When the card is presented, have the donor fill out his or her name and address and the date of the visit, both to prevent reuse of the card and to add names to your mailing list.

Promote the event with posters in hospitals, doctor's offices, supermarkets, and any cooperative high-traffic neighborhood stores. Be sure to send press releases to local media. Contact the Red Cross for information on high-iron foods to offer to donors.

Present customers with bounce-back coupons to say "thank you" and generate repeat visits.

Materials   Posters, press releases, bounce-back coupons.

Timing

Six weeks prior:

Begin contacting hospitals, doctor's offices, supermarkets, and stores to arrange their cooperation in displaying your posters.

Four weeks prior:

Prepare posters, bounce-back coupons.
Contact the Red Cross for high-iron food information.

Three weeks prior:

Print posters and bounce-back coupons.

Two weeks prior:

Discuss special food items with kitchen staff.

One week prior:

Distribute posters.
Discuss program with staff.

Start:

Begin serving dinner to donors.
Distribute bounce-back coupons.

264. Birthday Tactics

Recognizing customers' birthdays on a regular basis is a great way to make them feel special and to build and maintain a mailing list. Birthdays and food just naturally go together, and any customer who responds to your birthday offers is guaranteed to bring other customers along, including people who may never have patronized your business. It's easy, effective, and highly personal, and it should be part of every food-service business's marketing plan.

265. Birthday Parties

Objective Increase awareness, generate traffic, increase sales.

Target Existing customers and potential new customers.

This tactic is easily promoted via table tents stating that your restaurant is available for birthday parties. State that you will provide decorations, hats, and favors, as well as a birthday cake, at no additional charge. (You may want to include gratuities in the price.)

Require reservations at least one week in advance, and provide a special menu of all-inclusive party selections, with each selection having a different price point. For example: Birthday Dinner for four guests, $59.95; for six guests, $79.95; for eight guests, $99.95. If you prefer, you can simply provide per-person pricing.

Before you begin this promotion, be sure to discuss the special menu with your kitchen staff. It will be necessary to assign individual servers for the party to be sure that the program runs smoothly.

Materials   Table tents, special menus, party supplies.

Timing

Three weeks prior:

> Discuss the special menu with your kitchen staff.
> Prepare table tents, special menus.

Two weeks prior:

> Purchase party supplies.
> Print special menus.

One week prior:

> Explain promotion to staff. If you will be including gratuities in the price, your staff should be made aware of this.

One day prior:

> Set out table tents.

Start:

> Take party reservations.

266. Children's Birthday Club

Objective   Increase awareness, build mailing list, generate traffic, increase sales, stimulate trial.

Target   Families with children ages 6 to 13.

All children between the ages of 6 and 13 should be given a special "(name of your restaurant) Birthday Club" card to fill out. The card should include the child's name, address, age, and birthday, and it entitles the child to a free "Happy Birthday Giant Ice Cream Sundae" anytime within one week before or after his or her birthday.

Generate excitement by advertising that the children can choose any flavor ice cream with any toppings they want. List the flavors and toppings on the card so that kids can check them off for fun. Once the cards are redeemed, keep them in a monthly file, filed one month prior to the child's birthday, and be sure to add the names to your mailing list.

As the dates come up, birthday cards should be sent to the children saying: "Happy Birthday, (Name of Child)! (Your Restaurant's Name) is getting your free Happy Birthday Giant Ice Cream Sundae ready. It has 3 scoops of (ice cream flavors) and is covered with (list of toppings). Make sure you ask your family to bring you in between one week before and one week after your birthday. And if we don't see you before that special day, have a very, very happy (6th, 7th, etc.) birthday!"

Materials   Birthday Club cards, preprinted birthday cards.

Timing   This is a promotion that can be started as soon as you have your materials ready and run throughout the year. Just make sure that the ice cream flavors and toppings that you list on the cards are readily available at your restaurant. Make sure to discuss the program with your staff before you begin.

267. Birthday Club

Objective   Increase awareness, build mailing list, generate traffic, increase sales, stimulate trial.

Target   Existing customers and potential new customers.

Have your staff encourage diners who are waiting for their meals to fill out a Birthday Club registration card, located in take-one boxes on the tables. Guests return the cards to their server, who puts them in a Birthday Club collection box. Each week, the sign-up cards are sorted according to the month of the birthday, and at a specified time before the birthday, they trigger a birthday-card coupon mailing. Suggestion: Offer a free dessert, such as a cake for four to six people.

The birthday cards should read: "Congratulations on your Birthday. To make it even more special, (Your Restaurant's Name) has a cake waiting for you! Just call 123-4567 to let us know when you're coming in. And have a happy, happy birthday."

Both the sign-up card and the birthday card should be attractive two-color pieces. *Note:* Be sure to transfer the names of the Birthday Club members to your mailing list for other mailings.

Materials   Take-one boxes, Birthday Club registration cards, preprinted birthday cards, registration card collection box.

Timing

Four weeks prior:

> Design attractive take-one boxes, Birthday Club registration cards, and birthday cards.

Three weeks prior:

> Print registration and birthday cards. Order take-one boxes.

One week prior:

> Explain promotion to staff.

One day prior:

> Set out take-one boxes with registration cards.
> Set up collection box.
> Review program with staff.

One week after:

> Meet with staff to obtain feedback in the form of customer comments and staff suggestions.

268.   Family Tactics

Family tactics, per se, are designed to meet the general interests of the middle-American family. Some are targeted to the entire family unit, some are aimed at mother or father alone, and some are geared toward areas of interest to the children of the family—counting on the fact that this will also get their parents to come into your restaurant. The tactics here are usually general enough so that they could also be used to target other markets.

269. Mom's Night Out

Objective   Generate traffic, increase sales, stimulate trial.

Target   Existing customers and potential new customers.

This program is designed for restaurants in a trading area where there are a large number of working mothers within a three- to five-mile radius. It works especially well for families with children who remain at school for after-school programs and are picked up at about 5:00 p.m.

It is designed to encourage families to get together at your restaurant for dinner. Promote the program with newspaper ads, and give each mom who visits the restaurant before 6:30 or 7:00 (whenever your regular dinner traffic starts building) free soft drinks for the entire family. Make sure to state a minimum purchase requirement, such as $10.

Materials   Ads in local newspapers

Timing

Three weeks prior:

Prepare ads.
Purchase media.

One week prior:

Place ads.
Explain program to staff.

Start:

Begin giving free soft drinks with minimum purchases to families who dine before your set specified hour.

270. Family Feast

Objective   Increase awareness, increase community goodwill, generate traffic, increase sales, stimulate trial.

Target   Existing customers and potential new customers.

The week before Mother's Day is designated as National Family Week to celebrate the importance of family life in American society.

Create a promotion around this holiday week by offering a selection of predetermined dinner specials for families of four, six, and eight people. Determine a special price for each predetermined dinner selection, and offer these selections at the restaurant or as take-out.

Be sure to include bounce-back coupons, either presented with the dinner check or as bag stuffers for take-out items. Promote this program with radio and/or newspaper advertising that includes predetermined "family feasts" and their prices.

Use menu inserts and your communications board to promote the specials to diners who are already in your restaurant.

Materials   Newspaper ads, radio scripts, communications board notices, menu inserts, bounce-back coupons.

Timing

Three weeks prior:

Set program goals and determine costs.
Prepare radio script and/or newspaper ads.
Prepare menu inserts and bounce-back coupons.
Buy media.

Two weeks prior:

Print menu inserts and bounce-back coupons.

One week prior:

Explain program to servers.

One day prior:

Review program with servers.

Start:

Begin serving "family feasts" and distributing bounce-back coupons.

271.   Night on the Town

Objective   Generate traffic, keep staff busy, increase sales, promote activity during slow periods, stimulate trial.

Target   Existing customers and potential new customers.

Create a special dinner ambiance on two nights per week, preferably your two normally slowest nights, for a two-month period.

Place a large bouquet of fresh flowers on a table just inside the door between the lobby and the table area. Place fresh flowers on every table. Try to set up a partnership promotion with a local florist where the florist supplies the flowers in exchange for brand exposure on every table display and in your newspaper advertising.

Use half of the lighting you'd normally use, and put a candle on every table. Assign special staff to welcome customers and continuously check the service at each table. If you have a wait, consider passing out light hors d'oeuvres in the lobby.

Consider developing a special menu with "Night on the Town" pricing—and make sure that the price is slightly lower than normal to further encourage traffic on designated nights.

You may also want to use your newspaper advertising to offer a free glass of wine to "Night on the Town" diners.

Advertise weekly for at least the first two weeks of the promotion. Make sure to hang an attractive, descriptive poster during the promotion.

Materials   Newspaper ads, radio scripts, communications board notices, menu inserts, bounce-back coupons.

Timing

Four weeks prior:

> Contact local florist to arrange partnership promotion.
> Prepare newspaper advertising and poster.
> Prepare special menu (optional).

Three weeks prior:

> Buy media.
> Print poster and (optional) special menu.

Two weeks prior:

> Explain program to servers.
> Purchase candles and other decorations as you see fit.

One week prior:

> Reaffirm and review partnership promotion with florist.
> Place first newspaper ad.

One day prior:

Decorate restaurant.
Hang poster.
Review program with servers again.

Start:

Accept floral delivery and set out flowers.
Turn down the lights and light candles.
Set out (optional) special menu.
Begin serving "Night on the Town" dinners.

One week after:

Place second newspaper ad.

Four weeks after:

Evaluate results

272. Family Night

Objective Generate traffic, keep staff busy, increase sales, promote activity during slow periods, stimulate trial.

Target Existing customers and potential new customers.

This promotion, perfect for your slowest night, creates an at-home atmosphere in your restaurant by serving family-style.

Let the mother choose the entree from your regular menu, along with the appetizer and dessert, and serve the mother's choices on platters on the center of the table—family-style rather than as individual portions.

Offer free beverages to the table, also mother's choice. Serve soft drinks by the pitcher, coffee in a carafe or thermos server. Prepare family-sized cakes, pies, gelatin molds, and so on for dessert.

Materials Newspaper ad, table tents, menu inserts.

Timing

Four weeks prior:

Prepare newspaper ad, table tents, and menu inserts.

Discuss preparation of family-sized food portions with kitchen staff.

Three weeks prior:

Buy media.
Print table tents and menu inserts.

One week prior:

Explain program to staff.
Place ad in newspaper.

Start:

Advertise on table tents.
Place inserts in menu.
Begin serving family style.

One week after:

Evaluate program and take appropriate action.

273. Coupon Book

Objective　Increase awareness, increase community goodwill, generate traffic, increase sales, stimulate trial.

Target　Existing customers and potential new customers.

For this three- to four-week promotion, you should have as many retailers as partners as you can get together. The partners pay for retail advertising, and the restaurant pays for the cost of posters and coupon books. Try to get the cooperation of the most popular and frequently visited local merchants, such as dry cleaners, video stores, and drugstores.

Give every customer who has dinner at your restaurant during the promotion a coupon book good for deep discounts on family-oriented merchandise at the participating retailers. The participating retailers will, in turn, distribute buy-one-get-one-free coupons to those redeeming the coupons you have given out.

Display posters in your restaurant and at the participating retailers' locations. If you have a good deal of cooperation, it's best to run your newspaper advertising at the beginning of each week of the promotion.

Materials　Newspaper ads, posters, retail coupon books, buy-one-get-one-free coupons.

Timing

Six weeks prior:

> Contact local trading area retailers to arrange partnership promotion.

Four weeks prior:

> Get firm commitment from participating retailers and have them sign a written participation agreement.

Three weeks prior:

> Prepare newspaper ads, coupon books, coupons, and posters. Buy media.

One week prior:

> Place first ad in newspaper. Distribute posters and buy-one-get-one-free coupons to participants. Discuss program with staff.

Start:

> Display posters and distribute coupon books.

274. Celebrity Day

Objective Increase awareness, create excitement, generate PR, generate traffic, build your image, increase sales, stimulate trial.

Target Existing customers and potential new customers.

Arrange a day when a well-known local personality or sports figure will come to your restaurant. Develop a traffic-generating newspaper ad stating that any customer dining at your restaurant on the promised day will have an opportunity to meet the celebrity and get an autograph.

If the celebrity is big enough, consider using radio as well as newspapers to promote the event. With a sports figure, distribute flyers at local sporting events and schools at least one week in advance. With a TV personality, distribute flyers through advertising agencies specializing in marriage mail, where your coupon is mailed in an envelope with coupons from other businesses.

Since this type of event is likely to generate a lot of traffic, be sure to distribute bounce-back coupons to all customers who come in that day.

Materials   Newspaper ad, radio script (optional), flyers.

Timing

Eight weeks prior:

> Begin looking for a well-known personality who will cooperate. Make sure to have the person sign an agreement to attend on the set date.

Four weeks prior:

> Prepare newspaper ad, radio script (optional), flyers, and coupons.
> Arrange marriage mail.
> Order photographs of celebrity.

One week prior:

> Explain program to servers.
> Place radio and/or newspaper advertising.
> Confirm date with celebrity.

One day prior:

> Review program with staff.

Start:

> Begin handing out photos and coupons to customers.

275. Mystery Coupons

Objective   Increase frequency, generate traffic, increase sales.

Target   Existing customers and potential new customers.

For this tactic, distribute mystery coupons for four weeks and run the program for an additional four weeks. During the promotion, all diners receive a sealed envelope with a mystery coupon enclosed.

Depending on your type of food service, the mystery coupon could be for a free appetizer, dessert, order of French fries, soft drink, glass of wine, or some other item. The coupon is valid only if it is presented to the server, unopened, during the customer's next visit. The server opens the envelope, shows the mystery coupon to the customer, and redeems the coupon.

Structure the coupons so that most of them are for the least expensive foods and only a few are for the most expensive foods. Determine the specific number of each based on sales volume.

Materials Coupons, envelopes.

Timing

Three weeks prior:

Determine coupon items and the number of each.

Two weeks prior:

Print coupons.
Purchase envelopes.

One week prior:

Explain program to staff.

Start:

Review program with staff.
Begin distribution of "mystery" coupons.

Four weeks after:

Begin coupon redemption.
Evaluate program and take appropriate action.

276. It's Our Treat

Objective Increase awareness, increase community goodwill, increase sales, stimulate trial.

Target Potential new customers.

Contact your local Welcome Wagon or similar group and ask representatives to pass out "It's Our Treat" coupons to new residents, good for free dessert and coffee with the purchase of lunch or dinner.

You can also go through realtors in the area to distribute the coupons to new home buyers or renters in the area. Reward the distributors by asking them to attach their business cards to the coupons. When a designated number of coupons with their business cards attached have been redeemed, they will be contacted to come in for a free dessert and coffee for two. There are no other purchases necessary for the distributors.

Materials Coupons.

Timing

Three weeks prior:

Prepare coupons.
Contact Welcome Wagon and local realtors for distribution.

Two weeks prior:

Print coupons.

One week prior:

Distribute coupons.
Explain program to staff.

Start:

Review program with staff.
Begin redeeming coupons from new patrons.

One week after:

Call realtors whose coupons have been redeemed to offer them their free dessert and coffee.

277. Invitation to Dine

Objective Increase awareness, increase sales, stimulate trial.

Target Potential new customers.

Prepare an invitation for new members of the community to learn about your business and send it via direct mail to a list of new residents obtained through mailing list companies or your local realtor's office.

The invitation offer should be strong (i.e., a buy-one-get-one-free promotion or some other significant offer that is appropriate to your type of business). Include a name and address section on the invitation, and state that the invitation must be presented at the time of purchase. This will give you new names for your mailing list as well as ensuring that the same customers do not come in for your free offer more than once.

Have the invitations expire in one month, and have the manager sign and date each one. This gives a more personal feel to the piece. Additionally, set the piece apart from all that junk mail by designing it to look like a real invitation. Hand-address the envelope (no computer labels), and put only your return address, not your company name, on the back flap. Also, mail the invitation first class with a commemorative postage stamp, not by meter.

Materials   Invitations, envelopes, mailing list, stamps.

Timing   This is an ongoing promotion that does not require special timing. Simply prepare the invitations, generically, and fill out the date and signatures prior to mailing. If the promotion works well, request a new resident list every four to eight weeks and repeat.

278.   Special Appearance Day

Objective   Increase awareness, increase community goodwill, create excitement, generate PR, generate traffic, build your image, increase sales, stimulate trial.

Target   Existing customers and potential new customers.

Create excitement and generate business through the appearance of a special unit of the fire department, police department, or any other group that will attract a crowd.

Children and their families are always attracted to displays and rides on fire equipment and police equipment. You can promote this family event inexpensively by distributing flyers as doorknob hangers or marriage mail in the residential areas within a three- to five-mile radius.

Materials Flyers.

Timing

Twelve weeks prior:

Contact the appropriate organization to arrange the promotion.

Three weeks prior:

Confirm promotion with organization.
Prepare flyers.

Two weeks prior:

Print flyers.

One week prior:

Distribute flyers via doorknobbers or, better yet, marriage mailing.
Explain program to staff and delegate responsibilities for crowd control.

Start:

Review program with staff.

End of day:

Invite participating members of the organization in for free refreshments.

279. Have a Heart

Objective Increase awareness, increase community goodwill, generate PR, generate traffic, build your image, increase sales, stimulate trial.

Target Existing customers and potential new customers.

Contact the local chapter of the American Heart Association to determine which of your menu items could be identified as foods that are good for customers with heart problems, and identify those items on your menu with a small red heart. Put up a poster at the front of your restaurant to

alert customers of the meaning of the red heart in the menu: low cholesterol, approved by the American Heart Association.

When the program begins, send press releases to the local media explaining that your restaurant "has a heart" and that some menu items
have been approved by the American Heart Association, and consider
announcing that you'll donate $1 from each check to the local Heart As-
sociation office. Send press releases to doctors and hospitals as well, so
that they will perhaps recommend your restaurant to their patients.

After the program breaks, run small ads in your local newspaper to
promote it, if you can afford to do so. The entire program will increase
the value of your restaurant to the community and will give customers,
especially those with heart problems, an added reason to eat at the restaurant.

Materials   Red heart stickers, press releases, poster, ad.

Timing

Four weeks prior:

> Set program goals and determine costs.
> Contact the American Heart Association.

Three weeks prior:

> Purchase heart stickers for your menus.
> Prepare ad and buy media.
> Prepare and print posters.

Two weeks prior:

> Send press releases to media and medical personnel.
> Discuss program with kitchen staff and other staff.

Start:

> Place ad.
> Set out explanatory poster.
> Put hearts on menus.

22
Theme Nights

One way to generate excitement is to have theme nights that offer food, costumes, decorations, activities, or any other attractions that increase the level of entertainment and surprise. Here are a few suggestions. All of these should be promoted just as you would any other tactic: through in-store promotions and counter cards, table tents, mailing, emailing, media, and doorknobbers, and through local organizations.

280. European Nights

Have a local travel agent give talks on planning trips to specific areas of Europe. Conduct this promotion over several weeks, with each week focusing on a different destination: "France Night," "Italy Night," "Greece Night," and so on. Have the travel agent discuss airfares, sightseeing, and the travel packages available for the specific country. The travel agent will be glad to participate, as this will give him or her the opportunity to meet members of your community who are interested in travel.

Decorate the restaurant to fit with the particular country and offer special menu items from the featured country at a discounted price. As giveaways, get some euro coins.

281. Yoga Night

Hire an instructor from a local yoga studio or, even better, a yogi if there is one in your area who would be willing to come in for this promotion. Have this person explain the basic philosophy of yoga and demonstrate its exercises to your customers.

Decorate the restaurant with an East Indian theme and have a special menu, in addition to your regular menu, of Indian food available at a discounted price. This same idea might work with a tai chi or feng shui instructor. Then, of course, you would decorate your restaurant with a Chinese theme.

282.   Origami Night

Check with your local bookstore to see if it can help you find someone who is an expert in origami, the ancient Japanese art of paper folding. Hire this person to demonstrate the techniques of origami. Have colorful paper on hand to distribute to customers so that they can have fun trying the folding techniques.

Decorate your restaurant with a Japanese theme, using origami flowers, if they are available. Prepare a Japanese menu for the evening (in addition to your regular menu) and serve the special items at a discounted price.

283.   Hootenanny Night

Create an atmosphere of merriment and spontaneity—and a whole lot of fun for your staff and your customers. Hire a folk singer/guitarist to lead a sing-along. Hire a dance instructor to teach square dancing. If you can afford it and you have the room, hire a country band as accompaniment. Otherwise, use your P.A. system.

Decorate the restaurant with a "country" theme and offer a special menu of country foods: fried chicken, corn fritters, biscuits, and so on. Get as ethnic as you like to create authenticity. Offer these foods at a special price. Make sure your regular menu items are also available.

284.   Flower Night

Ask a dependable and talented local florist to treat your customers to a demonstration of the techniques of floral arranging. The florist will do this gladly, as it will give him or her exposure to local residents and members of the business community who are interested in flowers.

Make sure to place arrangements of fresh or silk flowers on every table, and be sure that every customer leaves with a flower in hand. Have a drawing for a nice floral arrangement and build your database at the same time. The florist who is demonstrating should give you the flowers for free, or at least at a substantial discount.

If your chef is willing, research edible flowers to add to the salads and use as garnishes for your regular dishes. Be sure to have the florist let your customers know that the flowers on their plates are edible.

285. Hire a Hypnotist

Hypnotism has a mystique that seems to automatically generate interest. Invite a hypnotist to your restaurant during a prearranged single-sitting dinner to talk to your customers about hypnotism and perhaps do some demonstrations. Serve free dessert and coffee to your customers.

286. Model-Building Clinic

During a specified weekend lunch period, ask the owner of a hobby shop in your trading area to arrange a question-and-answer session about the fine points of model building. Invite customers, with their children, to bring in their unfinished models to get specific advice about completing them. The hobby shop owner should speak for free, as this will give her or him a lot of exposure within the community. This applies to other hobbies, as well.

287. Hidden Treasure

Display a locked treasure chest full of prizes in your lobby. Allow the first 1000 customers who come into your restaurant for lunch or dinner to choose a key to the treasure chest at random and try to open it. Make sure that 999 keys do not fit the chest, so that you have only one lucky winner. This promotion should run during a one- to four-week period, depending on the traffic in your restaurant.

288. Little League Days

Sponsor a local Little League baseball team and have players come into your restaurant after every winning game for a free burger and soft drink. Give your team members free soft drinks even if they don't win, and extend that same offer to all other Little League teams. In all cases, require league members to come to your restaurant in uniform in order to receive their free food items.

289.   Eat and Compete

Make your restaurant the local place to relax and enjoy a game of checkers by placing a checkerboard and checkers on each table during the slower times of the day. Customers can enjoy a relaxing game while they have a late afternoon lunch or snack.

290.   Seniors Early Bird Lunch

Invite seniors who walk, jog, or play tennis in the morning to come into your restaurant for a special after-exercise "Early Bird Lunch." Develop a special menu with a selection of light, nutritional lunch items at an inexpensive fixed price. Make sure to include a selection of juices or other cold drinks.

291.   Plant It Beautiful

During the spring, offer a free packet of flower seeds to anyone who orders specific food items from the menu. Use this promotion to increase sales of food products that need a boost.

292.   Career Afternoon

At the beginning of the final semester of your local high school's year, set up a career counseling day when parents and students can come in to discuss potential career opportunities with career counselors from the local colleges or universities. Set a specific time for the event, close the restaurant to other customers, and offer the career counseling and a light lunch for students and parents at a set price.

293.   Look-Alike Contest

Advertise a contest in which teenagers can bring in a photo of a celebrity whom they think they look like. Take a Polaroid shot of the person bringing in each picture, and have that person fill out an entry blank giving his or her name, address, and phone number. Display all the photos of the celebrities and look-alikes. At the end of the promotion, have your staff decide on the three people who look the most like the celebrities. Call the winners.

Suggested prizes: first prize—free dinner for the entire family; second prize—free dinner for two; third prize—free lunch for two.

294. New Neighbors Days

Place a poster in your window stating that anyone who has just moved into the neighborhood is invited to come in to meet the management of your restaurant and receive a free dessert and beverage with the meal. Make sure to provide a bounce-back coupon for a percentage off an additional food purchase.

295. Caricature Night

Have a local artist on hand during dinner hours over one weekend to draw caricatures, at random, of customers. People will generally want to purchase these, so offer the drawings for sale and split the profit with the caricaturist. Arrange to keep the caricatures that are not purchased immediately and display them at your restaurant. This will encourage people to return to see their picture on display, and it will probably boost future sales of the caricatures as well.

296. Shopper's Lunch

If your restaurant is in a busy shopping area, during the holidays, especially around Christmas, Mother's Day, and Father's Day, offer parents a discounted, quick shopper's lunch. Coordinate the event with a special cafeteria-style children's section. Set up a showing of cartoons for the kids while they are eating so that their parents can enjoy their lunches in peace.

297. Jogger's Breakfast

Start the morning community ritual at your restaurant by holding an extra-early Jogger's Breakfast to encourage people to wake up, do their jogging, and come into your restaurant as they are, to join other local joggers for a quick, healthy breakfast before work.

To start off the program, invite a local fitness expert to come to the restaurant during the first morning you offer the Jogger's Breakfast to give joggers pointers and hold a question-and-answer session. Joggers are always anxious to learn more about their sport.

298.   Houseplant Care Luncheon

Invite members of the community who take a serious interest in house-plants to a special four-session luncheon series at your restaurant in which a local nursery or florist gives a clinic on the choosing and care of house-plants.

Sell tickets for the four-week event, which is best held during the lunch period on a day when your luncheon business needs a boost. Sell com-bination tickets for the four-session clinic and four lunches.

299.   Meal in a Wheel

Serve children's dinners in a Frisbee instead of on a plate. After dinner, kids get to keep the Frisbees, which of course include your restaurant's name, address, and phone number and a special saying, such as: "Have Fun at (Your Restaurant Name)." Kids will be begging their parents to bring them in for the free Frisbees.

300.   Kids Kups

Try a promotion in which you advertise that "Kids get to keep their cups." Serve children their drinks in colorfully decorated plastic cups with "Kids Kup" written on them. Include your restaurant's name, address, and phone number. Kids will want to use the cups at home, and your name will be in front of their parents every time the cup is used.

301.   Keep 'Em Comin' Coupons

To increase business during the usually slow months of January and February, try printing coupon booklets of eight coupons good for $5 worth of free food. Pass them out to customers during the month of November.

The first two are good for the period between Thanksgiving and Christmas, and the last six are good during the months of January and

February. You might consider calling the coupon booklet "Happy Holidays from (Your Restaurant's Name)."

302. Wine Showcase

If your restaurant is upscale, has a reputation for fine gourmet food, and is located in a wine region such as New York or California, try a (Name of Your State) Dinner. Make this one reservations-only, and limit it to the number of people you can handle in one seating. Serve your most extravagant five- to seven-course meal at a fixed price, with each course featuring regional wines.

303. Summer Days

During the summer months, feature a selection of at least five or six different salads, which change daily, at a special price. Throw in lemonade or iced tea and a citrus mousse, lemon cake, or key lime pie for dessert. Be sure to display a flower-laden cart full of the day's selection near the front door.

304. Sunday Storytelling Brunch

Hold a Sunday brunch for parents, and provide a "burger-and-fries" lunch for young children in a special section of the restaurant. Provide an ongoing storytelling session using popular Golden Books to keep the children busy while they are eating and the parents are dining. Purchase multiple copies of the inexpensive Golden Books, put a sticker on the front saying "Compliments of (Your Restaurant's Name)," and give them to the children as takeaways.

23

Drive-Through Tactics

If you have a drive-through at your restaurant, the following eight tactics can be used along with your regular in-store promotions. They can be ongoing, seasonal, or geared to other specific promotions, in addition to being promotional on their own.

Your drive-through is another vehicle that you can use to bring increased traffic, goodwill, and loyalty. Most of these ideas are so simple to implement that they should be considered a must for any drive-through restaurant. They're a way to keep your customers coming back again and again. And, through word of mouth alone, they're bound to bring you a host of new and lasting customers. Most important, they will help you stand out in the crowd.

305. Premium Distribution

Distribute automobile-oriented premiums with drive-through orders as a token of thanks for your customers' patronage. Do not stuff the premium into the bag, but have the drive-through staff hand it to customers and say, "We'd like you to have this (item) as a small thank-you for being our customer."

306. Product Discounts

Put a poster on your drive-through menu offering product discounts for carloads of more than four people. Make sure that your drive-through staff offers the discount, even if the customer doesn't notice the poster and doesn't ask for the discount. You determine the amount of the discount. My suggestion is 10 percent.

307. Bounce-Back Coupons

Distribute bounce-back coupons to drive-through customers, inviting them back for another visit. However, make the offer good for in-store dining only. Again, be sure that you do not stuff the coupon into the customer's bag, but have your drive-through staff hand it to the customer and say, "Thank you. And here's a coupon for (offer) the next time you have the time to dine inside our restaurant."

308. Cross-Coupon Program

Select a retailer in your trading area that also has a drive-through window. Banks are excellent, as they produce very high customer traffic. Suggest a regular cross-coupon program in which the other retailer hands out coupons (which you supply) for your drive-through, and you, in turn, hand out coupons (which the retailer supplies) for its drive-through.

Here's a suggested tag line for both coupons: "Now that you've visited our drive-through, why not try (name of cross participant)'s drive-through for (special offer)."

309. Radio-Knob Hanger

Customers are given punch cards with any in-store or drive-through purchase. The punch card has a string that fits over the car radio knob and contains five dots for punching. The first dot is punched when the card is given. Each time the customer makes a purchase, either in the store or at the drive-through, the next dot is punched. When all the dots have been punched, the customer may redeem the card for a free food purchase. Be sure to have an expiration date on the card to encourage frequent return visits.

310. Quick Cleanup

Place a large trash bin at the side of the drive-through with a sign telling customers to feel free to empty their trash in the bin while they wait for their order. Make sure the drive-through staff keeps an eye on the bin so that it's not overflowing.

311. Windshield Wash

Have a staff person on duty outside your drive-through window to clean the windshields of customers while they wait for their orders. Be sure the staff person is pleasant to the customers and thanks them for coming to your restaurant.

312. Radio Station Bumper Sticker Tie-in

Set up a program with a popular local radio station in which your restaurant distributes bumper stickers with its name on them to all customers, both inside the restaurant and at the drive-through window. Distribute a promotional flyer explaining the program along with the bumper stickers.

Every day, at a particular prime drive-time hour, the radio will announce the license plate numbers of two customers whose cars have your restaurant's bumper sticker. Have your drive-through staff make a note of the license plate numbers of all cars with your bumper stickers on them and send them weekly to the radio station. The radio station picks the license numbers at random.

Winners (those whose license plate numbers are announced on the radio) may come to your restaurant *on that same day only*, show proof of their license plate number, and receive a free dinner.

You may be giving away up to two free dinners a day, depending on whether customers hear their license plate numbers called or not, but the amount of exposure your name will get as a result of this promotion will be phenomenal.

24

Outrageous Ideas

The following section contains 52 outrageous ideas. Some of them are highly unusual. Some are very expensive. Others are totally simple.

Read them over and think about them for a while. Put the simple ones into practice as quickly as possible, as they can only improve your business. Then choose one of the more unusual ones and try to incorporate it into your business. It will give you an edge—make you stand out from the crowd—and lead to a myriad of other promotional possibilities.

313. Special Services and Amenities

- Provide waiter call buttons on tables.
- Set up child care on your premises while customers are dining.
- Set up adults-only, couples-only, families-with-kids, and singles-only rooms.
- Provide limousine service to and from the restaurant.
- Look into computerized menus.
- Hire kind, gentle maître d's and hosts.
- Provide special rooms where customers can bring their dogs.
- Open the kitchen to diners.

314. Money Matters

- Take applications for restaurant credit cards.
- Offer discounts for cash (like gas stations do).
- Begin frequent-diner bonus plans to earn free meals.
- Arrange an on-site ATM, along with discounts for cash.

- Give money-back guarantees to customers who are not satisfied with the food.
- Offer large discounts for infractions like miscomputed checks or rude service.

315. Reservation Policies

- Begin a centralized reservation service co-op with other area restaurants.
- Offer seating charts and ask for preferences (as in theaters).
- Make the bar bill complimentary if reservations are not honored within 15 minutes.
- Give free dinners if reservations are not honored within 30 minutes.
- Take credit card numbers with reservations and charge for no-shows.

316. Unusual Amenities

- Provide individual climate control and adjustable lighting at each table.
- Hire strolling masseurs.
- Provide portable phones and faxes at tables for business lunches.
- Give guests hot hand and face towels before and after meals.
- Set up VCR/DVD booths with earphones for patrons who are dining alone.

317. Food for Thought

- Provide calorie counts and cholesterol content on request.
- Leave pepper mills on tables.
- Pass out hors d'oeuvres while diners are waiting to be seated.
- Allow patrons with smaller appetites to order half-sized portions.
- Offer an unusual cuisine: Eskimo, Basque, or Zulu, for example.
- Allow customers to make special orders of their choice.
- Offer foods cooked without butter or salt.
- Offer home-style cooking and table service.

318.   Be the First in Your Neighborhood...

- To combine a record/video store and a restaurant.
- To open a rooftop restaurant with telescopes at tables.
- To open a 24-hour haute cuisine restaurant with casual dress suggested.
- To feature a special menu for diabetics.
- To open a Parisian-style cafe with outdoor seating.
- To hire CPAs for business lunches to combine lunch and income tax filing.
- To open a combination restaurant/Laundromat.
- To offer a complete macrobiotic menu.
- To open a combination bookstore/restaurant.
- To open an all-smoking restaurant where smokers are welcome!
- To open a feng shui café or restaurant.

319.   Revivals

- Give free refills on all soft drinks.
- Allow customers to bring their own bottle of wine. Charge corkage fees.
- Open a cafeteria.
- Have live music and a dance floor.
- Serve water without customers having to ask.

320.   Social Consciousness

- Donate 5 percent of the amount of every check to the homeless.
- Take daily leftovers to city shelters.
- Offer free rides to patrons who have consumed too much alcohol.
- Offer customers the option of donating a percentage of their bill to their favorite charity.

25

Nonprofit Tactics

Nonprofit is one of the fastest-growing business categories in the country. An estimated eight million people are employed in nonprofits, and many of them are borrowing marketing tactics from the for-profit sector.

The following are a few ideas that your nonprofit organization, civic group, charity, or other community-based group can use to increase your visibility, membership, and fund-raising.

321. Outreach Program: Bring Your Cause to the Masses!

Objective Increase awareness, increase community goodwill.

Target Potential business and community donors.

Outreach is a very effective way to introduce your organization to potential donors. This program is designed to develop partnerships with local businesses and other community organizations to spread the word, telling people in the surrounding community what you do. Your message will be delivered more easily and received more readily, if you select the right partners.

For example, restaurants that are interested in picking up business on customarily slow nights would most likely be willing to donate a specified percentage (20 percent is a good figure) of their total take on a particular night to your organization. To arrange this, call the restaurant manager and request that a fund-raising event be held there. In turn, you will promote the event, packing the restaurant with diners on an otherwise slow night. Everyone wins: The restaurant increases its business, and you reap the profits of a no-hassle fund-raiser.

Materials Flyers and discount coupons to hand out.

Timing

Two weeks prior:

Create flyers and discount coupons.

One week prior:

Post flyers.
Distribute coupons.

322.   Sampling as a Cross Promotion

Objective   Increase awareness, increase goodwill, raise money.

Target   Local businesses.

Ask local businesses and service professionals to provide your organization with coupons and other giveaways that you can offer to donors in exchange for their financial support. Conversely, have the participating businesses collect a small donation, perhaps $1, from their patrons. In this promotion, one hand washes the other.

To adapt this promotion to your nonprofit organization, first determine a type of product or service offered by local businesses that is easily sampled or is in some way related to your cause, then directly ask for that item or service to be given to you free. Stand by your promise to recognize the business as a donor and/or promote its business or service.

The key to the success of this promotion is that potential donors get something immediately to introduce them to your business partner. A hair salon could give you free samples of shampoo and conditioner with a special certificate inviting the donors to the shop as potential customers.

Other examples might be a bookstore giving away bookmarks, a dry cleaner giving away mini lint rollers, or even a dentist distributing tooth-brushes and toothpaste samples. Restaurants can provide menu flyers and bounce-back coupons to attract customers.

When you are using a product giveaway for your outreach program, remember to ask suppliers to provide you with the samples for free or at an extremely reduced rate. Remember, it's to their advantage to help you with this, because they, too, will benefit from the new customers you'll help generate.

Materials   Coupons, samples.

Timing

Four weeks prior:

Prepare list of businesses to solicit.
Collect giveaways.
Print posters.

Three weeks prior:

Plan fund-raising campaign.

Two weeks prior:

Distribute collection boxes.

One week prior:

Contact businesses to set up appointments to pick-up samples (or have them dropped off).

One day prior:

Display posters describing campaign.

Start:

Receive samples.

Six weeks after:

Evaluate results.

323.   Car Dealer Tie-In

Objective   Increase awareness, increase goodwill, raise money.

Target   Car dealerships in your trade area.

Have a car dealer donate a specified amount of money, such as $10, to your organization or cause for every person who comes in for a test drive and mentions your organization's name during an established time period. Make sure the dealer keeps a sign-in log of those who come out for a test drive on behalf of your organization.

Ideally, you want the dealer to really promote this event and put your organization's name in its advertising. Your organization should also promote the event as you would any other fund-raiser you host. The dealer should be anxious to participate because it will be guaranteed walk-ins that it wouldn't normally get—it might even sell a car! You get some much-needed cash for a good cause.

Materials   Flyers, advertising.

Timing

Four weeks prior:

> Contact local auto dealer as a partner.
> Make a list of prospective drivers.

Three weeks prior:

> Prepare advertising, flyers.

One week prior:

> Distribute advertising, flyers.

One day prior:

> Contact prospective drivers.

Start:

> Redeem gift certificates.

Six weeks after:

> Evaluate program.

324.   Spread the Wealth: Donate Lottery Tickets

Objective   People buy lottery tickets and turn them in to the organization, which gets to keep whatever's won.

Target   The community.

Begin an ad or public relations campaign asking people to drop off lottery tickets at your organization or mail them in. You just might be the lucky winner! This is a good idea to start when the jackpot reaches an exorbitant amount of money. Contact the press about this one.

Timing

Four weeks prior:

Prepare posters.
Create press release.

Two weeks prior:

Print posters.
Send press release.

One day prior:

Hang posters.
Send media alert.

Start:

Scratch off the lottery tickets or check the numbers as they come in.

325. Cow Chip Bingo

This is one of the most outrageous and fun fund-raisers. It raises about $10,000, and it always gets a lot of publicity.

Get a farmer to partner with you on this. The farmer donates a fenced-in one-acre field, a cow, some chalk, and, at the end, a cow chip. The field is marked off with chalk lines in a grid of one-foot squares (your local high school will have the equipment to do this), and you sell chances for $10 per square. The squares are identified on a graph or map, so each chance is tied to a specific square.

Once you've sold off all the squares, the farmer lets the cow into the fenced-in field, and when the cow drops its first chip, the person who bought a chance on the square that chip lands in wins a big cash prize and your organization gets to keep the balance of the money.

326. Ice-Melt Sweepstakes

This is another fun event that will attract a lot of attention and raise many thousands of dollars. It works only in northern climates, where ponds and lakes freeze hard every winter.

All you need is a cinder block, a clock, and a box. Sometime in the later winter or early spring, you set the cinder block in the middle of the town pond or lake. Next to it is a battery-operated clock that is enclosed in a box to keep it safe from the weather and set on a wooden pallet that will float. Attach a string from the block to the battery in the clock in such a way that when the cinder block falls through the ice, it dislodges the battery, and the clock stops.

Run a big promotional campaign selling guesses as to the exact time and date that the block will fall through the ice, the first sign of spring. The person who comes closest to guessing correctly wins a big cash jackpot, and your organization gets to keep the balance.

The excitement will build as spring gets nearer. Hold a big event to celebrate the winner and the end of winter.

327. That's Entertainment!

Objective   Increase awareness, raise money.

Target   Potential donors.

Approach your local theater, bowling alley, or movie house, or create a volunteer thespian troupe to provide an afternoon or evening of entertainment at a low-cost flat fee or no cost to your organization. Then sell tickets for the event, retaining all the profit from the proceeds. Everyone is looking for entertainment, and this is a simple way to give people what they want and make a buck at the same time. It's easy to do and usually gets great results. The people you are targeting are already interested in going out, so the hardest part is done.

328. Connect with a Restaurant or Caterer

Objective   Increase awareness, raise money.

Target   Restaurants and caterers.

Ask your local restaurants and caterers to create a lasting impression and become a popular place to go by adopting your cause and showing their support of the community.

In return for listing them as donors, restaurants and caterers can offer their nonprofit counterparts a part of the profits and assist in many different ways: by helping younger children (see Schools/Colleges); direct involvement with the community in promotions designed to aid the community (see Political/Civil); involvement with the local houses of worship (see Houses of Worship); and, of course, fund-raising promotions.

The worthy causes that are most popular or most particular to a community offer a great promotional opportunity for restaurant and similar businesses. It never hurts to ask for the support of these businesses. If they support your cause, they get to advertise it in their promotional materials.

329. Big Bucks

Objective   Increase awareness, raise money.

Target   All businesses and service professionals.

Ask local businesses to produce "Big Bucks" for distribution to area nonprofits (local charities and civic organizations, such as the Boy Scouts or the Lion Club) for resale to the public. Each "Buck" is worth $1 toward any purchase at the participating businesses.

Your organization or charity sells the Big Bucks for their face value of $1 and rebates a portion of that amount to the participating business for each Buck redeemed. This allows the charity to make a profit and still covers the partnering businesses' costs.

At the end of the promotion, return all unsold Bucks to the business. The promotion should run for six weeks, allowing for a four-week selling period and two additional weeks for redemption.

Materials   Letter to businesses, "Big Bucks" coupons.

Timing

Six weeks prior:

Set program goals.
Begin contacting businesses by letter to make proposal.

Plan advertising.

Five weeks prior:

Follow up letters with phone calls.

Three weeks prior:

Receive printed Big Bucks from participating businesses.

Two weeks prior:

Circulate ads/flyers outlining promotion.

One week prior:

Announce to press.

Start:

Begin redemption of Big Bucks and record sales.

Six weeks after:

Return any unsold Big Bucks. Get reimbursement for coupons redeemed.

End:

Discontinue discounts.
Send thank-you letters to participating businesses.

330. Million-Dollar Legacy (With a Twist)

Best For Church and community groups, nonprofits.

Objective Increase awareness, increase community goodwill, create excitement, generate PR, build your image, stimulate trial.

Target Businesses.

This is a clever, thought-provoking tactic that draws a lot of attention on a limited budget. Let residents and local businesses in the community make an investment in your organization. Ask them to make a specified donation, and have the dollar amount deposited with a local bank that is participating in the fund-raiser. The idea is to have the bank determine how much needs to be placed in the account so that it will yield about $1 million in a hundred years. The bank should be able to determine the exact amount of the deposit that would be necessary to ensure a result of $1 million at average interest rates. Make the account a trust payable to the organization, group, or cause. Have the bank draw up the trust.

Use advertising and organizational materials to promote the event to businesses and members of the community. Your advertising should explain exactly how the program will work.

Materials   Newspaper ads, press releases, posters.

Timing

Six weeks prior:

Prepare advertising and press releases.
Buy media.
Make initial contact with local bank to establish account.

Four weeks prior:

Begin advertising via mail, fax, email, and press releases.
Contact press and city officials for participation.

Two weeks prior:

Contact accountant to set up the fund-raiser.
Arrange radio and newspaper announcements.

One week prior:

Announce program.
Begin acting as a collection point for funds.

One week after:

Announce results.
Print a thank-you list of contributors.

331. Raffle Baskets

Best For   Church and community groups, nonprofits.

Objective Create excitement, generate PR, solicit donations.

Target Individual community members; merchants and businesses.

This program is implemented as a way to raise funds through the donation of goods and services by local merchants and other businesses. After soliciting donations, create attractive raffle baskets to display at a local community center or your organization. Offer people the chance to win the basket(s) of their choice by filling out raffle entry forms during a prescribed period of time. Offer a discount to those purchasing raffle tickets in quantity. For example, sell the tickets for $1 each or six for $5.

At the close of the raffle, which should coincide with another public event, hold a drawing and contact the winners. Publicize the event to the community and the media.

Materials Entry blanks, entry box, baskets and contents.

Timing

Four weeks prior:

Solicit basket items.
Select display site.

Two weeks prior:

Order or create entry blanks and entry box.

One week prior:

Create baskets to be displayed for one month or another prescribed time period.
Contact news media via phone and press releases.

Start:

Showcase baskets for one month.
Display posters, entry forms, and entry box in a visible location.

End date:

Compile all names and addresses of entrants on a computer for your donor mailing list.

332.   Donor Wall of Fame

Best For   Nonprofits.

Objective   Generate a strong, loyal donor base.

Target   Community members and local businesses.

Put together a list of donor candidates and directly solicit donations from them. As the checks come in, create a Donor Wall of Fame. Construct it in as prominent a place as appropriate. As you add names, mail a note of thanks signed by you and your team members: "Thanks for your support. People like you really make a difference!"

26
Opening Anniversaries

In the early sections of this book, I encouraged you to think of marketing as a way of life, and to do the hard work of looking at your business and coming up with a marketing plan. To make sure your marketing efforts are well thought out, are woven together to achieve the best result, and fit in with the other aspects of your business, plot out on a calendar a year of promotional tactics. Look at a year of typical holidays and other events that may suggest opportunities to plan promotions.

This and the following chapters offer several dozen promotions organized around specific dates and events. Select those that make the most sense for you. Then build in the lead times and other essential planning factors that will produce the winning result: increased sales.

333. Anniversary Tactics in General

Best For   Most business types.

Objective   Increase awareness, increase goodwill, generate traffic, build your image.

Target   Existing and potential customers.

For new businesses, first-year anniversaries are opportunities to remind people that you've made it this far and to build on the excitement and enthusiasm that you created during your grand opening. You can also take advantage of other anniversaries as well. Look at your business and see what makes sense. A fourth anniversary might seem odd, but five is a nice round number.

When running anniversary promotions, measure their success by comparing a particular period of time against the same period in the previous year or, if you've been open awhile, against two previous years. As you begin your new year, compare your sales and other measures against the first business month of the previous year.

Anniversary promotions should be designed to maintain and build top-line sales for subsequent years. You do this by stimulating additional frequency from your current customer base, and by attracting those customers who may have tried you during the previous year, but for some reason returned to your competition.

Make sure that all your anniversaries reaffirm your stability and credibility in your local trading area, and always treat them as important promotional opportunities.

Anniversary promotions, like grand openings, should run for an entire week, with the major promotional day falling on a weekend or other busy day.

Here is a general timetable for anniversary promotions. Specific tactics will be found later in the chapter.

Timing

Six weeks prior:

Review your trading area background study, giving special attention to upcoming community events. This will help you determine which other businesses have the potential to tie in with your anniversary promotion.

Five weeks prior:

Complete all anniversary plans.

Four weeks prior:

Order all promotional materials.
Plan media.

Three weeks prior:

Explain details to staff and begin operational readiness.

Two weeks prior:

Place all media.

One week prior:

Final staff briefing.
Announce a staff incentive program.
Do final recheck of all elements of promotion.

Open:

Display all anniversary materials.
Implement all activities as planned.

Note: When you are considering promotions for an anniversary celebration, many of the same programs applicable to a grand opening
can easily be applied:

High School Band
Ribbon-Cutting Ceremony
Celebrity Appearance
Direct Mail
Premium Giveaways
Fund-Raisers

Also, consider giving customers specially made products or premium gifts
with "Happy Birthday (your name)" on them.

334. Thank-You Promotion

Best For Most consumer-oriented businesses.

Objective Increase awareness, create excitement, generate traffic.

Target Existing customers and potential new customers.

Display a list of 100 names of regular customers on a bulletin board or
poster inside the business the night before your anniversary promotion
begins. When anyone who comes in during the anniversary-week promotion finds his or her name on the list, the purchase is on the house. In
a restaurant, if you are offering a free dinner, you may also want to offer
a free soft drink or dessert to the other members of the party.

Once the customer comes in, be sure to cross his or her name off the list. Use this opportunity to provide a "thank you for your patronage" card with a bounce-back coupon promoting future visits.

Materials   Newspaper ad, in-store poster or bulletin board, list of names, "thank you for your patronage" cards.

Timing

Three weeks prior:

Buy media.
Begin preparing newspaper ad.
Determine the names for your list.

Two weeks prior:

Print "thank you for your patronage" cards.

One week prior:

Prepare poster or bulletin board.
Explain program to staff.
Place ad.

Start:

Set out materials and posters.
Present "thank you for your patronage" cards.

One week after:

Evaluate results.

335.   Price Rollback

Best For   Retailers, restaurants, some service businesses.

Objective   Increase awareness, create excitement, generate traffic.

Target   Existing customers and potential new customers.

Create instant excitement and high value for a two-day period during the anniversary promotion week by rolling all prices back to a level last seen in the 1950s. Promote a 1950s theme with store decorations and staff attire.

To increase awareness, be sure to include today's prices. Generate high traffic by distributing bounce-back coupons good for up to two weeks after the anniversary promotion.

Materials   Newspaper ad, 1950s in-store decorations (such as old record album covers), posters, bounce-back coupons.

Timing

Three weeks prior:

   Buy media.
   Begin preparing newspaper ad.
   Explain program to staff. Ask them to collect album covers.

Two weeks prior:

   Print menus, posters, and bounce-back coupons.

One week prior:

   Place ad.
   Discuss details of 1950s attire with staff.

One day prior:

   Decorate.
   Set out new menus.

Start:

   Distribute bounce-back coupons to all patrons.

336.   Anniversary Sweepstakes Party

Best For   Retailers, restaurants, some service businesses.

Objective   Increase awareness, create excitement, generate traffic.

Target   Existing customers and potential new customers.

Run an anniversary sweepstakes during your anniversary week, offering your customers an opportunity to win valuable prizes just by filling out an entry blank (no purchase necessary). Notify winners by telephone, and ask them to return to your business to collect their prizes. Mail coupons to winners who do not come in to pick them up.

Suggested prize structure:

Grand Prize: trip, stereo, TV
5 Second Prizes: bikes, cameras
25 Third Prizes: store T-Shirts, premiums

All others: Coupons for free items/services

Place an ad in the local paper that includes an entry blank. Participants clip the ad, fill it out, and drop it in a box at your establishment. Make sure the ad has space for the person's address and telephone number as well as the name. Retain the entries to augment your mailing list. Display posters to generate awareness. Have a supply of entry blanks on hand for those who learn about the sweepstakes while they are in your establishment.

Invite a local figure to handle the drawing of the winners' names at a special event following the promotion. This will encourage entrants to be present and also promote credibility and goodwill.

Materials   Newspaper ad, entry blanks, entry box, posters, prizes.

Timing

Three weeks prior:

Buy media.
Begin preparing newspaper ad.
Explain program to staff. Ask them to suggest prizes.
Begin collecting prizes and premiums.
Arrange for person to handle drawing.

Two weeks prior:

Print menus, posters and coupons.

One week prior:

Place ad.

Start:

Display posters and prizes.
Set out entry boxes.

Sunday after:

> Hold special event to draw prize winners' names.
> Notify winners who are not present by telephone.

Monday after:

> Begin distribution of prizes.

One week after:

> Mail coupons to all entrants who did not come in to pick up their prize.

337. Anniversary Appreciation Week

Best For   Retailers, restaurants, some service businesses.

Objective   Increase awareness, create excitement, generate traffic.

Target   Existing customers and potential new customers.

Present a "thank you for your loyalty" bounce-back coupon good for free items, gifts, or meals to every patron during your anniversary week. Distribute the coupon to customers in your business during the full anniversary week, and give it a two-week redemption period.

Suggestions: Use a buy-one-get-one-free coupon or a free add-on item to another purchase.

Materials   Newspaper ad (optional), bounce-back coupons.

Timing

Two weeks prior:

> Explain program to staff.
> Print "thank you for your loyalty" bounce-back coupons.

Start:

> Distribute coupons.
> Two weeks after
> Redeem coupons.

27

Holiday Tactics

Holidays are traditionally a time when consumers are in a festive mood and receptive to anything that seems like fun. There are many physical and emotional nuances associated with holidays, especially major ones like Thanksgiving, Christmas, and New Year's.

The promotions you'll find here are intended to generate goodwill within the community and provoke feelings of nostalgia, festivity, generosity, and family. You'll find some promotions that are geared toward children and a large array of holiday promotions designed to attract high school and college students. These promotions should also be fun for you and your staff.

Take a look at the calendar and you'll find many traditional opportunities:

Jan. 1: New Year's Day

Jan., third Monday: Dr. Martin Luther King, Jr. Day

Feb. 2: Groundhog Day

Feb. 14: Valentine's Day

Feb., third Monday: President's Day

March 17: St. Patrick's Day

March 22–April 25: Easter

May, second Sunday: Mother's Day

May, last Monday: Memorial Day

June 14: Flag Day

June, third Sunday: Father's Day

July 4: Independence Day

Sept., first Monday: Labor Day

Oct., second Monday: Columbus Day

Oct. 31: Halloween

Nov. 11: Veteran's Day

Nov., last Thursday: Thanksgiving

Dec. 25: Christmas

In addition to these holidays, there are others that may not be celebrated by the public at large, but may have some promotional value to your business. These may include Chinese New Year, Jewish New Year (Rosh Hashonah), Chanukah, Kwanzaa, Bastille Day, Mardi Gras (New Orleans), Super Bowl Weekend, the Running of the Bulls, Ramadan, and so on.

338. One-Year Group Coupon Book

Best For   Some retailers, restaurants, entertainment businesses, some service businesses.

Objective   Increase awareness, generate traffic, increase sales, stimulate trial.

Target   Church groups, local clubs, civic organizations.

Generate patronage, orders, or parties for specific holidays from large groups. Research and determine the groups to target for this program, such as health clubs, sports clubs, scouts, church groups, women's groups, civic groups, or business groups.

Print an appropriate number of coupon booklets with each page specifically geared to a particular promotional event. For example, (1) Easter Special; (2) Memorial Day Special; (3) Labor Day Special; (4) Veteran's Day Special; (5) Thanksgiving Special; (6) Christmas Special; (7) Christmas Group Package; (8) New Year's Group Package.

Have designated staff members distribute coupon booklets as doorknobbers at the offices of all local area groups.

Materials   Coupon booklets, cellophane doorknob bags.

Timing

Six weeks prior:

Determine the groups you wish to target.

Five weeks prior:

Print coupon booklets and obtain doorknob bags.
Explain program to staff.

Four weeks prior:

Have staff distribute doorknobbers.

One week prior:

Begin confirming reservations.

Start:

Redeem offers.

Two weeks after:

Evaluate results.
Modify if necessary and repeat for future holidays.

339.　New Year's Pledge

Best For　Retailers, restaurants, some service businesses.

Objective　Increase awareness, create excitement, generate traffic.

Target　Existing customers and potential new customers.

This is a reaffirmation of your business's high standards by restating your promise of quality, service, and value.

Prepare a press release geared toward developing your image and promise of having good service. Send it to the editors of your local newspapers and try to encourage publication as close to New Year's Day as possible. Prepare a newspaper ad carrying the same pledge as the press release. It should also contain two coupons to entice customers to come to your business during the month of January. Place the ad just prior to or on New Year's Day.

Materials   Press release, newspaper ad.

Timing

Four weeks prior:

Buy media.

Three weeks prior:

Prepare ad and press release.
Explain program to staff.

Two weeks prior:

Send press release to local newspaper editors.

One week prior:

Place newspaper ad.

Start:

Redeem coupons.

340.   Super Bowl Sunday

Best For   Retailers, restaurants, some service businesses.

Objective   Increase awareness, create excitement, generate traffic.

Target   Existing customers and potential new customers.

Conduct a poll of your customers' picks to win the Super Bowl. During the week prior to the event, put the following advertisement on your reader board or posters: "Vote for Your Favorite Team and Win a Free (Item/Service/Beverage/Etc.)!"

Use the board to keep a running tally of votes as employees hand out individual bounce-back coupons printed with the offer and the names of the competing teams. Customers specify which team they're rooting for, and that team's name is punched out on the coupon. Only the winning coupons can be redeemed for the free gift.

Inform your local newspapers and radio stations about the promotion; you may get some free publicity. You may also want to produce flyers offering in-house specials during the Super Bowl as well as products with tie-ins or food products for eating in front of the TV. These pieces could be designed as doorknobbers to be hung throughout your trade area.

Materials   Coupons, flyers, communications board.

Timing

Three weeks prior:

Compile addresses from your mailing list.
Prepare and print flyers and coupons.

Two weeks prior:

Obtain doorknob bags.
Explain program to staff.

One week prior:

Have staff distribute doorknobbers.
Display communications board.

Start:

Distribute bounce-back coupons.

341.   Groundhog Day

Best For   Retailers, restaurants, some service businesses.

Objective   Increase awareness, create excitement, generate traffic.

Target   Existing customers and potential new customers.

Offer adults a free item or a hot beverage with every purchase, and offer children free hot chocolate. In addition, have a Groundhog Coloring Contest for children. Advertise in the local newspapers, and use a communications board during the event. Design a connect-the-dots groundhog handout or place mat for children. Name the groundhog the "(Your Business's Name) Groundhog." Hand out crayons to the children. Print contest rules as follows:

Children must be under 12 to enter.

Connect the dots and color the " _____ Groundhog."

Complete your entry form with your name, age, address, and phone number.

The winner will be announced on February 15 and notified by telephone.

Entries will be judged on neatness and artistic merit. Decisions of judges are final.

Suggested prizes: One first prize—a bicycle; three second prizes—a $25 gift certificate; 25 third prizes—a free children's item when accompanied by parent or guardian. Be sure to add the names and addresses to your mailing list for future promotions.

Materials   Newspaper ad, handouts or place mats, crayons, prizes, communications board.

Timing

Three weeks prior:

Design handouts or place mats.

Two weeks prior:

Print handouts or place mats and buy crayons.
Explain program to staff.
Buy media.

One week prior:

Place ad.

Start:

Display communications board.
Distribute handouts or place mats and crayons to children.

Two weeks after:

Call winners and present prizes.

342. Valentine's Day "How We Met" Contest

Best For Retailers, restaurants, some service businesses.

Objective Increase awareness, create excitement, generate traffic.

Target Existing customers and potential new customers.

Sponsoring a contest for the best story of "how we met" is a relatively inexpensive tactic when it is planned as a partnership promotion with a radio station and a travel agency. The winning couple receives a romantic trip for two, such as a cruise to the Caribbean.

Ask the editor of your local newspaper to serve as one of the judges, thereby almost assuring media coverage. Ask a high school principal, a retired person from the community, and a local politician to also serve as judges. Ask the participating radio station to read some of the better or funnier stories, which you will supply to the, station as they are received, between the first of February and the day before Valentine's Day.

Invite all participants (including the judges, the radio DJ, and the travel agent) to a free event or dinner at your business or restaurant on Valentine's Day Eve, and have the judging after the event. If you can, set this up as a remote broadcast from your business to announce the winner.

Place an ad in the local newspaper one week prior to the start of the contest and again at the start of the second week of the contest (optional). Be sure that the radio station agrees to provide continuing coverage of the promotion during the entire 14-day period.

Provide entry blanks that ask for the couple's name, address, phone number, and email addresses and give the rules and regulations of the contest. Advertise that the entry blanks are available to be picked up at the travel agency, the radio station, or your business, and require that all entries be hand-delivered to your business. When you accept entries, log them in and transfer the names, addresses, and phone numbers to your mailing list.

Materials Two newspaper ads (one optional), entry blanks.

Timing

Six weeks prior:

Begin working on partnership promotion participants.

Five weeks prior:

> Invite judges. Some of these people have busy schedules and need several weeks advance notice.

Four weeks prior:

> Prepare entry blanks. Be sure to check with a local attorney for the rules and regulations governing this kind of contest.
> Buy media.

Two weeks prior:

> Discuss program with staff.
> Print entry blanks.

One week prior:

> Buy logbook for entries.
> Distribute entry blanks.
> Place first ad.

Start:

> Collect and log in the entries.

One week after:

> Place second ad.

Fourteen days after:

> Have dinner and judging.
> Announce prize winner.

343. Valentine's Day Free Kisses

Best For Retailers, restaurants, some service businesses.

Objective Increase awareness, create excitement, generate traffic.

Target Existing customers and potential new customers.

Offer "free kisses" to your customers. Using newspapers, radio, and your reader or specials board, advertise that you will be giving away free kisses on Valentine's Day. Pick up a case or two of Hershey's Kisses, but keep your customers' curiosity high by not mentioning the real kiss in your ads. Curious customers will have to come into your store to find out what kind of kisses you're giving.

Materials   Newspaper ad, radio script, Hershey's Kisses, reader or specials board.

Timing

Four weeks prior:

Locate a supplier for Hershey's Kisses in your area (Sam's Club or Costco, for example) and make the purchase.

Three weeks prior:

Buy media.
Prepare ad and radio script.

Two weeks prior:

Explain program to the staff.

One week prior:

Place media.

Start:

Distribute "kisses" to your customers.
Set out reader or specials board.

344.   Sample Radio Script for Kisses Event

Thirty-second spot:

Live announcer:

"This (day of the week) is Valentine's Day, and we are giving free kisses to our (name of business) customers.
"We're not kidding!
"Kisses for Mom, for Dad, for the entire family—even a sweet kiss for your Valentine!

"Come on in and enjoy our famous (service/product/food, etc.) and great prices. You'll find some special prices that would make even Cupid blush.

"At (name of business) you always get a good price and great service and free kisses—because you're special.

"So, come on in (day of the week), and don't forget to say, 'How about a kiss?' (Name of business and address)."

345. Sweetheart's Day

Best For Entertainment businesses, restaurants, some service businesses, some retailers.

Objective Increase awareness, create excitement, generate traffic.

Target Existing customers and potential new customers.

Offer a dinner for two, bowling for two, theater for two, or anything with a romantic aspect to it at a discount. Promote this event through local papers, student papers, windshield flyers or doorknobbers, and flyers on college bulletin boards. Add a little romance by giving a red rose to every woman who comes in on Valentine's Day.

Materials Newspaper ad, flyers, cellophane bags for doorknobbers, roses.

Timing

Three weeks prior:

Buy media.
Prepare ad and flyers.

Two weeks prior:

Print flyers.
Explain program to staff.

One week prior:

Place ads.

Start:

Distribute flyers.

346. Love Poem Contest

Best For Retailers, restaurants, entertainment businesses, some service businesses.

Objective Increase awareness, create excitement, generate traffic.

Target Existing customers and potential new customers.

This tactic should be done as a partnership promotion with a local jeweler and a local hardware supplier. The winner receives a fine piece of jewelry for his loved one, donated by the jeweler, and a surprise masculine gift, such as a set of tools, donated by the local hardware supplier. Keep the man's gift a secret until the end of the promotion.

This promotion can create a lot of excitement, as most men are not likely candidates to have their poetry openly publicized. Its uniqueness, and the fact that women will be prodding their husbands and boyfriends to participate, is what makes this promotion so much fun.

Run this promotion for the two-week period prior to Valentine's Day, with the winner's poem being published in the local newspaper along with a picture of the winner and his loved one. Ask the local newspaper editor, the head of the high school/college English department, and a retired citizen to judge the poems.

Provide entry blanks that ask for the participant's name, address, phone numbers (work and home), and email address. The entry blanks should clearly spell out the rules and regulations of the contest and should be advertised as being available to be picked up at the jeweler or at your store. Completed entries should be hand-delivered to your business. Be sure to log in the entries as they are received, have the person sign the log, and transfer the information to your database.

The night before Valentine's Day, invite the judges and cross-participants to a free cocktail party at your business for the reading and judging of the poems. If the winner isn't present, phone him that evening, and have him come in with his loved one on Valentine's Day to collect the prize. Have the participating jeweler and hardware supplier present, as well as someone from the press. Present the prize—and the special masculine prize for being "not only a great poet but a great sport." If possible, photograph the couple with yourself and the other participants for publication the next day.

Materials   Two newspaper ads (one optional), entry blanks.

Timing

Six weeks prior:

> Begin working on partnership promotion participants.

Five weeks prior:

> Invite judges (some people need several weeks advance notice).

Four weeks prior:

> Prepare entry blanks. Be sure to check with a local attorney for the rules and regulations governing this kind of contest.
> Buy media.

Two weeks prior:

> Explain program to staff.
> Print entry blanks.

One week prior:

> Buy logbook for entries.
> Distribute entry blanks.
> Place first ad.

Start:

> Collect and log in the entries.

One week after:

> Place second ad.

Fourteen days after:

> Have event and judging.
> Telephone prize winner.

Valentine's Day:

Have winner and participants come in and present prizes.

347. Lincoln's Birthday—Gettysburg Address

Best For   Retailers, restaurants, entertainment businesses, some service businesses.

Objective   Increase awareness, create excitement, generate traffic.

Target   Existing customers and potential new customers.

This tactic takes very little effort on the part of your business, but it has a great payoff, both for your business and for the community in general. You receive greater awareness, and the kids receive the reward of a well-learned history lesson.

Offer students who memorize Lincoln's Gettysburg Address free items or gifts during the week of Lincoln's Birthday. Teachers or parents validate your flyer-coupon for gifts after the student has recited the Gettysburg Address to them.

Contact history teachers at local schools and arrange for complete classroom participation. Start the program a week prior to the redemption week to give students a chance to memorize the address.

Materials   Flyer-coupon with Gettysburg Address printed on it.

Timing

Three weeks prior

     Contact history teachers to arrange classroom participation.
     Prepare flyer-coupon.

Two weeks prior:

     Print flyer-coupons.

One week prior:

     Distribute flyers to schools.
     Explain program to staff.

Start:

Redeem signed coupons.

348. St. Patrick's Day Less Green for Green

Best For Retailers, restaurants, entertainment businesses, some service businesses.

Objective Increase awareness, create excitement, generate traffic.

Target Existing customers and potential new customers.

Decorate the business appropriately and have your staff wear as much green as possible. Offer traditional treats, snacks, or foods, and create a larger-than-usual selection of green items.

Offer a special discount on all green items for the entire week. Promote the activity through a newspaper ad and your store's posters and reader or specials board.

Materials Newspaper ad, in-store displays, decorations, reader or specials board.

Timing

Three weeks prior:

Discuss promotion and items with staff.
Prepare newspaper ad and point-of-purchase materials.

Two weeks prior:

Print materials.
Discuss promotion and clothing with staff.
Buy media.

One week prior:

Place ad.
Buy decorations.

Start:

Decorate.
Set out reader or specials board.

349.   St. Patrick's Day Discount

Best For   Retailers, restaurants, entertainment businesses, some service businesses.

Objective   Increase awareness, create excitement, generate traffic.

Target   Existing customers and potential new customers.

This discount is good only on St. Patrick's Day. As in the "Less Green for Green" promotion, decorate your store appropriately and have your employees wear as much green as possible.

Offer refreshments and snacks, all dyed green. Offer a special discount on certain items for the entire week. Offer a coupon good for a discount to anyone wearing green.

Materials   Decorations.

Timing

Two weeks prior:

Discuss promotion and clothing with staff.

One week prior:

Buy decorations.

Start:

Decorate.

350.   National Secretaries Week

Best For   Retailers, restaurants, entertainment businesses, some service businesses.

Objective   Increase awareness, create excitement, generate traffic.

Target   Existing customers and potential new customers.

National Secretaries Week is the third week in April. This promotion is geared toward honoring secretaries with a special, such as a buy-one-get-one-free, a gift, or some other incentive.

The newspaper ad for this tactic is what makes it unique. Except for your logo, name, and address, the entire ad should be written in shorthand, which has long been out of use (but you can find books in your library that explain it). The idea is not only to attract secretaries, but also to attract curiosity among other readers.

After your ad has been prepared for print, make sure to prepare your staff and place a translation of the ad on your staff bulletin board.

Materials   Shorthand newspaper ad, translation for staff.

Timing

Three weeks prior:

> Prepare ad and have it translated into shorthand.
> Buy media (the newspaper will probably want to see a translation).

Two weeks prior:

> Repeat the ad on a poster or communications board, in shorthand, advertising the special in advance.
> Discuss program with staff.
> Provide translation for staff bulletin board.

One week prior:

> Place ad.

Start:

> Provide gifts or begin honoring buy-one-get-one-free or other incentive.

One week after:

> Evaluate program.

351.   Mother's Day Marine Corps Tribute

Best For   All business types.

Objective Increase awareness, create excitement, increase goodwill, generate PR, generate traffic.

Target Existing customers and potential new customers.

Mother's Day is an all-purpose holiday on which you have a chance to show your respect for the sacrifice and commitment of motherhood. With a minimum of creativity, you can come up with a host of great ideas. Here's one that was a huge success in a setting you would not have chosen.

Rensi Motorsports Racing Team, a leading NASCAR racing outfit, is owned by an ex-Marine, Ed Rensi, who wanted to see if he could help the Marine Corps in its recruiting efforts. He recently told one of my marketing conferences how he did it. You can do the same thing in your town, probably on a smaller scale.

> The United States Marine Corps was formed 280 years ago, an institution that has remained true to its values. They have three primary missions: recruit young men and women who are capable of being Marines; win battles; and return those young men and women back to the civilian corps as better citizens.
>
> To do this they have to recruit 43,000 new Marines a year. Mom is an instant disqualifier. Johnny comes home from school and says,' I talked to a Marine Corps recruiter today and I want to join the Marine Corps.' Mom grabs her heart, falls back in her chair, and says, 'How can you do this to me?'
>
> The Marine Corps recognizes how important Mom and the parents are in the decision-making process. So at a race in New Hampshire one Mother's Day, we wanted to make a statement to potential Marine Corps families. We bought 40,000 red carnations and had about 40 Marines in their crisp, full-dress uniforms come to the racetrack and stand in front of the entrance gates.
>
> Every woman who walked into the stadium who looked like she might be a mother was presented with a carnation. The Marine who handed her the carnation came to attention, gave her a smart salute, and said, 'The Marine Corps wishes you a Happy Mother's Day.'
>
> On the car we had entered in the race that day we painted "Happy Mother's Day Mom, United States Marine Corps."
>
> For that $4,000 expenditure for carnations we generated almost $3 million of print coverage from the New York border into New England. We generated more than $2 million worth of radio and television air time. A total of $5 million of marketing value was created for an outlay of $4,000. The good will generated was immeasurable.

Hoo-aah!

352. Mother's Day Violets Are Blue

Best For   Retailers, restaurants, entertainment businesses, some service businesses.

Objective   Increase awareness, create excitement, generate traffic.

Target   Existing customers and potential new customers.

Using a newspaper ad, invite people to bring their mothers to your establishment, where Mom will receive a free African violet. This tactic makes a great partnership promotion with a local florist.

Prepare a bounce-back coupon and present it to all visitors on Mother's Day to encourage the families to return within one month.

Have the florist donate the African violets and adorn them with a ribbon that says, "Happy Mother's Day from (Your Name) and (Florist's Name)." African violets last for a long time and are very easy to care for. Every time Mom waters her plant, she will be reminded of your name, the florist's name, and your generosity.

Materials   Newspaper ad, bounce-back coupons, African violets, imprinted ribbons.

Timing

Four weeks prior:

   Attempt to arrange a tie-in with a florist.

Three weeks prior:

   Prepare newspaper ad.
   Have ribbons printed.
   Prepare bounce-back coupons.

Two weeks prior:

   Discuss promotion with staff.
   Buy media.
   Print bounce-back coupons.

One week prior:

   Place ad.

Start:

> Hand out bounce-back coupons.
> Distribute African violets.

One to four weeks after:

> Redeem bounce-back coupons.

353. Mother's Day Jeweler's Tie-In

Best For Retailers, restaurants, entertainment businesses, some service businesses.

Objective Increase awareness, create excitement, generate traffic.

Target Existing customers and potential new customers.

Contact the manager of a jewelry store. Ideally, you'll know one already as one of your customers. Explain to the manager/owner that you would like to send 500 of your customers over to his or her store. That should get some attention! Then further explain that you want one real diamond and 499 fakes given to you. The real diamond should have a value of $500. (That costs the jeweler only a small fraction of the retail value.)

Advertise that all customers visiting you on Mother's Day will receive a free diamond, while they last. The catch is that in order to find out if the diamond they get is real, your customers have to go to the jewelry store to have it evaluated. The jewelry store loves this because it gets 500 potential customers walking through the front door at very little cost.

You can mention the promotion in your regular advertising or simply promote it within your location with posters and counter cards. This is also a great tie-in for any business that wants to attract the wedding industry, such as a bakery, disc jockey, limo service, tux shop, bridal shop, or photographer.

Materials Newspaper ad, posters, check presenters.

Timing

Four weeks prior:

> Arrange tie-in with a jeweler.

Three weeks prior:

> Prepare newspaper ad.
> Prepare posters.
> Prepare check presenters.

Two weeks prior:

> Discuss promotion with staff.
> Print posters.
> Print counter cards and other location materials.

One week prior:

> Place ad.

One day prior:

> Discuss promotion with staff.

Start:

> Distribute diamonds to customers.

354.   National Police Week

Best For   Many retailers, restaurants, entertainment businesses, some service businesses.

Objective   Increase awareness, increase community goodwill, generate PR, build your image.

Target   Local police forces.

During the second week in May, which is National Police Week, offer a complimentary gift, freebie, or meal to all members of the local police force in recognition of their dedication to duty and their efforts to protect the community.

Issue an invitation to the local precinct stating that any police officer who comes in during that week will receive a gift or freebie. In addition, use your communications board (or posters) to advertise the promotion. This will be noticed by locals as well as by the police, and will ensure good public relations.

This is the type of promotion that often gets media attention, so be sure to send a press release to the local newspaper.

When police officers arrive, present them with a bounce-back coupon to promote a future visit.

Materials Letter-style invitation, press release, communications board, posters (optional), bounce- back coupons.

Timing

Three weeks prior:

  Prepare invitation, bounce-back coupons, and press release.

Two weeks prior:

  Mail invitation.
  Send press release to local newspapers.
  Explain program to staff.
  Print bounce-back coupons.

One week prior:

  Display communications board (posters) with promotion description.

Start:

  Give freebies to police.
  Distribute bounce-back coupons.

One week after:

  Evaluate program.

355. Father's Day Weekend Campout

Best For Lodging businesses, some entertainment businesses, restaurants.

Objective Increase awareness, create excitement, generate traffic.

Target Parents—existing customers and potential new customers.

This program was designed specifically for the hotel/motel industry, but it also works well as a partnership promotion between restaurants and hotels or motels without food service, and for certain other businesses that have space available.

Create a "camping out" atmosphere in a large ballroom, a conference area, or, if available, a protected outdoor area. Set up tents and bring trees and bushes (artificial if necessary) to create the feeling of camping out in a forest. Invite children between the ages of 6 and 13 to a free overnight stay in your "camp," including complete supervision, with parents staying at the hotel or motel at a reduced rate.

Offer a special Father's Day dinner or other incentive, also at a reduced rate, or make the weekend a two-day, one-night package. Include the cost of food for the children and serve franks, beans, burgers, and other such foods, cooked on a barbecue if possible.

With a partnership promotion, the restaurant contributes a portion of the decorations for the "campground" and/or has some of the restaurant staff provide supervisory help in exchange for the Father's Day dinner being at the restaurant. The restaurant can also supply the food, on a cost basis, for the kids' barbecue.

Arrange no-cost entertainment for the children. Scout groups will be happy to provide talks and demonstrations during the day. The Red Cross will show how to perform CPR. The police K-9 Corps can bring their dogs and put them through their paces. In the evening, try to get a local theater group to put on a children's performance.

This program should be promoted through newspaper advertising and direct-mail flyers. With a partnership promotion, the mailing list of the restaurant should also be made available.

Materials Newspaper ads, flyers, mailing list, "campground" decorations, supervisory staff.

Timing

Six weeks prior:

Begin planning all details of promotion.
Begin contacting potential partners.

Four weeks prior:

Prepare newspaper ad.
Prepare flyers.

Secure mailing lists.
Print flyers.
Plan entertainment for children.

Three weeks prior:

Mail flyers.
Plan and purchase "campground" decorations.
Hire or delegate supervisory staff.
Buy media.
Arrange children's entertainment.

Two weeks prior:

Place first newspaper ad.

One week prior:

For cross-promotion, arrange delivery of "camp" food.
Discuss program with staff.
Place second newspaper ad.

One day prior:

Decorate "campground."
Deliver "camp" food (if cross-promotion).

356. Father's Day Cake

Best For   Restaurants, some retailers.

Objective   Increase awareness, generate traffic, increase sales.

Target   Existing customers.

Use an attractive poster to announce a Father's Day special that includes a gift of a family-sized "Happy Father's Day" cake. You can acquire the cakes from a local bakery, and possibly do a partnership with the bakery in return for including its flyers, handouts, and posters in your business.

Include a bounce-back coupon good for a special offer on a return visit. Distribute flyers in parking lots and other areas, and start the program running 2 weeks prior to Father's Day.

Materials   Flyers, posters, bounce-back coupons.

Timing

Three weeks prior:

Prepare flyers, posters, and coupons.

Two weeks prior:

Print flyers, posters, and coupons.
Discuss promotion with bakery.

One week prior:

Discuss program with staff.
Distribute flyers.
Display posters.

Start:

Distribute bounce-back coupons.

357.   Labor Day Weekend Salute to Workers

Best For   Most business types.

Objective   Increase awareness, create excitement, generate traffic.

Target   Existing customers and potential new customers.

This holiday is the perfect time to show your community how much you support its hard-working members. On Labor Day, offer a 20 to 25 percent discount on all purchases when customers show their union card, business card, or employment I.D. Extend a 10 percent discount to workers' families as an added show of appreciation.

Place ads in the newspapers of large corporations and union bulletins. Distribute payroll stuffers to local area businesses.

Materials   Newspaper ad, payroll stuffers.

Timing

Eight weeks prior:

Contact large corporations and unions to get publication dates.
Purchase media (this will often be free for this type of promotion).

Six weeks prior:

Prepare ads and place as necessary.
Contact local area businesses about the payroll stuffer program.
Prepare payroll stuffers.

Three weeks prior:

Print payroll stuffers.

Two weeks prior:

Distribute payroll stuffers.

One week prior:

Explain program to staff.

Start:

Begin giving discounts.

358. High School Back-to-School Special

Best For Businesses catering to teens.

Objective Increase awareness, increase community goodwill, increase
frequency, generate traffic, increase sales, stimulate trial.

Target Local high schools.

Advertise in local high school newspapers at the beginning of the school
year. The ad should carry a coupon, valid for no more than two weeks,
for a free item or gift.
   Prepare bounce-back coupons for "Buy Any Item—Get a Second One
at Half Price." Give these bounce-back coupons to students who redeem

the initial coupons. The bounce-backs will encourage return visits by multiple students sharing the coupon savings.

If the program works well for you, repeat it two or three more times during the year on special occasions, such as the end of a marking period, midterms, finals, or SATs.

Materials   Newspaper ads, bounce-back coupons.

Timing

Three weeks prior:

Contact the local school newspapers to discuss the promotion.
Prepare ad and bounce-back coupons.
Buy media.

Two weeks prior:

Print bounce-back coupons.

One week prior:

Explain program to staff.

Start:

Place ad.
Redeem coupons and distribute bounce-back coupons.

Two weeks after:

Evaluate program and repeat if successful.

359.   Quick College Year Promotions

Best For   Businesses catering to college students.

Objective   Increase awareness, increase frequency, generate traffic, increase sales, stimulate trial.

Target   College students.

Along with your back-to-high-school promotions, make sure in September that you are taking advantage of any college audiences that may be within your trading area. In Chapter 29 you will find a list of 23 tactics, each with a unique idea for catering to a college crowd, that will take you through the school year.

360. Grandparent's Day

Best For Restaurants, food-service businesses, some entertainment businesses.

Objective Increase awareness, increase community goodwill, generate traffic, build your image, increase sales, stimulate trial.

Target Existing customers and potential new customers.

Have your customers fill in their names and their grandparents' names and addresses on invitations. The invitations should read: "(Name of customer) requests the pleasure of your company at (name of your business) on Grandparent's Day, (the date of the first Monday after Labor Day)." Send out the invitations during August. Use table tents, counter cards, and posters for in-store advertising.

On Grandparent's Day, offer old-fashioned prices to make it a family affair. Advertise in local papers at least three weeks prior to the promotion. Offer an additional $1 discount to any grandparent who can show a picture of his or her grandchild/children.

Your ads should be geared not to the grandparents, but to their children and grandchildren, as they are usually the ones who make the arrangements for this day. Be sure to add the grandparents' names and addresses to your mailing list.

Important: Many grandparents will be alone on this day. It will promote goodwill for your establishment if you contact local senior apartment complexes and nursing homes and offer transportation for those grandparents who wish to attend your special Grandparent's Day celebration. Offer them a special area where they can eat or be together, and make sure your staff is especially nice and attentive to them. Extend the offer of $1 off for pictures of their grandchildren to them as well.

Have one member of your staff delegated to photograph all grandparents in attendance, with their grandchildren if applicable, and present the picture to them, bound into a folder with your business's name and address and logo. This will be a wonderful memento and will also assure a return visit to your restaurant.

Materials   Newspaper ad, invitations, Grandparent's Day menu with "old-fashioned" prices, Polaroid camera, imprinted photo folders, extra staff to provide transportation.

Timing

Eight weeks prior:

Begin planning all details of promotion.
Prepare invitations, envelopes, folders, ad, table tents, and posters.

Six weeks prior:

Contact local senior apartment complexes and nursing homes and arrange details.
Print invitations, envelopes, folders, table tents, posters, menus.

Four weeks prior:

Discuss promotion with your staff.
Display table tents and posters.
Begin distributing invitations to be filled out.
Add names to your mailing list.
Buy media.

Three weeks prior:

Arrange transportation.
Designate staff member with Polaroid camera to take pictures.
Place ad.

Two weeks prior:

Explain guest care to staff.
Purchase film.
Repeat advertising.

One day prior:

Review program with staff.

Start:

Offer grandparents a discounted meal.

361.   Halloween Trick-or-Treat Special

Best For   Most retailers, restaurants, entertainment venues.

Objective   Increase awareness, increase community goodwill, generate traffic, stimulate trial.

Target   Existing customers and potential new customers.

On Halloween, during the day and at night, offer trick-or-treaters under 12 a special children's gift or a meal for only $1 if they appear in costume and are accompanied by a parent.

Run a newspaper ad announcing your special during the week prior to Halloween. Distribute flyers for two weeks prior to Halloween in your store and in your surrounding trading area. Place cards, posters, table tents, and so on, welcoming trick-or-treat guests and their families.

Have a staff member take photos of the kids in costume and put up a display on the wall of your business. The kids will encourage their parents to return.

Materials   Newspaper ad, flyers, table tents, posters, camera and film (if necessary).

Timing

Four weeks prior:

   Prepare newspaper ad, flyers, table tents.

Three weeks prior:

   Buy media.
   Print flyers and table tents.

Two weeks prior:

   Discuss promotion with your staff.
   Display in-store promotional materials.
   Begin distributing flyers.

One week prior:

   Purchase film (if necessary).

One day prior:

Review program with staff.

Start:

Photograph children and display photos.

362. Halloween Haunted House

Best For Most business types.

Objective Increase awareness, increase community goodwill, generate PR, generate traffic, build your image, increase sales, stimulate trial.

Target Existing customers and potential new customers.

Every year at Halloween, either a civic group or a radio station in your area will sponsor a Halloween Haunted House. It is often used as a fund-raiser, with part of the proceeds of the admission tickets being given to a charity. If you participate in the haunted house, it will be a good vehicle to distribute coupons for your business. Coupon holders will redeem the coupons at a later date, generally coming in with non-coupon holders, who will, of course, pay the regular price.

The sponsoring organization provides the location, decorations, and personnel to run the operation. You can become a primary sponsor of the event by offering Halloween Night Haunted House Survivor Coupons, good for free items or gifts at your business.

The sponsoring group will probably have relationships with area printers who regularly handle this event, and they may print your coupons and in-store materials at a reduced rate.

You can offer the coupon as part of the admission ticket by printing a two-part ticket, or simply present the coupon to Haunted House visitors as they leave the house.

Materials Coupons, point-of-purchase material, communications board.

Timing

Eight weeks prior:

Contact local civic groups and radio stations to arrange participation.

Three weeks prior:

Plan and print coupons.
Display P.O.P. material.

One week prior:

Display participation announcement and the location of the
Haunted House on your communications board.

28

Thanksgiving and Christmas Tactics

The period from Thanksgiving to Christmas is an important period for most retailers and other businesses and offers the best opportunity for you to introduce your business to the most people in the shortest time. Don't miss out on some basic and creative promotional opportunities to increase your customer base and build on the customer base you already have.

363. Thanksgiving Food for Charity

Best For   Most business types.

Objective   Increase awareness, increase community goodwill, generate PR, generate traffic, build your image, increase sales, stimulate trial.

Target   Existing customers and potential new customers.

During the month of October, research the local community and determine a charity that you would like to tie in with for this all-November event. The ongoing promotion will identify your business as concerned and involved in the local community.

Charitable promotions such as this often bring offers of free media from local newspapers and radio stations. Do not overlook this promotional opportunity if it comes your way. If it does not, contact the charity and ask it to contact the local media. The media may be more receptive to giving free publicity to the charity.

Create an interesting display in your business and supply a drop box for donations. If you have limited room for storage, contact the local Boy Scouts or 4-H Club. These groups will probably be happy to assist by picking up donations on a regular basis and taking them to an air-conditioned storage area that you rent for the month. When people come in to make their donations, give them a coupon as a "thank you" that will entice them to return at a later date.

If they are willing and able, have the Boy Scouts or the 4-H Club members distribute flyers door-to-door explaining the program. The addition of a second nonprofit organization to the promotion will greatly increase your chances for free media coverage. Accept donations of money as well, but only in the form of checks made out to the charity you have chosen.

The day before Thanksgiving, create an event at which you will make the donation to the charity. Try to get a local D.J. to do a radio remote from your business for four hours prior to the presentation to encourage last-minute donations. If they have helped you, the Boy Scouts and 4-H Club members should also be on hand for the event. A representative from the charity should, of course, be present.

If the promotion goes as well as it should, consider making it an annual event. If you can decide this immediately, have the D.J. announce it over the radio. It will give your establishment great credibility within the community.

Materials   Coupons for donors, in-store poster, flyers, press releases, newspaper ad.

Timing

Three weeks prior:

> Contact charity you wish to tie in with and explain the program.
> Contact the Boy Scouts or 4-H Club to see if they will assist with the event.
> Prepare copy for ad, coupons, posters, and flyers.
> Contact D.J. to do radio remote.

Two weeks prior:

> Print flyers, coupons, and posters.
> Place ad, if free media have been offered to you.
> Send out press release.

One week prior:

> Explain program to staff.

Display posters.
Distribute flyers.

Start:

Set up display and drop box.
Accept donations.

End:

Determine whether program is successful enough to repeat each
year.

364. Merry Christmas Greeting

Best For   Most business types.

Objective   Increase awareness, increase community goodwill, generate
PR, generate traffic, build your image, increase sales, stimulate trial.

Target   Existing customers and potential new customers.

Send Christmas cards to your entire customer list during the month of
December. In addition, prepare a special mailing for a select group of
locals, such as the police chief, the mayor, heads of organizations, heads
of houses of worship, scout leaders, school principals, and so on. These
should be people that you would like to have as regular customers, people
that you could count on to help you in future promotions.

Prepare a card for these people with a picture of a bottle of wine or
some other item appropriate to the season against a festive background.
The inside could read, "We've reserved a complimentary (gift) for you
and a guest. Please join us for a specially priced (meal, entertainment,
service, item) any time during the month of January or February. We
look forward to serving you."

Of course, if the invitation is accepted, make sure your staff gives special attention to the guest and makes the special gift or item available.

Materials   Custom Christmas cards, house mailing list, special mailing
list, bottles of wine (partner with your local wine distributor) or some
other item.

Timing

Six weeks prior:

Order Christmas cards.

Four weeks prior:

Secure select group mailing list.

Three weeks prior:

Mail cards (first-class mail).
Discuss program with staff.

Two weeks prior:

Stock item or wine.

One week prior:

Review program with staff again. Make sure staff members understand how they are expected to treat special guests.

Start:

Give guests special attention and complimentary items.

Six weeks after:

Evaluate promotion's success.

365. Visit from Santa Sweepstakes

Best For Most business types.

Objective Increase awareness, increase community goodwill, generate PR, generate traffic, build your image, increase sales, stimulate trial.

Target Existing customers and potential new customers.

Offer an appearance by Santa, including a bag of gifts for the children, at the winner's home on Christmas Eve.

Find an experienced Santa (through department stores, the Jaycees, or the Salvation Army) with his own costume who can accommodate you by visiting the family after they are through with their Christmas Eve jobs. If you can't find a suitable Santa, consider doing it yourself. If you do so, be sure to make your costume reservation early.

If you begin early, you can tie in with a local department store or toy store to contribute the bag of gifts. In exchange, name the contributor in your promotional advertising. Be sure to budget for a variety of gifts and confirm the correctness of the gifts by informing the contributor, in advance, of the ages and sexes of the winning children.

Wrap an empty box with Christmas wrapping paper to use as your Sweepstakes Entry Box. Entry blanks should ask for the parent's name, address, and phone number and the number of children, with their sexes and ages. Check your customer mailing list after the entry blanks are received and add any names that you do not already have.

Hold the drawing about a week before Christmas, preferably on a Sunday, to give yourself plenty of time to contact the winners and inform the gift donor of the sexes and ages of the children.

Promote this program through newspaper advertising and in-store displays, beginning at least three weeks before Christmas.

Materials Newspaper ad, counter cards, table tents, posters.

Timing

Six weeks prior:

> Begin to look for department stores or toy stores that will contribute gifts.
> Begin interviewing "Santas"

Four weeks prior:

> Prepare newspaper ad.
> Prepare and print table tents, posters, and entry blanks.

Three weeks prior

> Buy media.
> Explain program to staff.
> Prepare entry box and set out.
> Place ad.
> Set out posters and table tents.

Two weeks prior:

Reconfirm Santa.
Stay in touch with contributing partner.

One week prior:

Draw name of winner from entry box and inform winner.
Inform contributing store.

Start:

Have Santa deliver gifts to winners.

366.   Christmas Bonus Payroll Stuffer

Best For   Most business types.

Objective   Increase awareness, increase community goodwill, generate PR, generate traffic, build your image, increase sales, stimulate trial.

Target   Existing customers and potential new customers.

Contact the managers of various area businesses and offer discount buy-one-get-one-free coupons as an extra Christmas bonus gift for their employees. Design the coupons in the form of a gift certificate, and encourage their distribution by offering business managers a gift certificate good for the same offer.
      When customers redeem their certificates, present them with an additional bounce-back coupon to encourage a return visit.

Materials   Gift certificates for buy-one-get-one-free, bounce-back coupons.

Timing

Four weeks prior:

Prepare offer and design and print certificates.
Begin contacting local area businesses for promotion.
Design bounce-back coupons.

Three weeks prior:

Print bounce-back coupons.

Two weeks prior:

Distribute certificates to local area businesses.

One week prior:

Discuss program with staff.

Start:

Begin redeeming certificates.

One week after:

Begin redeeming bounce-back coupons.

367. Christmas Santa Claus

Best For Most consumer-oriented businesses.

Objective Increase awareness, increase community goodwill, generate PR, generate traffic, build your image, increase sales, stimulate trial.

Target Existing customers and potential new customers.

Arrange for a volunteer from a local community organization to play the part of Santa. Or, you or one of your staff can play Santa. Be sure to reserve a costume well in advance of the holiday.

Schedule Santa for a four-hour appearance during a busy period on the two Saturdays immediately before Christmas. Decorate the entire business, and set up an area for the Santa where he and the children will not be in the way of other patrons or your staff. Schedule one staff person to serve as Santa's helper to keep children in line and entertained while they are waiting for Santa.

Pass out peppermint sticks to the children, and distribute coupons for their next visit. This is also a good time to promote the sale of gift certificates.

Materials Newspaper ad, posters, flyers, gift certificates, Santa, Santa suit, decorations. Santa's helper could also take Polaroids of children with Santa as giveaways, or you could enlist the service of a local professional photographer, who would take photos of the children to sell to the parents and split the profits with you.

Timing

Six weeks prior:

> Prepare copy for ad, posters, and so on.
> Arrange for Santa or reserve costume.

Four weeks prior:

> Print materials, posters, flyers, gift certificates.
> Buy media.
> Buy store decorations.
> Try to arrange for participation by a photographer, or prepare Polaroid and film for Santa's helper.

Three weeks prior:

> Discuss program with your staff.
> Decide on area for Santa and children.
> Set out table tents and posters.
> Begin selling gift certificates.

Two weeks prior:

> Distribute flyers (in parking lots and other areas).
> Purchase peppermint sticks for children.
> Place ad.

One week prior:

> Confirm Santa or Santa costume.
> Assign a staff member as Santa's helper.

One day prior:

> Pick up costume.
> Decorate store or restaurant for promotion.

Start:

> Santa appears at your business.

One week later:

> Review promotion with staff.

29

Quick College-Year Promotions

Best For Food, beverage, entertainment, sports, and other youth-oriented businesses.

Objective Create excitement, build loyalty, increase frequency.

Target College-age students.

The following is a schedule of 23 tactics, each with a unique idea to cater to a college crowd, that will take you through the school year. Your only requirement is a nearby college or university campus.

These are only a fraction of the possible promotions that can be used to celebrate various real and creative holidays during the year. They are meant as suggestions to get you thinking about other possibilities. Don't forget: When you are dealing with a college crowd, you cannot be too outrageous!

Most of these promotions focus on food and beverage, which college students consume a lot of. Even if yours is a nonfood business, such as a bowling alley, movie house, skating rink, or sports facility, consider using food and beverages to attract an audience.

Be sure to keep the atmosphere pleasant, homey, and friendly—and, most important, do not impose too many rules and regulations regarding students' behavior and dress. Students tend to frequent the places where they feel most comfortable and where they can get the best product or food at the best prices. Keep these students happy and they will remain loyal to your establishment throughout their college careers—and, if they are locals, forever!

329

368. September—Hula Hoop Day

Hold a day-long hula hoop contest. Award the winner free food or other prizes for a week, and give the two runners-up free food for the day.

369. September—Grandparents' Day

Invite students to bring their grandparents to campus. Offer free dinners, bowling, tickets, or something else to grandparents who are accompanied by students.

370. September—Ice-Cream-Cone Anniversary

Make this one a week-long celebration. Hold an ice-cream-cone-eating contest. Have outrageous flavors of the day. Offer specials on ice-cream cones and feature a five-scoop cone, which, if it is eaten without dropping a scoop, is given free.

371. October—National Apple Month

Decorate with a special apple display and feature apple pies and other apple dishes at discounted prices. Hold an apple-dunking contest and give the winner a bushel of apples.

372. October—Oktoberfest

Serve nonalcoholic beers, German sausages, sauerkraut, and other German foods in addition to your regular menu, or as a special event if you don't ordinarily serve food. Encourage students to try the German foods by offering them at a special discount.

373. October—National Pasta Week

Set up a pasta bar with different pasta dishes—tricolored pastas, spinach pasta, artichoke pasta, and so on—and a variety of sauces. Decorate with red-and-white-checked tablecloths and candles in wine bottles, and play Italian music.

374. October—Halloween

Celebrate All Hallows' eve with a storyteller, a costume contest, and pumpkin food specialties. Offer a free dinner for two, or some other reward, for the best costume.

375. November—Mickey Mouse's Birthday

Offer free items or food to anyone with a Mickey hat or any Mickey memorabilia. Get a projector and screen and show Mickey Mouse cartoons all day. This is great for a movie theater.

376. November—Thanksgiving Day

Hold a real Thanksgiving feast—appetizer, soup, salad, main dishes, desserts—for a fixed price. Have an afternoon sitting, an early evening sitting, and a late evening sitting. Take reservations. Serve family-style, prayers included.

377. December—Christmas Day

Decorate with inexpensive gift-wrapped presents and give these to students who have not gone home for the holidays. If you wish, you can offer them free items or desserts with their meals as an added gift.

378. January—Hat Day

Have your staff and customers wear different kinds of hats—hats of every description. Offer free items or food to customers who sport the wildest hats in exchange for loaning their hat to you for the balance of the school year. Decorate the restaurant with the hats to make this a memorable occasion and bring students back in.

379. January—Super Bowl

Ask female staff members to dress as cheerleaders. Show the game on a rented giant-screen TV. Have football trivia contests before the game. Serve snack foods like hot dogs and burgers at discounted prices.

380. February—National Heart Month

Bring your menu to the Red Cross to identify items that are heart-healthy. Mark those items with small red heart stickers, and offer special prices on those items for the entire month.

381. February—Valentine's Day

Get your local pizza place to make heart-shaped pizzas and your local bakery to make heart-shaped cakes decorated with hearts. Offer two-for-one specials to couples. Give red carnations to women customers.

382. March—Mardi Gras

Traditionally held just prior to the beginning of Lent, Mardi Gras is a great time to invite students to your business for a masquerade ball and a feast of southern-style food.

383. March—St. Patrick's Day

Serve a special Irish dinner. Play Irish music. Have an Irish dance instructor present, and have a contest for the Wildest Irish Name on Campus.

384. March—National Pig Day (March 1)

Celebrate with an all-you-can-eat "pig out." Offer bacon, pork chops, sausages, and pork roasts. Show Porky Pig cartoons. Have your staff wear pig noses. End the evening with a pig-calling contest.

385. March—Ides of March Toga Party (March 15)

Have customers dress in togas, and dress your staff in bed sheets and laurels. Set up a huge T-shaped table and have customers serve themselves punch in large wine goblets. Make the party last an entire evening, with the staff replenishing the food as diners come and go.

386. April—April Fool's Day

Discount different items or services, but don't tell your customers which ones are discounted until after they order. Have your employee or server tell them, "April Fool!" Offer a free dessert or other item as a reward. Call your fish dish "Ship of Fools," your special of the day "Fool's Gold," and your salad bar "Fool Hearty Bar."

387. April—National Guitar Day

Play live guitar music and coordinate your products, food, or services: Spanish guitar–Spanish food; country guitar–country food. Invite students to bring their guitars and participate.

388. April—Shakespeare's Birthday (April 23)

Hold an Elizabethan festival. Have the staff and the patrons dress as minstrels and ladies-in-waiting. Serve traditional British food and drink. Have a Macbeth or King Lear contest. Give away beer mugs (with your name imprinted, of course) as prizes for the best recitations.

389. May—National Photo Day

Sponsor a Food Photo Contest. Entries should be photographs of anything that is food related–food on a table, food-service establishments, food being eaten, food being harvested, and so on. Display the entries at your restaurant. Have students put their name, address, and phone number on the back of each submitted photo. Have a well-known local photographer serve as judge. Give the winner a nice camera as the grand prize.

390. June—Donut Day

Offer free homemade donuts. Hold a donut-eating contest or some other crazy event to go along with this off-the-wall holiday.

30
e-Marketing

Technology has had a remarkable effect on the traditional neighborhood. It has expanded the neighborhood's borders and lengthened your reach. Promotional techniques that rely on email campaigns are sometimes considered impersonal—the opposite of neighborhood marketing. But neighborhood marketing and technology don't have to contradict each other.

When used well and thoughtfully, email campaigns and web-site strategies can produce effective results.

Fishbowl, a leader in email marketing for the hospitality industry, recently reported the success of a national chain that built an email list of more than 2500 names per store. The company uses the list to send monthly emails that provide news, announcements, and promotions. It also sends each guest a gift when the guest joins, a birthday gift, and a surprise gift each year. The results have been amazing—the chain estimates that this program produces at least $15,000 per year in incremental sales per store.

But email is tricky. While you can mail a million brochures through the post office and not get a single complaint, if you send a mass email, you will have hundreds or thousands of angry recipients. This is an area in which it is helpful to spend some time with a professional, especially if you are going to use a web site along with email, which is strongly advised.

Here are some basic rules and ideas to help you take advantage of the reach of technology-assisted campaigns while staying true to the neighborhood marketing philosophy.

- Always get a customer's permission before sending anything by email. Encourage customers to sign up for your email list while they're visiting your location, and have a sign-up form on your web site.
- Make customers feel appreciated by using email marketing sparingly and personalizing your messages as much as possible. Bombarding

guests with frequent messages will land your campaigns in every guest's virtual trash can.

- Have some messages with special offers come from the email address of the store manager. This makes a powerful statement, and the personal touch impresses guests.
- Check into the latest technology that is available to help you assess guest frequency. By tracking credit card transactions, you can get a much better idea of how often guests are really coming in, and how much they're spending when they're there.

391. Collecting Email Addresses

Objective Build emailing list.

Target Existing customers and new customers.

You may already be building a mailing list, either in the store or through direct mail, events, and other promotions, but are you using that opportunity to collect email addresses? If you aren't, adding one simple line to your response form can dramatically increase the value of your database. In fact, some people are more likely to join a list if they can provide an email address rather than a home address, so you have the opportunity to build an even larger list.

If you have an email club, newsletter, or some other means of communicating via email, let customers know what they can expect to receive from you.

Rules for collecting email addresses:

- Ask for permission to send emails.
- Let customers know what they will receive via email.
- State your privacy policy (for example, "We won't rent or sell your information to anyone"), and don't cheat!
- Tell customers that they can "unsubscribe" from your list at any time.
- Send customers a confirmation when they join your list.
- Send ongoing communications to keep your business top-of-mind.

Materials Existing direct-mail bounce-back offers, in-house enrollment forms, mailing list, gift certificate order forms.

Timing   Include this in every communication you do.

392.   Tell-a-Friend Campaign

Objective   Build emailing list, create excitement, generate traffic, stimulate trial.

Target   Existing customers.

Once your house email list is established, get your loyal customers to spread the word about your business. Develop an email campaign that asks the existing list members to provide the email addresses of five of their friends. In exchange, you will give each friend a free gift or product just for trying you out. If you add an incentive for the list member who is referring friends, not only will you stimulate new trial by non-list members, but you will increase the frequency with which your existing list members patronize your business.

Once the friends receive the offer to try your business (you'll know that they responded because they'll provide your employee with the email coupon to redeem the offer), be sure to ask them to join the email list.

Materials   Email postcard to house list, online collection area for friends' emails, email gift certificate for the referred friends, email thank-you coupon for list members (optional).

Timing

Three weeks prior:

Design email message and broadcast it to list members.

One day prior:

Train staff to accept certificates and track redemptions.

Start:

Mail gift certificate to the email addresses collected and to the list members (if selected).

Four weeks after:

Evaluate program.

393. New Product/Service Announcement via Email

Objective Create excitement, generate traffic.

Target Existing customers.

Once you have an email list, use it to generate traffic by letting your loyal customers know about new items, products, or services. Send an email message to your existing list members to announce your new product or service, and provide a picture and a coupon if that item is ordered or purchased. Include a minimum purchase requirement. Track the coupons you receive and send customers a survey to get their input on the new item.

Materials Email postcard to house list, posttrial survey (either in-store or through email).

Timing

One week prior:

Design email message to list members.

One day prior:

Train staff to accept certificates and track redemptions.

Start:

Email the announcement/offer to list members.

One week after:

Email survey to those redeeming certificates.

394. Nontraditional Event Promotions via Email

Objective Create excitement, generate traffic, promote activity during slow periods.

Target   Existing customers.

Use your email list to generate excitement and traffic with a special "your business only" promotion. Celebrate Tax Day ($10.40 off any purchase), Arbor Day (save a tree, donate a book), Grandparent's Day, or Texas Independence Day. Your options are unlimited.

Announce this one-day event, and throw in a special offer if you like.

Materials   Email postcard to email list, in-store signs to promote the event.

Timing

Two weeks prior:

Design email message to list members.

One week prior:

Train staff to honor offer (if applicable).

Five days prior:

Email the announcement/offer to list members.

395.   Hear Me Roar—Customer Satisfaction e-Surveys

Objective   Build your image, increase goodwill.

Target   Existing customers.

Customers love to give feedback. Since you probably have comment cards, but find them hard to analyze and summarize, why not survey your guests via email? Create an online survey and send it out via email. You can have all feedback received automatically collected and summarized it for quick and easy analysis. You can either have a survey created on your web site or use a third-party service to host your survey. A simple survey with five to eight questions is perfect, and you'll be surprised at how many responses you'll receive. Make sure to add an incentive for respondents, such as a free gift, a special offer, or even a drawing, and you'll see a rise in responses—and in traffic, too!

Some burning questions include

- How often do you patronize the business?
- How would you rate our products? Excellent, Good, Fair, Below Average, Poor
- How would you rate our service? Excellent, Good, Fair, Below Average, Poor
- Would you recommend our business to a friend?
- How far from our business do you live?
- If you could change one thing about our business, what would it be?

Materials Email postcard, survey.

Timing

Two weeks prior:

Design email message and online survey.

Start:

Email survey to list members.

One week after:

Train staff to honor offer (if applicable).

Send thank-you offer or select prize winner (if applicable).

Two weeks after:

Evaluate responses.

396. News They Can Use

Objective Build customer loyalty.

Target Existing customers, email list, web-site visitors.

One of the most effective ways to use a web site is to make sure that there is something new on it, something that is of value to your audience, every day or every few days.

A municipal official who was running for re-election in a suburban community near Philadelphia had her web-site manager post a news item on the site every night. Sometimes it was a press release from the campaign, sometimes it was a link to an article about the campaign, but often it was news of a general but local nature that was tied to her issues, which were principally sprawl, water quality, schools, and taxes.

Initially, her web-site traffic was modest. But word began to spread, and by the time of the election, web traffic had soared, and people were checking her web site several times a day to see if there were any hot developments. When the campaign got so busy that it didn't have time to post the news, visitors complained!

In a business setting, the power of this tactic cannot be underestimated. Consider that your audience is made up of your neighbors. What do they care about? Highway closings, school news, taxes, odd events, sports results, and useful tips.

To use this tactic, you may want to hire a local writer to spend an hour each day scouring the local press for news items. At the same time, post news about what is happening in your business: the birth of a popular employee's child, an employee who won an award, a new product or service, helpful hints on how to use your products, news and tips about what is happening in your business category. Are you in the food business? Give your visitors the latest nutrition news about carbohydrates. Do you operate an art-supply store? Tell them about local gallery openings, and show some local art. Are you in the insurance business? Talk about changes in the law, important court decisions, overlooked risks, and so on.

By keeping your web site fresh, you will boost your traffic and your sales.

397. Reach Out and Email Someone

Objective   Increase awareness, stimulate trial.

Target   Other businesses in your neighborhood.

Just as you can send an employee out with samples to neighboring businesses, you can use email to reach out specifically to customers in your trading area. Instead of mass emailing, this tactic is highly focused and personal. Often you can reach customers that you would never be able to track down by telephone or get to open your mail. And if the email is successful, it will be forwarded to others.

Depending on what type of business you operate, take your Yellow Pages and begin to search for the web sites that other businesses in your neighborhood maintain. Each time you find a local business that could be a customer, or whose employees could be your customers, send a personalized email, using a template that you've set up ahead of time.

The subject line is key. You have 42 characters to work with, and your subject line should be just as compelling as a book title because, like a book, you want the recipient to be compelled to read the message inside.

Here's a trick to make sure your email gets read: Begin the subject line with the name of a real person at the business. For example, if you are a painting contractor, your subject line might read: "Mr. Smith—Need a fast, reliable painter?"

Your message should be personal, short, and direct. For example, if you were writing to a real estate broker, you might say: "As your neighbor, I wanted to let you know that I'd be happy to give an estimate for any of your customers who might be selling their homes and need to freshen the walls. We're a family-owned business, right around the corner, bonded, with great references. If you ever need a fast, reliable painter, I'd welcome the chance to give you an estimate."

Make sure to give your full name, address, telephone number, mobile phone number, and fax number at the bottom. If you reach out to 20 prospects a week this way, in a year's time you'll have made yourself known to 1000 potential new customers and an untold number of others to whom your email was forwarded. Make sure to keep a record of the email address of every individual you contact this way, and create a database that you can use for follow-up marketing. Note those who responded, even if only to say thanks. Follow up with a postal mailing and a special offer.

398. Cross-Linking Web Sites

This is a basic tactic that many businesses overlook. It is part and parcel of networking and cross-promotion. Find local businesses that serve your audience and don't compete with you. Offer to place a link to their web sites from yours, and vice versa. In doing so, look for opportunities to make special cross-promotions, just as you do in-store. If you own a bookstore, cross-promote with a store that sells recorded music. If you sell clothing, why not cross-promote with a dry cleaner? If you sell cars, cross-promote with a car wash. Remember to offer a coupon or discount of real value in your promotions, such as a 50 percent discount on a book if you bring in a register tape from the music store, and vice versa.

Most web-site hosts offer tracking services, so you can tell just how many visitors you have from a promotional partner's site.

399.   Community Announcements

You can offer local nonprofit community groups the opportunity to include brief announcements about their upcoming events and fund-raisers on your web site and in your emails in exchange for sponsorship links on their web sites or ads in their newsletters, or for giving out coupons and brochures at their events and meetings.

By including community news in your emails, you will show your audience that you are involved in your neighborhood in a constructive way. This will build goodwill with your existing customers, and they will feel that your emails are more than just promotions.

400.   Become a Community Resource

Many government, community, trade, affiliation, and other institutional web sites include lists of neighborhood resources. Make sure that you are listed on and linked to every one of these web sites that you can be linked to. Visitors' bureaus, chambers of commerce (make sure you join!), real estate brokers and associations, and so on consider these resource lists valuable because it makes their sites "sticky," meaning that visitors tend to stay longer and become more engaged as they search for information.

401.   Email News and Press Releases

Whenever you have a legitimate press or news release about your business or an upcoming community event you are involved with, make sure to send it to the local media by email. News organizations increasingly prefer email (without attachments, please) because they can cut and paste the copy directly into their page layouts. Your email press release has a better chance of getting printed than anything you send on paper.

If you don't have a media email list, create one. Go to the web sites of your local newspapers and radio and television stations, look up the email addresses of the editors or the reporters who cover your neighborhood, and create an address list to which you can mass-mail your notices. Keep it current and accurate.

Don't abuse this avenue. If you send junk mail that isn't legitimate news, it won't be long before your messages are trashed without being read. Look for opportunities to promote yourself and your employees.

Subject lines are all-important here. Start your subject line with: "News: Local bagel shop introduces low-carb bagels" or "Editors: Local pet store sells 1000th ferret." Keep these emails short, giving just the facts. If you can afford it, hire a local copywriter or freelance writer to product them.

Index